CULTURAL POLITICS

Writing Ireland

CULTURAL POLITICS
general editors Jonathan Dollimore and Alan Sinfield

Writing Ireland: colonialism, nationalism and culture
David Cairns and Shaun Richards

Poetry, language and politics *John Barrell*

The Shakespeare myth *Graham Holderness*

Garden-nature-language *Simon Pugh*

in *preparation*

Opera, ideology and film *Jeremy Tambling*

Teaching women *Ann Thompson and Helen Wilcox (editors)*

Drama in South Africa *Martin Orkin*

The politics of romanticism *Nigel Leask*

Empire boys *Joe Bristow*

Georgette Heyer and Jane Austen: representations of regency England
Roger Sales

Writing, postmodernity and femininity *Carolyn Brown*

Strategies of contemporary women writers *Maggie Humm*

Teaching Shakespeare *Stephen Glynn (editor)*

Counter-cultures in 1980s popular music *Steve Redhead*

Gender, race, Renaissance drama *Ania Loomba*

Pre-Raphaelite art and literature *Marcia Pointon (editor)*

Bakhtin and cultural criticism *David Shepherd and Ken Hirschkop (editors)*

Gay culture and politics *Simon Shepherd and Mick Wallis (editors)*

Lesbian identity in twentieth-century women's writing *Gabriele Griffin*

Writing Ireland: colonialism, nationalism and culture

David Cairns and Shaun Richards

MANCHESTER UNIVERSITY PRESS

distributed exclusively in the USA and Canada by ST. MARTIN'S PRESS, *New York*

Published by Manchester University Press,
Oxford Road, Manchester M13 9PL, UK
and Room 400, 175 Fifth Avenue, New York, NY 10010, USA
Distributed exclusively in the USA and Canada
by St. Martin's Press, Inc.,
175 Fifth Avenue, New York, NY 10010, USA

Reprinted 1990

British Library cataloguing in publication data
Cairns, David
Writing Ireland: colonialism, nationalism and culture
— (Cultural politics).
1. Ireland — Politics and government —
1558– 2. Ireland — Civilization — 19th and 20th
centuries
I. Title II. Richards, Shaun III. Series
320.9417 JN1415

Library of Congress cataloging in publication data
Cairns, David, 1948–
Writing Ireland: colonialism, nationalism, and culture/by David
Cairns and Shaun Richards.
p. cm.—(Cultural politics)
Bibliography: p.
Includes index.
ISBN 0-7190-2371-8: $35.00 (U.S.: est.). ISBN 0-7190-2372-6
(pbk.): $15.00 (U.S.: est.)
1. Ireland—Civilization. 2. Ireland—Politics and government.
3. National characteristics. Irish. 4. Nationalism—Ireland.
I. Richards, Shaun. II. Title. III. Series.
DA925.C17 1988
941.5—dc 19
88-1540
CIP

ISBN 0-7190-2372-6 *paperback*

Photoset in Linotron Joanna by
Northern Phototypesetting Co, Bolton

Printed in Great Britain
by Hartnolls Limited, Bodmin, Cornwall

Contents

Acknowledgements

We would like to record our thanks to the people who have helped us in our work on Ireland's cultural politics and this project in particular. Our research has developed in tandem with our teaching on a final year interdisciplinary option course and our students' interest and enthusiasm have been a constant stimulus to further work. North Staffordshire Polytechnic has been generous in its support of our research through Travel Grants, provision of wordprocessing facilities and Research Grants. Dr John Shelton, Head of Humanities, has been supportive throughout our work and has sought to smooth our path in many ways. In the Polytechnic Library, Mrs Ann Jardine's tireless efforts on our behalf in tracing texts and periodicals have been much appreciated.

The advice and encouragement of the Series Editors of Cultural Politics, Jonathan Dollimore and Alan Sinfield, has been invaluable at all stages, likewise, John Banks, Manchester University Press Editor, has been most helpful. Declan Kiberd was kind enough to offer to read the manuscript and his thoughtful comments, particularly on Chapters 1 and 4 were succinct and useful. Needless to say, neither he nor the Series or Press Editors bear any responsibility for acts and omissions in the final text.

Lucette Richards undertook the onerous task of reading the manuscript for typing errors which she did with speed, accuracy and good humour. For both of us, the forbearance and support of our families during the past year have been the key factors in making this work possible and our gratitude is marked in the

For our families

1

What ish my Nation?

'Beginnings', wrote Edward Said, 'have to be made for each project in such a way as to *enable* what follows from them' (Said, 1985b, p. 16). Our beginning lies with the reality of the historic relationship of Ireland with England; a relationship of the colonized and the colonizer. In this study our foremost concern is with the ways in which the making and re-making of the identities of colonized and colonizer have been inflected by this relationship; a process which has taken place through discourse: 'a linguistic unity or group of statements which constitutes and delimits a particular area of concern, governed by its own rules of formation with its own modes of distinguishing truth from reality' (Weeks, 1982, p. 111). Although the main focus of our study is the nineteenth and twentieth centuries, a necessary prelude is an outline of the originary moment of the colonial relationship and its aftermath; consequently, our examination of the cultural engagements of the English and the Irish peoples begins in the sixteenth century at a crucial moment for English State and cultural formation.

The medieval colonization of Ireland from the twelfth century onwards had taken the form of piecemeal displacement of the native rulers by Anglo-Norman noble families, a process loosely supervised by the English monarchy. This colonization had subsequently been checked in the fourteenth century by plague and Scots invasion, blows from which the medieval colony never recovered. In the fifteenth and early sixteenth centuries the Yorkists and the first two Tudors had been content with a policy of restrained expenditure and containment but, as Steven Ellis has argued, 'the loss of Calais [1558] finally ended the dreams entertained by Kings like Henry VIII to recreate Henry V's continental empire and forced the monarchy to concentrate on the British Isles' (Ellis, 1985, p. 15). Simultaneously, he notes, attempts at conquering the 'celtic fringes' of the British Isles were 'influential ... in shaping the characteristics of *English* [our emphasis] nationality as it developed in Tudor times. Before the Reformation, the Tudor territories were united principally by a common allegiance to the English crown [and] ... a generally wide sense of "Englishness" prevailed. After the breach with Rome, however, and the growing consciousness of differentiation from continental Europe which accompanied the Elizabethan idea of an elect nation, a narrower definition of Englishness emerged' (p. 319).

In part, the emergence of this 'narrower definition of Englishness' may be traced not only to the loss of continental Empire, but also to the impact of the Reformation and to rapid overseas expansion. The fragmentation of Christendom, together with encounters with new civilizations, posed serious challenges to understanding for contemporary writers, problems immeasurably compounded by those changes in the nature of language and representation to which Michel Foucault has drawn attention. Foucault has argued that, prior to the sixteenth century, the pre-classical *episteme*, or mode of acquiring knowledge, was based upon resemblance and finding affinities and similarities. He has suggested that 'the fundamental supposition was that of a total system of correspondence (earth and sky, planets and faces, microcosm and macrocosm) and each particular similitude was then lodged within this overall relation' (Foucault, 1970, p. 55). In contrast, acquisition of knowledge within the classical *episteme* was based upon difference: 'The activity of the mind ... will ... no longer consist in drawing things together, in setting out on a quest for everything that might reveal some sort of kinship, attraction, or secretly shared nature within them, but, on the contrary, in discriminating, that is establishing their identities.... In this sense, discrimination imposes upon comparison the primary and fundamental investigation of difference' (p. 55). In the case of later sixteenth- and seventeenth-century England, the conjunction of shifts in ways of acquiring knowledge with colonial expansion, in Ireland and elsewhere, requires that we be aware that writing by Englishmen about Ireland and the Irish may not only have served to broaden English knowledge of the neighbouring island and its inhabitants, but also to define the qualities of 'Englishness', by simultaneously defining 'not-Englishness' or 'otherness'.

Michael T. Ryan has applied Foucault's ideas about the pre-classical and classical *epistemes* in an examination of writings from the Age of the Reconnaissance on the peoples of the Americas and has shown that within the pre-classical *episteme* these 'new' peoples were assimilated into European frames of reference through the category of 'paganism'. What was specific in their practices, beliefs and appearance was seen as being of only minor significance in comparison to the similarities that could be discovered between their cultures and those of ancient pagan civilizations, and of the Eastern and near Eastern World. In this way the unknown became reassuringly familiar (Ryan, 1981). The process which Ryan describes vis-à-vis the New World had taken place much earlier in the case of Ireland, through, for example, Giraldus Cambrensis' twelfth-century texts *The History And Topography of Ireland* and *The Conquest of Ireland* (Cambrensis, 1982, 1978), and texts written by the medieval English colonists who had followed Giraldus (Canny, 1973, p. 584), in which the Irish were made known to the wider world as a people descended from the ancient Scythians, who in many districts were wholly pagan, and in others only partly converted to Christianity, and who were in urgent need of the Faith. In recounting fabulous happenings, the habits of the natives and the topography of the island, Giraldus' *History* illustrates Foucault's contention that in the pre-classical *episteme* 'there is a non-distinction between what is said and what is read, between observation and relation ... [to know] ... one has to collect together in one and the same form of knowledge all that has been recounted, either by nature or by man, by the language of the world, by tradition or by the poets' (Foucault 1970, pp. 39-40). Seen in this light, Giraldus' writings may be viewed as attempts to know the Irish and Ireland within the framework of the pre-classical *episteme*. Such knowledge was intended to justify the expansion of Angevin temporal power, by reference to the overriding necessities of securing Irish conformity to the spiritual power of the universal Church, and the extension of the Faith, but it was not founded on a conception of the Irish as irremediably, and therefore permanently, inferior. Their conquest would be the first step on their road to full absorption within the community of humanity and their conversion/conformity was both the prime requisite and external sign of acceptance.

During the sixteenth century both classical and pre-classical *epistemes* coexisted for a time and consequently texts and part-texts from the pre-classical *episteme* (such as those of Giraldus) were drawn upon by writers who formed their understanding within the terms of a classical *episteme*, in which knowledge was constituted on the basis of difference rather than similarity. In the new *episteme*, Giraldus' texts, together with others such as Geoffrey of Monmouth's *History of the Kings of Britain* (*circa* 1136) and Bede's *Ecclesiastical History* (*circa* 731), provided the basis for a new historiography of the English people, providing the discourses which underwrote both 'a narrower definition of Englishness' and new practices of colonization. Consequently, when Edmund Spenser reproduced observations on the Irish recognizably derived from Giraldus it was, however, within a framework quite different from that of the originator.

In the context of a demonstration of some of the procedures whereby sixteenth-century men sought to conceive of identity as self-made, Stephen Greenblatt has said of Spenser's *The Faerie Queene* that 'Ireland ... pervades the poem' (Greenblatt, 1980, p. 186). In Greenblatt's study of English 'Renaissance Self-Fashioning' two enabling institutions are central to the process: the Court, with its cult of *Gloriana*, and secondly 'a perception of the not-self, of all that lies outside, or resists, or threatens identity' (p. 177). Greenblatt argues that neutralization of the 'other' is required for the success of the process of 'securing the principle of difference which is necessary to fashion the self' (p. 177), a process which he discerns in the destruction of the 'Bower of Bliss' in Book 2, Canto 12 of *The Faerie Queene*. Here, 'otherness' takes the form of Acrasia, personifying the temptations of ease and sexual pleasure. But the violence meted out to Acrasia, exemplar of the temptations which would lure the would-be self-fashioner into the abandonment of his project, indicates a perceived need to combat the continuing strong influence of the notion of assimilation, in order to establish difference as a new principle.

Acrasia's confinement in 'chaines of adamant' (Spenser, 1965, p. 276), symbolizes the dilemma of the construction of identity based on difference – she cannot be destroyed for her continued and identifiable presence as 'other' is required for the continuing reproduction of the identity of the self of Guyon, the Knight of Temperance. For Spenser himself a crucial stage in the process of self-fashioning, through identification of the 'other', took place in the course of his experiences as a New English colonist in late sixteenth-century Ireland, and in particular in his consideration of the policy to be followed towards the Native Irish. This consideration took the form of a dialogic treatise written at approximately the same time as *The Faerie Queene*, *A View of the Present State of Ireland*, where Spenser takes up many of the categories, descriptions and imputations which Giraldus had used, to argue that the Irish could only be brought into civility by the extirpation of their culture. The *View* takes the form of a dialogue between the representatives of two positions: Irenius, the authorial voice in the dialogue, and Eudoxus, 'the good humanist [who] should be truly convinced by the man of action, Irenius, that his was the only way of bringing about the permanent reform of Ireland' (Brady, 1986, p. 47).

In the *View*, Irenius/Spenser takes the supposed descent of the Irish from the ancient Scythians as conclusive proof that they are a barbaric race who must be broken by famine and the sword before they can be remade as biddable and law-abiding. For Spenser, 'cultural trauma ... was the necessary precondition to all social and political reform' (Brady, 1986, p. 30). Until the later sixteenth century the orthodox English position on the treatment of the Native Irish was that, given firm government, they could be reformed, their culture and customs being merely surface features overlaying a basic humanity. In contrast, Spenser argued that the laws and customs of the Native Irish reflected values and priorities which were incompatible with assimilation. Whereas earlier proposals had concentrated on removing only the top strata of Native Irish society, the chiefs and warriors, Irenius/Spenser's proposals were for root and branch treatment of the whole population, treatment which he advocated should also be extended to the Old English, the descendants of the medieval colonists (Spenser, 1934, p. 133; Canny, 1973 p. 597-8; Brady, 1986, p. 28). Moreover, he saw the refusal of the Irish to conform willingly to what he regarded as self-evidently superior English practices, and in particular their refusal to accept Protestantism, as proof of their barbarity so that, notwithstanding their Christianity, the Irish were to be considered as comparable to the natives of the New World and thus liable to similar treatment: 'They are all Papists by their profession, but in the same so blindly and brutishly informed for the most part as that you would rather think them atheists or infidels' (Spenser, 1934, p. 109. Canny, 1973, pp. 585-6).

The particular threat that the Native Irish posed for the New English, as the arrivals of the late fifteenth and sixteenth centuries (such as Spenser) were known, was that of cultural pollution. The New English argued that the culture of the Irish had led to the degeneration of those exposed to it – a threat exemplified for Spenser, amongst others, by the 'Irish' traits, such as language and customs, displayed by the Old English who had intermarried freely with the Native Irish and so ceased, in New English eyes, to be really English: 'is it possible that an *Englishman*, brought up naturally in such sweet civility as England affords could find such liking in that barbarous rudeness [i.e. the customs of the Native Irish] that he should forget his own nature and forgo his own nation?' (Spenser, 1934, pp. 62-3; Greenblatt, 1980, p. 184). The perceived consequence of the pollution by Irish culture was that the Old English had 'degenerated and grown almost mere [i.e. native] Irish, yea and more malicious to the English than the very Irish themselves' (Spenser, 1934, p. 62).

Spenser's argument in the *View* was that the Native Irish were fundamentally 'other'. Assimilation was impossible, for the Irish would pollute the New English as they had the Old English. But the Irish must be remade to labour for the New English since the flow of yeoman families from England was insufficient. Thus, for Spenser, coercion had to be yoked to incorporation to form an integrated set of urgent proposals for unmaking the Irish and refashioning them into a quiet and godly people. Spenser's knowledge of the Irish was secured by the principle of difference, itself founded upon maintaining the distance which separated the English from the Irish. As in *The Faerie Queene*, destruction of the 'other' would undermine the process of self-fashioning. Hence, like Acrasia, the Irish must have their cultural vitality maimed in order to remove the threat of cultural pollution, but they must remain as 'other' to continue to make possible the fashioning of 'Englishness' and to labour for the New English. These circumstances rendered impossible the potential for assimilation which existed in the pre-classical *episteme* and Spenser substituted for it the possibility of incorporating the Irish as second-order citizens; a strategy which maintained the positional superiority of the New English. Spenser's approach to this issue was not unusual; similar arguments can be found in other New English texts and particularly in the polemics and justifications of late sixteenth- and early seventeenth-century clergy of the Church of Ireland, which spoke of the polarization rather than the unity of humanity. As Alan Ford has suggested, in late sixteenth century Ireland, in 'rebutting Catholicism, the [Protestant] polemicists helped to create for members of their own church a new consciousness of their own beliefs and distinctiveness' (Ford, 1986, p. 64).

Protestant polemics may have given encouragement to members of the Church of Ireland, but the effects on their intended targets – Native Irish and Old English – were minimal. Forced to reflect upon the failure of proselytization and preaching, Protestant Church of Ireland divines put forward an explanation which derived from the Calvinist theology to which Spenser was personally sympathetic (Brady, 1986, p. 44 and n. 78) and which viewed humanity as separated into the saved and the damned, where salvation stemmed from hearing and attending to the Word of God: 'Only those whom God chose, the elect, could, through God's grace, which worked on their will and understanding, transcend their inherent sinfulness. Without this grace conversion was impossible' (p. 67). Faced with the refusal of the majority of Native Irish and Old English to conform to Anglicanism, some of their would-be evangelizers argued that this showed that there were 'few or none amongst them who were chosen by Christ' (p. 68). Thus Spenser's arguments about the barriers separating the Irish and English on the cultural plane were mirrored on the theological.

This separation of the elect and the fallen, the English and the non-English, derived in Spenser's works not only from his loathing for Irish culture but from his fear of the ease with which the English/elect might be defiled by this contamination as, in his opinion, had happened to the Old English. What is remarkable in the *View* is not the boundless confidence of the Elizabethans in an expansionist, imperial, future, but fear of impending collapse, and recognition of the fragility of the newly developing 'narrower definition of Englishness' once translated onto foreign soil, coupled with apocalyptic expectations that the final battle between the legions of the righteous and those of Anti-Christ was imminent. As Carol B. Ziener has pointed out, anxious Englishmen in the late sixteenth and early seventeenth century found in the Church of Rome 'the very epitome of the orderly nation they wanted so much to be' and while they 'could not deny that they would [ultimately] win, for this would be to deny either that God was on their side or that God was omnipotent – treason or heresy; they could, however, doubt that Rome would be willing to lose' (Ziener, 1971, pp. 51-2).

English doubts about the short-term outcome of the struggle between righteousness (English State Protestantism) and superstitious idolatry (Catholicism) were magnified amongst beleaguered New English Protestants in Ireland. As Ford and Lennon have shown, the response of the New English was to draw cultural and religious indicators together to efface in their own minds the differences separating Old English and Native Irish and to lump them together as 'other' (Ford, 1986, Lennon, 1986). The works of Spenser and his contemporaries display a shift from the pre-classical *episteme* to the classical *episteme*, with the result that, during the seventeenth and eighteenth centuries, the understanding of the Native Irish and the Old English held by the New English required the latter to treat the former as subjects fit only for domination – hence the comparatively insignificant attempts that were made at conversion to Protestantism. This understanding, and the *episteme* upon which it was based, necessarily meant that the assimilation of the Irish into a dominant English culture on terms of equality became unthinkable. Instead, the Irish were to be incorporated within the New English dominated colony as permanently subordinated inferiors. From the later sixteenth century, the cultural products which celebrated the supremacy of Englishness were based upon difference and discrimination and ensured that the positional superiority of the English was produced through the 'otherness' and inferiority of alien peoples of which the Irish were one (Greenblatt, 1980, Chapters 2 and 4).

The process of describing the colonized and inscribing them in discourse as second-order citizens in comparison with the colonizers commenced with the invocation of the judicial and military power of the State, but subsequently the colonizers attempted to convince the colonized themselves of their irremovable deficiencies and the consequent naturalness and permanence of their subordination. The wish of the colonizer that subjection should be willingly accepted rather than require constant recourse to coercion, can be seen in *Henry V*, the culmination of Shakespeare's second tetralogy, itself a dramatization of the process involved in the constitution of the unified nation, particularly as the process is expressed in the constitution of the unified and ordered subject who, to emphasize the power of the process, is the monarch himself. The transformation of Hal into Henry, particularly through the rejection of Falstaff, is a highly charged realization of the denial and repression of the 'other' attendant upon the constitution of the ordered subject and nation. What Shakespeare dramatizes is the originating moment of nationhood when the nation 'becomes conscious of itself, when it creates a model of itself. [This] model defines the unified, the artificially schematised image, that is raised to the level of a structural unity' (Lotman, 1978, p. 227).

Declan Kiberd has gone so far as to argue that: 'The notion "Ireland" is largely a fiction created by the rulers of England in response to specific needs at a precise moment in British history' (Kiberd, 1985, p. 83). What Kiberd identifies is the position of superiority from which the colonizer speaks, a position so entrenched that no aspect of the identity of the colonized can safely be assumed to be inherent. A number of recent analyses of the reciprocity between colonizer and colonized have concluded that colonial discourse establishes the colonized as the repressed and rejected 'other' against which the colonizer defines an ordered self and on to which all potentially disruptive psycho-sexual impulses are projected (Bhabha, 1983; 1984; Nandy, 1980; 1983). The colonized are thereby constrained to assert a dignified self-identity in opposition to a discourse which defines them as, variously, barbarian, pagan, ape, female; but always subordinate and inferior. Hence, 'positional superiority' puts the colonizer in a whole series of possible relationships with the colonized 'without ever losing him the relative upper hand' (Said, 1985b, p. 7).

'Culture', Uri Lotman has argued, 'requires unity'; a unity acquired by the introduction of order and the elimination of contradictions (Lotman, 1978, p. 227). It is incorrect, however, to speak of the elimination of contradictions. This may be an ideal, it may even be attempted, but the production of unity never arrives at a final point for, as Greenblatt has argued, it always needs a re-definition which only the presence of an excluded (rather than eliminated) 'other' can provide. This formulation may be clarified by reference to those of Shakespeare's History Plays which were themselves the final manifestation of a new form of English historical writing; a form distinguished by being 'intensely nationalistic' and 'deliberately propagandistic' (Ribner, 1979, p. 2).

Henry V dramatizes the might and the mercy of the English Nation State as it resolves the action as the victory at Agincourt is crowned by Henry's kissing the French Princess in the recognition that she is his 'sovereign queen'. The result of this betrothal, it is hoped, will be that the contending kingdoms should share an equal unity and 'Christian-like accord' (Act 5, Sc. ii). Philip Edwards has argued that the resolution of this imperial war is a piece of dramatic wish-fulfilment: that a contemporary cause of discord, namely Ireland, should come to an equally satisfactory conclusion (Philip Edwards, 1979, pp. 74-86). Shakespeare's patron, Southampton, had embarked in the Essex Expedition against Hugh O'Neill, Earl of Tyrone, in 1599 and *Henry V* would seem to have been written in the months of hope between that Expedition's setting out in the April, and its ignominious return in the autumn of that same year. The Chorus's prologue to Act V directly compares the triumph of Henry to the expected triumph of Essex, and in terms which coincide more closely with the realities of such campaigns than does Henry's dispensing of mercy. 'Rebellion', it is hoped, will be 'broachèd on his [Essex'] sword' (Act V, Prologue); an abstraction of rebellion and its suppression which is given an expression closer to the actuality of the Irish experience in the threat issued in the play to the citizens of Harfleur that their infants will be impaled on spikes. Behind the marriage which binds Henry to France, just as behind the mercy dispensed to Harfleur, there lies the reality of the sword. Unity of the Nation State will be achieved either by incorporation of the discordant elements or by their elimination.

While the play dramatizes an idealized resolution of Anglo-Irish discord in the unity of marriage, and threatens in dialogue the alternative of massacre, there is also a more direct engagement with the problems of 'internal colonialism' which, in their expression, suggest that they have already been resolved. The famous scene at the English camp when English, Welsh, Scots, and Irish Captains meet in an encounter whose main function is to dramatize their united presence in an army constantly referred to as English (Act 3, Sc. ii), reveals that just as in the marriage which unites England and France, so in the union which produces the English Nation State, there is a relationship which is 'structured in dominance'. What simultaneously unites and divides the Captains, or at least distinguishes between them, is the English language. Fluellen the Welshman substitutes 'p' for 'b' and utters 'look you' at intervals, Jamy the Scot has even more deviations from 'standard' linguistic expectations with his frequent use of 'gud' and mispronunciation of 'marry', while Macmorris the Irishman is the very embodiment of the 'stage Irishman'; pugnacious and argumentative, expressing all in repetitious 'mispronunciations': 'O, tish ill done, tish ill done! By my hand, tish ill done!' (Act 3 Sc. ii). These Celts are united in their service to the English Crown. Their use of the English language, however, reveals that 'service' is the operative word, for in rank, in dramatic importance, and in linguistic competence, they are comical second-order citizens. They are, moreover, disputatious, and the argument between Fluellen and Macmorris, which is resolved by Gower's admonition, is further dramatic evidence of the harmony which England has brought to the fractious occupants of the Celtic fringe. Shakespeare's dramatization of the harmonious incorporation of such disparate elements into the English State reaches its peak in Macmorris's famous question: 'What ish my nation?' (Act 3, Sc. ii). As Philip Edwards argues, Macmorris's outburst is a denial of such separate status, brought on by the sensed implication in the words of Fluellen, that while the Welsh may speak from within the united State, Macmorris is a member of a separate and therefore marginal group. 'What ish my nation?' is therefore a rhetorical question to which the answer is supplied by Macmorris's service in the English army. The achievement, on a mass scale, of Macmorris's incorporation would represent a triumphant conclusion to the process of unmaking advocated by Irenius/Spenser as a prerequisite for the fashioning of godly and biddable second-order citizens. The process of self-fashioning required the continued presence of an 'other' so that the maintenance of subtle points of differentiation from the colonizer would continue to reproduce, not only the subordination of the colonized, but the superordination of the colonizer.

The function of dramatizing the internal relations between the various peoples who together constituted the emergent 'English' Empire may readily be grasped. As Hayden White has argued: 'A given culture is only as strong as its power to convince its least dedicated members that its fictions are truths' (White, 1972, p. 6). White's use of the term 'fictions' in this context seems to be derived from that of Frank Kermode when he observed that 'Fictions can degenerate into myths whenever they are not consciously held to be fictive' (Kermode, 1966, p. 39). The distinction that Kermode draws between the two terms is that fictions are a means of finding things out and they are consequently open to change while myths 'are the agents of stability' (p. 39). The Shakespearean 'fiction' of *Henry V* is, then, the expression of a politically advantageous 'myth' and indeed is expressed in terms which are themselves subsequently utilized for overtly political purposes. James I of England whose accession to the throne came only four years after the composition of *Henry V*, also expressed the indissolubility of the nation in terms of a marriage: 'I am the husband, and the whole isle is my lawful wife' (Philip Edwards, 1979, p. 84). This merging of the marginal with the mighty is equated by James with the fate of the brook which flows into a river which, in turn, flows on into an ocean: 'so by the conjunction of divers little kingdoms in one are all these private differences and questions swallowed up' (p. 84).

Culture, then, requires the drive toward – if not the achievement of – unity. But the contradictions that are necessarily excluded as a means of its achievement are quite literally those elements which contra-dict, speak against and speak otherwise than the dominant group. While Henry can be seen to court the French Princess in her own tongue and she replies in English, the same degree of linguistic parity is not extended to the Celtic Captains, for their position in the contemporary world of Elizabethan England was potentially, and actually, far more disruptive than that of a nation whose separate status was now an acknowledged if not welcomed fact of political life. The Welsh, Scots and Irish must, therefore, be seen to speak English as evidence of their incorporation within the greater might of England, but they must speak it with enough deviations from the standard form to make their subordinate status in the union manifestly obvious. What cannot be acknowledged is their possession of an alternative language and culture, for to do so would be to stage the presence of the very contradictions which the play denies in its attempt to stage the ideal of a unified English Nation State. The resolution in the play is seen to be achieved by marriage rather than by massacre, by incorporation rather than by exclusion, but the inclusion of the Celts within the English State, of which the army is a paradigm, is as a result of an equally devastating act of cultural elision. The victims in the process of the march towards unity are those who contradict, and so implicitly question, the dominance of the incorporating power. Shakespeare's work engages with the process of colonial discourse at the moment of its mobilization to deal with Ireland, but the position of the colonized, namely Macmorris, is seen as one of proud inclusion. In this sense, the play, despite its references to the slaughter of Irish rebels, is an idealization of an actuality which stubbornly refused to conform. In the relationship of colonizer and colonized inclusion is available at the cost of de-culturation: distinctiveness is only possible at the risk of genocide.

The rôle of language, supported by the threat of physical power in colonial relations, finds even clearer expression in *The Tempest*, the Shakespearean play which, more than any other, has been read in the context of colonial discourse (Barker and Hulme, 1985; Brown, 1985; Griffiths, 1983). Language is indeed revealed to be the 'perfect instrumenyt of empire', as Antonio de Rebrija stated in 1492 (Barker and Hulme, 1985, p. 197); through his knowledge of Prospero's tongue Caliban is not only capable of being commanded to fetch in fuel, but also capable of comprehending the physical consequences of disobeying. The only resistance that Caliban can muster is to curse Prospero, but the very curse is itself a confirmation of his subjection: 'The red plague on you / For learning me your language!' (Act 1, Sc. ii). Imprisoned by language and power Caliban is the paradigm of the colonial subject in colonial discourse: a 'monster' who both threatens the virginity of Miranda and, through his abortive rebellion, the life of Prospero. The conclusion to be drawn from such a presentation is the necessity of Caliban's subjection to the (self) protective power of Prospero who must be constantly alert to the threat of treachery on the part of his slave.

Shakespeare's presentation of Caliban as possessing a consciousness chafing under the restraints and injustices of his position has a marked similarity to the view of Franz Fanon, one of the most influential of anti-colonial writers, who argued that the independent consciousness of the colonized maintained its discrete existence within the subjugated body: 'he is overpowered but not tamed; he is treated as an inferior but not convinced of his inferiority' (Fanon, 1965, p. 42). The position implicit in Fanon's formulation is that, just as the colonized are subjected by force, so will a superior force lead to liberation. While the reality of force in colonial relations can never be denied, the problem in Fanon's analysis resides in his assertion that the colonized are not convinced of their inferiority: a reduction of the colonial enterprise to might alone and a failure to engage with the rôle of culture in forming consciousness.

Louis Althusser's classic formulation on the process of the constitution of the subject: 'all ideology hails or interpellates concrete individuals as concrete subjects' (Althusser, 1971, p. 173), is the development of a political thesis from Jacques Lacan's idea of the 'structure of misrecognition' which Althusser pinpoints as being 'of particular concern for all investigations into ideology' (Althusser, 1971 p. 219). The moment at which the infant gazes at itself in a mirror is, in Lacan's words, 'an identification ... namely, the transformation that takes place in the subject when he assumes an image' (Lacan, 1977, p. 2). Althusser recognized that the failing of classic Marxism, such as that adapted to the colonial situation by Fanon, was that it reduced the power of the State to that of its repressive force alone. The reality, he argued, was that power could not be maintained without control over what he termed 'Ideological State Apparatuses': those social institutions which embrace the domains of religion, culture, education, familial relations, etc., and are distinguished from 'Repressive State Apparatuses' in that they 'function "by ideology" ' (Althusser, 1971, p. 145). Just as there is a need for the productive skills of (capitalist) society to be maintained, so, argues Althusser, is there a need for the working class to be confirmed in the 'naturalness' of its subordinate status. In other words there must be a reproduction of the subordinate class's submission to the rules of the established order. The 'misrecognition' which then occurs is consequent upon the subordinate class's (or people's) acceptance and adoption of the image proferred by the dominant group.

The issue, then, is consciousness, and Althusser is explicit in his view that what is at stake is 'the production of a new consciousness in the spectator [subject]' (Althusser, 1979, p. 151). Elements of such an analysis had already been sketched out by the Italian Marxist Antonio Gramsci, who in 1916 had outlined the principle on which much subsequent theory was to rest: that far from being the object which responded to changes in the means of production, 'Man is above all else mind, consciousness' (Boggs, 1976, p. 59). 'Nothing that exists is natural', argued Gramsci, 'but rather exists because of certain conditions' (Gramsci, 1971, p. 158). If consciousness of the created nature of conditions is lacking there will be no change, for the existence of the *possibility* of freedom is not of itself sufficient for its actual achievement, a prior requirement for which is that the possibility is recognized for what it is. Not only must the moment be recognized, there must also be the ability to use the moment correctly and the desire to want to use it. Gramsci argued that it is essential for the liberation of any class (or people) that they create a 'counter-hegemony' to combat the hegemony, or ideological control, of the dominant class (or colonizer). This critical function is to be carried out by the individuals who Gramsci labels the intellectuals, and it is in these twin concepts of 'counter-hegemony' and 'the intellectual' that Gramsci's centrality to the study of colonial discourse is to be found.

Gramsci identified the moments at which the possibility of liberation occurred as being produced when the rulers have failed in some major political undertaking for which they have enlisted the consent of the people – such as a war – or when the people 'have passed suddenly from a state of political passivity to a certain activity, and put forward demands which taken together ... add up to a revolution' (Gramsci, 1971, p. 210). The situation of Ireland in the early nineteenth century constituted just such a 'crisis of authority' but, as Gramsci argued, although these moments of crisis may see the rulers dependent on unmasked coercive force, that does not necessarily mean that 'the people' are capable of defining and advancing their own interests. Such advances have to be prepared for by intense labour in the cultural domain so as to create a new consciousness (the counter-hegemony) on which can be based choices and actions which will be effective in the particular situation. Here, the rôle of the intellectuals is crucial, for while there may be an emergent consciousness in 'the people' they will only become capable of producing a counter-hegemony if aided by the intellectuals, who must, even if not born into the people, be united with them in an 'organic' relationship: 'One cannot make politics-history without this passion, without this sentimental connection between intellectuals and people-nation' (p. 418).

While the hegemony of the dominant group may be fragmenting, and opposition to its power manifesting itself in the writings of intellectuals claiming an organic relationship with the people, that counter-hegemony may be either 'transformist' or 'expansive'. Expansive hegemony is essentially that generated by the 'sentimental connection' between intellectuals and people-nation which Gramsci posited as the essential first step towards freedom. While one group will dominate and seek to maximize its own expansion, 'the development and expansion of the particular group are conceived of, and presented, as being the motor forces of a universal expansion' (p. 182). Transformist hegemony, in contrast, is conceived of in essentially negative terms; it does not advance the broad interests of the whole class-alliance functioning, instead, by incorporating subordinate groups (or significant individuals from those groups) into the ranks of the leading group with the effect of neutralizing potential challengers to the leading group by depriving them of their intellectuals. Expansive hegemony, however, creates a national-popular will through the genuine adoption of the interests of the people. In analyzing the hegemonies and counter-hegemonies which developed in nineteenth- and early twentieth-century Ireland two key formulations, developed by Edward Said, are the 'strategic location' of intellectuals, defined as 'the author's position in a text with regard to the ... material he writes about' and 'strategic formation', defined as: 'a way of analyzing the relationship between texts and the way in which groups of texts, types of texts, even textual genres, acquire mass, density, and referential power among themselves and thereafter the culture at large' (Said, 1985b, p. 20).

The concept of hegemony, Gramsci's term for the pervasive force by which a class (or people) are convinced of the naturalness of their situation, the rôle of the 'organic' intellectuals in revealing their 'misrecognition' of their situation and aiding them in the formulation and articulation of their own counter-hegemony, along with the centrality of consciousness in the process, coalesce in the concept of culture; the very site of the struggle for hegemony. As Gramsci recognized, it was essential for any collective action that 'a single cultural "climate" ' (Gramsci, 1971, p. 349) be achieved, for it was only through that "cultural-social" unity' (p. 349) that 'dispersed wills, with heterogeneous aims [would be] welded together with a single aim, on the basis of an equal and common conception of the world' (p. 349). It is for the intellectuals to work towards the crystallization of this 'cultural-social unity', for 'Critical self-consciousness means, historically and politically, the creation of an élite of intellectuals' (p. 241). The precise nature of the unity to be created is especially pertinent as it is what Gramsci terms 'national-popular', and it is this expression of the 'people-nation', normally found as nationalism or patriotism, which must be achieved by a hegemonic class; it must "nationalise" itself in a certain sense' (p. 241). The struggle for hegemony is then the issue in a people's bid for self-determination: 'A social group can, and indeed must, already exercise "leadership" [i.e. be hegemonic] before winning governmental power (this indeed is one of the principal conditions for the winning of such power)' (p. 57).

If culture is the site on which the struggle for hegemony takes place, then discourses are the primary cultural means through which individuals become *subjects*. Discourses, each governed by its own rules, which give both coherence and effectiveness, supply the forms and thematic materials through which individuals are 'hailed' or 'interpellated' into a particular social or political position, but this is not a once-for-all occurrence (Althusser, 1971, pp. 170-7). The struggle to interpellate individuals into particular groups, and thereby into accepting a particular outlook upon life, society, history, goes on unceasingly. Individuals may be de-interpellated from one group and re-interpellated into another, and the means through which this constitution of the subject takes place is through discourse. The whole of the struggle for hegemony is founded upon the struggles of contending groups to interpellate individuals into a particular form of subjectivity, thence into a given group, and subsequently to maintain and develop that interpellation. But discourses are not available solely to the subjects of one particular group, discourses are uniformly available to all subjects who have acquired the skills necessary to perceive them. Those individuals who articulate the rules of a discourse are initially empowered by them, but because such rules, like the discourses they sustain, are uniformly available, the capacity to interpret them is also uniformly available. This may result in the situation of the framers of the rules being trapped and overcome by the operation of the same rules from the operation of which they had earlier benefited. Hence Michel Foucault's insistence that 'discourse is the power which is to be seized' (Foucault, 1981, p. 53), and it is Foucault's dictum and subsequent question which is of particular relevance: 'How does the struggle for the taking over of the discourse take place between classes, nations, linguistic, cultural or ethnic collectivities?' (Foucault, 1978, p. 15).

The essential force and relevance of Foucault derive from his assertion that discourses are 'practises that systematically form the objects of which they speak' (Foucault, 1972, p. 49). Our point of reference, he asserts, should not be language and signs but war and battle: 'the history which bears and determines us has the form of a war rather than that of a language: relations of power, not relations of meaning' (Foucault, 1980, p. 97). Thus, as in the case of Elizabethan England, discourses function at specific historical moments in response to urgent needs; they have a 'dominant strategic function' (p. 195). The example Foucault gives in support of his contention refers to his own study, *Madness and Civilization*, but the relevance to the colonial situation is readily apparent: 'This [need] may have been, for example, the assimilation of a floating population found to be burdensome for an essentially mercantilist economy: there was a strategic imperative acting here as the matrix for an apparatus which gradually undertook the control or subjection of madness, mental illness and neurosis' (Foucault, 1980, p. 5). Discourses, then, constitute groups, or peoples, as those acted upon, defined, and frequently rejected by the articulators of the dominant discourse. Foucault sees this as the defining characteristic of discourse and the task he proposes is 'to discover how it is that subjects are gradually, progressively, really and materially constituted ... We should try to grasp subjection in its material instance as a constitution of subjects' (p. 97).

Current understandings of Native Irish society in the sixteenth and early seventeenth centuries view it as politically fragmented and responses to the aggressive colonizing of the New English as particularistic (O'Dowd, 1985; Cunningham 1985; Canny 1982). Hence, at any time up until the mid-seventeenth century. Native Irish responses to the New English advance were neither geographically or socially uniform: in the late sixteenth century the Native Irish élite of Munster was partially accommodatory to New English advances, while in Ulster and near to Dublin, extremely hostile. Furthermore, there is evidence of a socially differentiated response to the New English and to cultural attempts at incorporating the Native Irish, so that at the lower levels of Native Irish society those who earned wealth, rather than exacted it, adopted some at least of the ways of the English – and with sufficient willingness to cause the native élite considerable unease as they observed the cultural and material ground on which their traditional leadership rested being undercut (Ó Tuama and Kinsella, 1981, p. xxvii, p. 117).

Recently, insights into cultural formation in early modern Ireland have come from the bardic poetry of the period, which has been read 'against the grain' to supply an understanding of the forces at play in a time of rapid internally and externally generated economic and social change (Dunne, 1980). In the process, historians have suggested that although levels of artistic achievement may have been qualitatively high in certain pieces, overall the texts and poems of the later sixteenth and early seventeenth centuries display only occasional evidence that the bards and poets, the foremost intellectuals in Native Irish society, appreciated the magnitude of the changes that were occurring within their social world. Rather than resisting such changes the intellectuals in Native Irish society attempted to locate the New English and their activities within traditional frameworks for handling the incursions of aliens, in particular the framework supplied by the *Leabhar Gabhála*, the *Book of Invasions*, which from the twelfth century had 'provided a convenient explanation and a comfortable *modus vivendi* for the distinct ethnic groups which ... made up Irish society at that time.... The popularity of the *Leabhar Gabhála* in the early seventeenth century, as indicated by the new editions prepared and transcripts made, suggests that such an approach still had appeal, and that the political connotations of the *Leabhar Gabhála* had lost little of their original significance' (Cunningham, 1986, p. 156). The *Leabhar Gabhála*, however, was both a shield and a sword; while on one hand it demonstrated that invaders were invariably absorbed into Native Irish ways, to skilled New English controversialists, such as Sir John Davies, it provided 'proof' that in Irish law, custom and culture, rights of conquest were overriding. Davies went as far as to assert that the history of invasions demonstrated that the contemporary 'problem' of Ireland derived from the lack of thoroughness with which previous invasions had been pursued (Canny, 1982, p. 106).

Some writers in Gaelic were aware of the deficiencies of the cultural-political positions inherent in the *Leabhar Gabhála*, as Geoffrey Keating's careful attempts to refute Davies, Spenser, Cambrensis and others show. But that this awareness should be demonstrated by Keating, an Old English priest, rather than by a member of the Gaelic intelligentsia, suggests that at this point intellectual leadership was passing from the bards and poets to the Counter-Reformation Catholic clergy. While writers such as Keating sought to rebut New English polemics, sixteenth- and seventeenth-century bards and poets met the advance of the New English with ineffectual vituperation or an indifference born of a belief in their ultimate absorption. Alternatively, some saw them as potential patrons, writing love poetry for the wife of a New English landlord as the mid seventeenth-century poet Piaras Feiritéar did (Canny, 1982, p. 106), or supporting the claims to nobility of arrivistes as did Fear Flatha Ó Gnímh for the MacDonnels of Antrim (Cunningham, 1986, p. 154). Among the Gaelic intelligentsia both indifference and accommodation had their adherents, as surviving poetry shows, but the extent to which the bards and poets had ceased to lead in Native Irish society is shown by their preoccupation with the long aesthetic competition known as *The Contention of the Poets* (Canny, 1982, p. 99 and n. 31; Cunningham, 1986, p. 164) which absorbed the attention of many of them at precisely the moment that New English attacks on them were at their fiercest for, as Liam De Paor has argued, the 'shrewder Elizabethan and Jacobean officials had singled out this class [the bards and poets] for attack, seeing in it a most important moral resource for the society they were trying to subdue' (De Paor, 1986, p. 171).

The deficiencies of Gaelic intellectuals at this crucial moment goes some way towards explaining how and why Catholic clergy, from both Native Irish and Old English backgrounds, came to cultural-political prominence at this time. There were other factors at play, however. The endurance of Catholicism in Ireland from the sixteenth century can partly be attributed to the failures in approach and inconstancies of purpose manifested by Protestant proselytizers but, in addition, while

European Catholic observers considered the Irish Catholic Church a ramshackle affair its adherents found much in it which they could support and its clergy, on the whole, remained loyal to Rome. In England, by contrast, there were always sufficient clergy prepared to go along with the State's giddy reversals of religious policy to make available the personnel to staff the ecclesiastical administration. In particular, after 1558, this allowed the State the opportunity, while the existing clergy held the breach, to arrange for the education and training of more committed and more theologically and academically able successors. Even in England, the process of turning towards Protestantism and against Rome required the vigilance and energy of the State for nearly forty years. In Ireland, however, under looser executive supervision, many of the existing clergy found it possible to make minor concessions to the State's requirements and to maintain for those they served a substantial measure of continuity in ritual and dogma. More importantly, the clergy who refused to conform were only intermittently harassed and in some areas were openly tolerated with the support of the local élite, so that they were able to continue to educate the sons and daughters of many prominent Irish and Old English families as Catholics. Denied higher education in England (or, after 1592, Trinity College, Dublin) because of the exclusion of recusants from Oxford and Cambridge, the sons of these families (mostly Old English) became the students of the continental seminaries, particularly Alcala, Louvain, Douai, and Salamanca, which were to send them back to Ireland to buttress Catholicism towards the end of the century. During the 1560s, family by family, those prominent amongst the Old English took the decisions about the education of their children which decided their future. In opting for Catholicism, many of these families chose to accept a division between themselves and the New English which affirmed their own existence as a community and, more speculatively, in their own eyes perhaps, confirmed in an important respect a further way in which the New English were newcomers. These individual family decisions were, however, of import for the wider community of the Old English 'because of their long-felt need to ensure survival as a colonial élite in hostile surroundings the members of the privileged order [i.e. the upper ranks of the Old English] were extremely closely bonded', ties cemented by close intermarriage (Lennon, 1986, p. 84). In this way the pressures attributable to New English arrivals caused the Old English to adhere more firmly to old ways and to seek support for their position not from the Crown – to which they had historically turned for succour – but from the continental powers of the Counter-Reformation.

By the end of the sixteenth century the educational decisions of the 1560s were bearing fruit in the shape of highly trained intellectuals, Catholic clerics, prepared for the tasks of refuting error and comforting the faithful. These individuals were drawn from both the Native Irish and Old English communities and, in writing religious materials for the support of their faith in Ireland, many took the decision to write in Irish in order to reach the widest possible audience. Systematic production of religious materials calculated to appeal to all levels of intellect, from popular poetry and scurrilous gossip about Luther's relations with nuns, to high-minded theology and learned philosophical and historical treatises, shows that the Counter-Reformation clergy, both while in Ireland and when writing from abroad, proceeded on a broad front, providing materials to promote a common 'popular-religion' to 'guide the people and keep it linked with the leading group' (Gramsci, 1971, p. 421). The form of the discourses produced by these Counter-Reformation Old English and Native Irish intellectuals is revealing, for their determination to advance their case took the form of refuting English and New English characterizations of the Native Irish as bestial and savage. Their discourses were, therefore, essentially negative and defensive – and hence Irish identity came to be founded upon the denial of English assertions, as may be seen in the attention that contemporary writers such as Keating paid to refuting Giraldus. This defensiveness manifested itself with increasing frequency during the seventeenth century as the situation of the Native Irish and Old English (or New Irish as they are termed by the mid-seventeenth century in documents of the Confederation of Kilkenny) came to be regarded as capable of redress only with external intervention – either temporal or supernatural – producing a deep pessimism which, drawing upon traditional modes in Irish literary expression, came to see the tribulations of the Irish as divine retribution for moral failings (Canny, 1982, p. 106; Kelly, 1985; Chatterjee, 1986).

By 1641, as the Old English and Native Irish began to coalesce under the pressure of New English and English attacks, the old Gaelic culture crumbled, displaced by the dynamic cultural force of Counter-Reformation Catholicism. At this point, the formation of a significant part of the social and cultural elements upon which the nineteenth and twentieth century struggles for identity in Ireland were to be based was completed. These formations, in which intellectual leadership was taken up by the Catholic clergy, were to be consolidated throughout the eighteenth century by the repression of the Catholic Irish by the Penal Laws. But as recourse to main force and the State's repressive apparatuses demonstrates, the colonizer had failed to persuade the colonized to accept their subordinate status willingly. In such circumstances, as Fanon noted, the colonized was 'overpowered but not tamed' and, aware of the potential of this threat to their Ascendancy, throughout the nineteenth century and after, a succession of Anglo-Irish intellectuals sought to produce forms of sentimental connection which would make it possible for the Ascendancy to assume the leadership of the people-nation – with their material and cultural dominance preserved. It is to the opening engagements in this long war of position that we now turn.

2

Pages like this our field

The major event of recent European history which was to have a profound effect on the politics of early nineteenth-century Ireland was the French Revolution, whose ideals of liberty, equality, fraternity had a particular resonance in a country in which the majority of the population were politically disenfranchised and economically disadvantaged. In the words of Wolfe Tone, a leading figure in the United Irishmen's rising of 1798, the objective of the movement was: 'To unite the whole people of Ireland, to abolish the memory of all past dissensions, and to substitute the common name of Irishman in place of the denominations of Protestant, Catholic and Dissenter' (Deane, 1986, p. 60). The defeat of the United Irishmen did not mean the end of their ideals and Dr William Drennan, coiner of the principles of the United Irishmen, was a founder in 1810 of the Belfast Academical Institution, among whose aims was demonstrably the continuation of revolution by other, educational, means as articulated in Drennan's wish that: 'a new turn might be given to the national character and habits, and all the children of Ireland should know and love each other' (O'Driscoll, 1976, p. 16).

Such a radical importation, though defeated militarily, alarmed those whose sense of political and cultural stability was most directly threatened, particularly as the succeeding years brought what the political establishment could only see as an accumulation of menaces: the dissolution of Grattan's Parliament; Catholic Emancipation (1829); the 1832 Reform Bill; the Repeal movement; and the increasing sense that the British Government was prepared to withdraw the support which was fundamental to the survival of the Irish aristocracy. It is within this tense time that the cultural polemic of Thomas Davis and Sir Samuel Ferguson has central significance as they both responded to, and created, the demands of an emergent nationalism; a force which, for both men, could neither be conceived of, nor advanced, separately from a concept of culture. The urge towards an assertion of a denied national identity occurred across Europe in the years following the French

Revolution – and in particular through an engagement with an indigenous folk culture. What is most striking, however, in the case of both Davis and Ferguson, is the extent to which the strategic location of each is declared by the fact that they were speaking from, and to, the very class whose advantaged position was now threatened. It is the reality of their relationship to the Anglo-Irish which must be remembered, but in order to understand more fully what the upheavals catalogued above meant for that class it must be given a clearer outline.

As Anthony Malcolmson observes: 'The Anglo-Irish Ascendancy was ... a narrow social and political élite ... In religion they were not only Protestant but Anglican, in distinction to Protestant Dissenting families of Scottish origin ... the humbler English settlers in Ireland belonging ethnically but not socially to the Anglo-Irish Ascendancy ... The Anglo-Irish Ascendancy could be defined as comprising those who themselves sat in the Irish Parliament or who exercised significant influence over the return of the 300 members of the House of Commons' (Malcolmson, 1978, pp. xvii-xix). This point is confirmed by L.P. Curtis Jnr., who concludes that the Anglo-Irish Ascendancy comprised between 2,000 and 3,000 families (Curtis, 1970, p. 37). The Ascendancy-dominated Parliament of the 1690s had passed a series of penal statutes against the Catholics, laws which, even if they were not always rigorously enforced, still hampered the practice of Catholicism in the late eighteenth century and placed substantial disabilities in the way of Catholic landowning (Connolly, 1982, pp. 6-12). Vis-à-vis the Protestant dissenters – of whom the Presbyterians were the most numerous – no such formal bans were applied and there was a small number of dissenting M.P.s, but the influence of the dissenters was limited by the fact that few were large landowners in a society where wealth derived almost entirely from land, from agriculture, or from servicing agriculture's needs, and in which political power was a function of that wealth.

Marilyn Butler's study of Maria Edgeworth defines the rôle which resident landlords were expected to play in rural Ireland as approximating in many respects to that of their English counterparts (Butler, 1972, p. 78 ff.). They were expected to dispense patronage and justice, to arbitrate in local disputes and to perform their functions as the leading figures in an unwritten but acknowledged 'moral economy'. Butler's account of the reception accorded to the liberal Richard Lovell Edgeworth's unlooked-for impartiality in the administration of law, in which we can see correspondances with E.P. Thompson's observations on Whig hegemony in contemporary England, suggests that the Anglo-Irish

Ascendancy used their access to the power of the law, in their capacity as Justices of the Peace, to bind together a hierarchical alliance of Protestants, separated by sect, but united by the willingness of the Ascendancy to connive with them in resisting Catholic redress of grievances (Thompson, 1985, p. 262; Butler, 1972, p. 116 and p. 137 ff.). This ability of the Anglo-Irish Ascendancy to bind together Protestants of all denominations in an alliance cemented by anti-Popery, also depended on a continuing and well-documented fear on the part of Protestants that Catholics waited, unblinkingly, for an opportunity to re-enter into despoiled properties (Elliott, 1978, p. 408, 411; Beames, 1975; Donnelly, 1978).

The failure of the United Irishmen movement at the end of the eighteenth century, and with it its projects for the proclamation of a Republic based on non-sectarian political (but not social) egalitarianism (Elliott, 1982), was due to government counter-measures, misfortune, and their own administrative incompetence. Their hope for a non-sectarian alliance of all the Irish would not only have dissolved the Ascendancy of the Anglo-Irish but would also have removed the basis upon which Protestants outside the Ascendancy understood their positions to rest. The vigour with which the combination of the United Irishmen and Defenderism was put down by Protestant Militias throughout Ireland, indicates that in the 1790s the majority of Protestants saw their position as insecure, guaranteed only by repression of the Catholics; a tradition which was to be reproduced by the institutionalization of Protestant sectarianism in the Orange Order. The order became a vital, popular organization which spread throughout Ireland and England in the 1800s, serving until 1829 as a significant political and cultural bridge between plebeian Anglicans and their social superiors (Hill, 1984).

After the Union, popular Protestant cultural responses in Dublin to the perceived threat of Catholic Emancipation took the form of a revived enthusiasm for the cult of King William III. In the eighteenth century, the King's birthday and the anniversaries of the victories at the Boyne and Aughrim had been occasions for celebrating the rights of individual (Protestant) liberty. In the early nineteenth century the cult, centred on his statue in College Green, turned more on King William's achievements as the vanquisher of Popery (Hill, 1984, p. 36). Higher up the social scale, members of the Corporation and the gentry formed organizations to demonstrate their resistance to the process initiated by Emancipation and the Reform Bill. In the contemporary journal *Saurin's*

Newsletter Protestant Ascendancy was now defined as the 'just dominion of light over darkness, of truth over error, the ascendancy of liberty and reason over despotism and arbitrary power, the supremacy of the religion, the arts, the civilization, of protestant Britain over the fanaticism, the ignorance, and barbarism of Rome' (McDowell, 1952, pp. 110-11). Tories put their faith in the Union and emphasized that the 'true principles of the protestant ascendancy are allegiance to the British king, obedience to the British government, the preservation of the British connexion, the maintenance of the laws and constitution of Great Britain in church and state' (p. 110).

The explicit identification with Irish culture which occurs in the writings of Ascendancy intellectuals during this period raises the issue of the responses possible for members of a colonial élite who, for ideological reasons, reject the position of superiority vis-à-vis the colonized into which they have been born. Albert Memmi's concept of 'the colonizer who refuses' (Memmi, 1974, p. 39) is qualified by his observation that conscious rejection does not ensure the erasure of unconscious attitudes and assumptions which frequently surface and reveal the 'refuser' to share many of the fundamental assumptions of the class which has been nominally rejected. Memmi's concept highlights both the possibility of the desire to disassociate oneself from the class of one's birth and the almost insurmountable problems involved in so doing. As Conor Cruise O'Brien defines the 'Irish race', it is made up of those who are of native Irish stock, Catholic, and who hold some of the general political opinions of people of that origin and religion, and also those of settler stock and Protestant religion 'to the extent that these cast in their lot with people in the first category, culturally, or politically, or preferably both' (O'Brien, 1972, p. 51). Such an act of cultural and political deracination is posited as a necessity if entry into the nation of the 'other' is to be achieved. Memmi suggests the fundamental imposssiblity of success, but one must be alert to the possibility that the moves of the colonizers towards the politics and culture of the colonized are motivated by the desire to achieve influence through an act of association and appropriation rather than identification and (self)absorption. The fundamental questions which define the intellectuals' strategic location are: have these intellectuals joined in sympathy with the people-nation; is their attempt to create a new cultural hegemony expansive or transformist?

Writing to a friend in 1858 Sir Samuel Ferguson declared 'I am an Irishman and a Protestant', but then, more problematically, went on: 'I was an Irishman before I was a Protestant' (O'Driscoll, 1976, p. 15). What these terms could actually mean in the conflictual moment of the early nineteenth century is fundamental to an understanding of not only Ferguson and Davis, but also Yeats and his fellow Revivalists. As Malcolm Brown asserted so succinctly, it is to Ferguson that one must go so as 'to penetrate the confusing mists that envelope Yeats's "Irishness" ' (Brown, 1973, p. 16.).

Lady Ferguson stated that 'Ferguson was not at any period of his life a "party"-man. As an intelligent student of history, past and present, he held definite views as to the policy, foreign and domestic of the empire .... The foremost place in his love belonged, however, to Ireland' (Lady Ferguson, 1896a, p. 237). Despite such disclaimers of sectional interest – which can, moreover, be found in Ferguson himself – an examination of *Blackwood's Edinburgh Magazine* and the *Dublin University Magazine* in which virtually all his early work appeared leads to the inevitable conclusion, as Lady Ferguson unwittingly reveals in her acknowledgement that her husband loved both the Empire and Ireland, that Ferguson was far from being detached from the factional politics of his day.

Ferguson's first poems to be published in *Blackwood's* appeared over the months February 1832 to December 1833, and the edition of January 1833 printed a poem by Ferguson, and an unattributed article entitled 'Ireland No.I', whose complementarity to one another forcibly suggests that Ferguson was both a poet and also a Protestant propagandist. The authors of articles in *Blackwood's*, and the *Dublin University Magazine*, were concerned with the crisis created by Emancipation and Reform which spelled, they believed, the demise of Empire, Church, and the class founded upon them. Articles with titles such as 'The Present Crisis' from the first edition of the *Dublin University Magazine* in January 1833, or 'The Coming Crisis' from an edition in July of that year, rehearse the idea that Protestantism is threatened and, if overthrown, will lead to the State being 'Buried in the quicksands of rebellion, anarchy, and irreligion' (Anon., 1833b, p. 247). The *Blackwood's* article, 'Ireland, No.I', makes explicit the dependency between English Conservatives and Irish Protestants upon which the future well-being of England and Empire was founded. Ireland, however, was 'prey to its own furious and ungovernable passions; ruled by an ignorant and ambitious priesthood; seduced by frantic and unprincipled demagogues' (Anon., 1833a, p. 67). Consequently, stern measures had to be employed for, as the article argued vociferously, it is only because of England's lenient government of its colony that the 'leprosy' of unrest had fermented to the point that the whole Empire was threatened.

Fundamental to the argument is a view of the Irish identical to that found in Spenser: the Irish are 'semibarbarous and impassioned', 'they have passions whose excitation they could not withstand'. Prior to the commencement of a developed English colonization at the end of the sixteenth century the whole land was 'savage and unknown' and most of the Irish 'are still almost in a savage state'. What is clearly required to cope with this race whose ingratitude is demonstrated by their rebelliousness is some action to 'vindicate the authority of the law against an insurgent people' (p. 78). Ferguson's poem 'An Irish Garland' which appears as a post-script to the article is overt in its expression of the forces ranged against one another in contemporary Ireland. On the one hand there are the Gentlemen 'Whose honour'd flag in ninety-eight / Put foul rebellion down' and ranged against them the Jackasses 'Whose ears, though cropp'd in ninety-eight / Now flout our skies again' (Ferguson 1833a, p. 87). As the use of 'our' makes plain, Ferguson's strategic location is on the side of the Gentlemen and opposed to the Jackasses whose association with France, irrationality, and violence, makes clear that they are the poetic equivalent of the 'demagogues' from whose tyranny, as the article argues, the people must be delivered 'in spite of themselves' (Anon. 1833a, p. 81). The task of demonstrating who is to be the people's saviour is Ferguson's concern throughout his own *Dublin University Magazine* articles which have been described as 'a unique and invaluable clarification of the Irish ideological atmosphere' (Brown, 1972, p. 15).

The fundamental issue which Ferguson addresses in 'A Dialogue Between The Head and Heart of An Irish Protestant' is the consequence of the leniency of the Whig government towards the Catholics, 'for if Catholic emancipation produce repeal, so surely will repeal produce ultimate separation; and so sure as we have separation, so surely will there be war levied, estates confiscated, and the Popish church established' (Ferguson, 1833b, p. 588). What exercises Ferguson is the position of the Anglo-Irish who are described as 'the acknowledged possessors of nine-tenths of the property', yet are now deserted by the Tories and hated by the Papists: 'plundered in our country-seats, robbed in our town houses' (p. 591). With such a developed sense of marginalization and potential exclusion Ferguson's objective is to argue a place for the Anglo-Irish based on their claims to Irish nationality, for he recognizes that 'our opponents have, in their Irish blood, a stronger claim to credit for disinterested nationality than we who are, generally speaking, comparatively "strangers" ' (p. 589). This perception, put forward by the Heart, is vigorously disputed by the Head in terms which are fundamental to Ferguson's argument; as the English nation has been built on successive waves of invaders so too it must be with Ireland: 'They were all Irishman in turn, and WE are Irishman now' (p. 589).

Central to Ferguson's case is the fact that his emotional response to Ireland is so strong that the fact of love is guarantee of the Irishness of the most recent wave of invaders, the Anglo-Irish who, as he argues in an article of 1836, are the natural culmination of a progression towards perfection: 'Race after race has now beeen transplanted into our social garden, and all now is ready for the final engraftment' (Ferguson, 1836, p. 658). The images of careful husbandry are crucial to Ferguson's strategy and, when he is obliged to acknowledge the near-genocidal dimension of colonialism he despatches its brutalities to the mists of time while still making no excuses for what he presents as a recognized necessity: 'Extermination, in process of time, came to be no longer the necessary concomitant of civilisation' (p. 658). The problem is that the Catholicism of the Irish stands as a barrier to recognition of the essential unity which love of country should bring in its wake, and it is to the correction of this religious division which Ferguson directs himself. Only if the 'deluded' people could be freed from 'the Irish priesthood [who] hold the hearts of their seduced victims in even firmer bondage than their minds' (Ferguson, 1833b, p. 590), could a nation be created.

The Ireland which Ferguson envisages is a Protestant nation which will include the Native Irish, whom he is prepared to persecute to save them from the error of Catholicism and enable them to join with the Anglo-Irish 'as free, loyal, and united Protestants' (Ferguson, 1833b, p. 593). Ferguson's love for his 'Popish countrymen' is given 'in spite of themselves', for they have to be weaned away from superstition and idolatory and prepared for the nationhood that they are temperamentally incapable of creating on their own. Ferguson reiterates the concept of the Irish as savage and primitive, characteristics which have kept them in a state of 'tyranny and blind savage levity' (p. 592), and from which they are only to be liberated by the Ascendancy which is seen as the only class capable of conceiving and creating a nation. The struggle is to convince the people of this truth and, as Ferguson prophetically observes: 'We must fight our battle now with a handful of types and a composing-stick, pages like this our field, and the reading public our arbiter of war' (p. 592).

The most complete example of the overt relationship between culture and politics in this period is Ferguson's four-part review of James Hardiman's *Irish Minstrelsy; or, Bardic Remains of Ireland*, a collection of poetic translations from Irish into English which had been published, with notes on the poems, in 1831. The review, published in the April, August, October, and November of 1834, stands as one of the clearest, and earliest, examples of what the late nineteenth-century polemicist D.P. Moran termed the 'Battle of Two Civilizations' (Moran, 1905, Chapter 6). The opening lines of the review establish the combative tone: 'Oh, ye fair hills of holy Ireland, who dares sustain the strangled calumny that you are not the land of our love? ... Who is he who ventures to stand between us and your Catholic sons' good-will?' (Ferguson, 1834a, p. 456). As in the 'Dialogue' the proof of Irishness is the sense of emotional attachment which he, as a Protestant, feels for the land itself, a love which is perfectly prepared to embrace all who share that response but which can equally express itself as hostility towards those who dare suggest that the Catholics and the Protestants, the Milesian and the Anglo-Irish, have incompatible claims, in which those of the former must always have precedence. In general terms Ferguson is continuing the excoriation of the 'demagogues' such as O'Connell vilified by *Blackwood's* and the *Dublin University Magazine*, but the particular target is Hardiman himself; in part for what Ferguson describes as the 'spurious, puerile, unclassical – lamentably bad' quality of the translations, but far more because of what Ferguson perceives to be the political implications of this poetry which, as annotated by Hardiman, is only expressive of, and available to, the Irish descended from indigenous Gaelic stock (Ferguson, 1834c, p. 453).

If Hardiman's literary excavations sowed dissension then Ferguson sought to create unity. Consistently, throughout the 1830s and 1840s, Ferguson fervently embraced all enterprises which might create a sense of nation which avoided the dissension and divisions of recent centuries by locating the locus of national consciousness in a distant past which could provide a still point at which contemporary differences could be resolved: 'a green point of neutral ground, where all parties may meet in kindness and part in peace' (p. 467). A clarification of this 'neutral ground' is found in his response to the government-funded Ordnance Survey of Ireland: 'may we not take it as an auspicious omen of the happiness and peace yet in store for us, and which must follow as an inevitable result of the continuance of a unity thus happily begun?' (Lady Ferguson, 1896a, p. 66). Ferguson's stress on the antiquarian research carried out as part of the Ordnance Survey was linked to his sense that knowledge of the land and ancient history of Ireland 'will enable us to know one another and the land we live in, and every spot of it; that such knowledge may beget mutual confidence and united labour'

(Ferguson, 1848, p. 361). Such expressions have been taken as evidence of Ferguson's ecumenical spirit, but those to whom the appeal for unity is directed are 'the Protestant wealth and intelligence of the country' (Ferguson 1834a, p. 457). As F.S.L. Lyons so delicately phrased it: '[the] concern with the ancient civilization of Ireland was perfectly genuine, though it was not wholly disinterested' (Lyons, 1979, p. 28).

In an explicit declaration of his cultural strategy Ferguson alerted his readers to the fact that 'their wealth has hitherto been insecure, because their intelligence has not embraced a thorough knowledge of the genius and disposition of their Catholic fellow-citizens' (Ferguson, 1834a, p. 457). What was being advocated was little less than an act of cultural appropriation: an attempt to structure discussion and interpretation of the cultural products of Ireland's past – as revealed by the work of the eighteenth-century antiquarians of the Royal Irish Academy and supplemented in the nineteenth century by the work of the Ordnance Survey – to ensure that this emerging strategic formation of texts could be mobilized to the advantage of the Ascendancy. Ferguson's project was a union of the Anglo-Irish and the Irish people which was always conceived of in terms of the advantages which would accrue to the former, for it would be naïve to argue that Ferguson conceived of a partnership of equals: unless the Irish abandoned that which sustained their sense of a separate identity – Catholicism – for all that was required to found a unified nation was 'scriptural education' (Ferguson, 1834c, p. 448). Throughout these writings of the 1830s and 1840s one finds echoes of the discourse of colonial difference, of the colonized as a less evolved form of humanity. 'On the one side', he wrote in 1836, you can lay your hand on 'barbarism, on the other on the perfection of civilization' (Ferguson, 1836, p. 658). The side of civilization, occupied by the Anglo-Irish, was the only hope that Ireland had of seeing 'the sour berry of savage life ... mellow into the sweet fruits of art and industry' (p. 658), for they, as Ferguson perceived them, were leaders in every sphere of scientific and literary activity, indeed 'there was never a time when that all-important body were so deeply, so devotedly engaged' (p. 675).

Identification with Ireland's past and present through assertion of an emotional attachment to the land acquired through right of conquest, together with sequestration of the national culture was therefore essential to Ferguson's objectives, but Hardiman – 'politically malignant and religiously fanatical' (Ferguson, 1834b, p. 153), motivated by 'the spirit of petty anti-Anglicism' (Ferguson, 1834d, p. 515), had taken the poetry and appropriated it to the nationalist cause. Ferguson went on the offensive, and the best example of his tactics is his alternative reading of 'Róisín Dubh', a poem best known in the version by Mangan in which the political allegory claimed by Hardiman is more overt. The fact that the poem can bear such a reading as imputed by Hardiman is vigorously disputed by Ferguson with the counter-claim that it is 'the song of a priest in love, of a priest in love, too, who had broken his vow' (Ferguson, 1834b, p. 158). A political reading, argued Ferguson, is clearly 'fictitious', and he skilfully denied politics as he simultaneously denigrated Catholicism and advanced Protestantism as the religion which was more in keeping with human actuality: 'We sympathise with the priest's passion, we pity his predicament; but we despise his dispensatory expedients, and give him one parting advice, to pitch his vows to the Pope, the Pope to purgatory, marry his black rose-bud, and take a curacy from the next Protestant rector' (p. 159).

Ferguson's interventions were founded on the notion that, to counter political mobilization of the past by the Catholics, the Anglo-Irish must 'embrace the genius of their fellow countrymen', in order to convince them of less mobilizing interpretations of their history. His project was to enter into the study of the Irish past in order to set the rules of its discourse. Once this was accomplished, the identification of the Anglo-Irish and the masses could be underpinned by culture and this would enable the successful proselytization of the Irish and their winning from Popery.

Where Ferguson sought to achieve cultural pre-eminence for the Anglo-Irish through use of a strategic formation comprising materials accumulated by antiquarianism and the Ordnance Survey, Thomas Davis, in contrast, attempted what at first sight appears as an expansive hegemony which, in embracing Anglican, Dissenter and Catholic would have advanced their perceived mutual interests. Whereas for Ferguson the Anglo-Irish Ascendancy represented unquestionably the repository and source of political authority and virtue in Ireland, Davis viewed the Ascendancy's interests (the landlords' interests) and those of other Protestants as mutually exclusive; consequently, much of his writing and praxis was directed towards constructing a political position for Protestants which was not dependent upon landlord support, and therefore did not suffer from the liability of having to support the landlords' case against the tenants. Eschewing a position oriented towards protection of the landlords' interests, Davis adopted the language and politics of the populist Repeal Movement, led by the Catholic barrister Daniel O'Connell, disseminating his ideas through journalism, ballad poetry and the establishment of Repeal Reading Rooms; venues where rural and urban members of the Repeal movement could gather to read materials which were either the products of Davis and his colleagues or referred to by them in their journalism or poetry as supporting their positions.

Davis's attempts to produce the possibility of inserting the Protestants into a cross-class, cross-sectarian alliance, were predicated on the relegation of sectarian belief to a matter of private conscience. If the sects were displaced from their central rôle in the production of identity, it was his belief that the production of an overarching cultural product, 'the nation', and support for it, nationalism, could function in their place as a single active interpellative agency, the forerunner of which he saw in the National Schools (Boyce, 1982, pp. 160-3). The means by which Davis sought to make his 'nation' and displace religious discourses as interpellative processes were popular education and the provision of popular literature, but in a society where Catholic and Protestant clergy and laity were acutely sensitive to issues of proselytization and faith, and each sect vigorously strove to resist encroachment by the other, a positive outcome of Davis's expansive project was dependent upon a radical restructuring of sectarian relations.

The first elements of Davis's programme were sketched out in his early essays 'An Address Delivered Before the Historical Society Dublin' and 'Udalism and Feudalism'. In the first, addressed primarily to Protestants, Davis pointed to the passing of one of the main conditions which had underpinned the Ascendancy's political superiority – the virtual exclusion of Catholics from access to higher education. Previously, he argued, 'the body of competitors for political power were of the aristocracy; for they inherited a monopoly of education, that which summons men to distinction. You also belong to what are called the upper classes in Ireland. But you will have competitors from whom your ancestors were free' (Davis, 1914, p. 8). In these changing circumstances Davis believed that his duty was to convince the younger Anglo-Irish that their duty was not to turn to employment in England or the Empire, but to choose Ireland as their field of action: 'your hearts are with your countrymen – yours is a generous ambition to lead *them* [our emphasis], not their foes' (p. 8). He continued: 'You must strip for the race. You will have competitors from amongst the people. The middle classes of Ireland are now seeking, in spite of the most perverse opposition chronicled in the annals of even our Anglo-Irish bigotry to establish provincial colleges – schools for their own education. When the men of the middle classes come into the field they will compel the men of the upper classes ... to fight a hard battle for their literary laurels and political renown. Prepare for that time' (pp. 8-9). Noting that with the expansion of the National Schools even the lowest levels of Irish society were acquiring education Davis concluded: 'If you would rule your fellow countrymen you must be greater than they ... I tell you, gentlemen of Trinity College, the peasant boys will soon put to the proof your title to lead them' (p. 9). The only way to lead them, he argued, was for his audience to acquaint themselves with Irish literature and history and, in answer to the rhetorical question 'what is the utility of history?'; he retorted: 'Is it nothing to warn us against the brilliant vices of an aristocracy? Is it nothing that its beacons gleam to keep the people from *beginning* (sic) to shed blood?' (p. 29).

Where Tories like Ferguson anticipated with trepidation that democracy would follow from Emancipation and Reform, Davis confidently embraced the prospect and, paraphrasing de Tocqueville, he urged: 'if you would qualify Democracy for power you must purify their morals and warm their faith' (p. 45). It was to this purpose that he commended his audience: 'GENTLEMEN YOU HAVE A COUNTRY. The people among whom we were born, with whom we live, for whom, if our minds are in health, we have most sympathy, are those over whom we have power – power to make them wise, great, good. Reason points out our native land as the field for our exertions ... To act in politics is a matter of duty everywhere; here of necessity' (pp. 46-7). To express the need for the upper classes to enter into *Irish* politics was not sufficient. His audience might be convinced by Davis's arguments, but they would still labour with the problem that to be Protestant, even more, to be Anglican, identified them with the landlords. Davis's essay 'Udalism and Feudalism' was designed to point the way towards a means of removing that obstacle and to setting out a social and economic programme distinct from both landlord domination and English Political Economy which Davis also condemned.

The theses of 'Udalism and Feudalism' were: the Irish landlord class was indefensible; large-scale capitalist agriculture and manufacturing industry alike were unacceptable morally and unsoundly based economically; hence the most productive and ethical system of tenures was peasant proprietorship – udalism. Davis demonstrated that England's social system was at its apogee in the seventeenth century and had declined subsequently as agriculture had become a series of 'huge manufactories of grain and cattle for the landlord' and the English people doubly degraded by becoming either agricultural or industrial labourers, the latter typified as 'a withered blotched thing, querulous as a sick noble or desperately calm, stunned with noisy mill-work' (Davis, 1914, p. 75). Davis argued that the economics of mass-manufacture were insecurely based, and predicted for English manufacturers an impending crisis of over-production after which 'the [English] people will fall back on the land, their native property and ultimate resource' (p. 75).

In these essays Davis set out the elements of his programme for an Irish nationality and society, to which later articles only added developments. Later writings take it as read that the dismissal of aristocracy and its system of tenures, 'landlordism', and the support for 'udalism', would produce a nation of peasant proprietors; the ideal form of society. Alert to the penetration of the concepts and cultural products of English Political Economy into Ireland, and that any countervailing notion of identity would have to deal with their influence, Davis wrote to one of his colleagues:

> Modern Anglicanism, i.e. Utilitarianism, the creed of Russell and Peel as well as the Radicals, this thing, call it Yankeeism or Englishism, which measures prosperity by exchange value, measures duty by gain, and limits desire to clothes, food, and respectability; this damned thing has come into Ireland under the Whigs and is equally the favourite of the Peel (sic) Tories. It is believed in the political assemblies in our cities, preached from our pulpits (always Utilitarian and persecuting) it is the very apostles' creed of the professions, and threatens to corrupt the lower classes, who are still faithful and romantic. To use every literary and political engine against this seems to me the first duty of an Irish patriot who can foresee consequences. Believe me, this is a greater though not so obvious a danger than Papal supremacy.
>
> (Duffy, 1881, pp. 299-300)

Davis's response to this threat was on two levels. Firstly to provide arguments which would refute the notion that England was the model of economic development which Ireland must follow. Secondly to provide an alternative set of popular cultural products to those which streamed from the presses of England. His intended cross-class, cross-sectarian alliance would be bound together by a secular nationalism and a definition of the Irish as all those who regarded Britain and the British as 'other'.

Davis's early essays provide the key to understanding the strategy he later followed in *The Nation*. This journal, which Davis, Charles Gavan Duffy and John Dillon jointly founded in October 1842, became the chief mass circulation organ of the Repealers with a weekly circulation in the region of 10,000 copies and an estimated readership of 250,000

(O'Tuathaigh, 1972, p. 188; Feeney, 1982, pp. 154-5). In its 'Prospectus' Davis addressed 'a nationality which may embrace Protestant [i.e. Anglican], Catholic, and Dissenter, – Milesian and Cromwellian, – the Irishman of a hundred generations and the stranger within our gates'; hence, the motto of *The Nation*, to foster Irish Nationality and make it 'racy of the soil', pointed to a nationality based on residence and willingness to acknowledge Irish rights and duties (Duffy, 1881, p. 80). In *The Nation* Davis set out to identify and celebrate his defined characteristics of nationality through articles, editorials, poetry and, particularly, ballads. The French writer Augustin Thierry had written in 1819 that the 'national spirit of the Irish' was to be found in songs where, 'inspired by the muse of independence ... are recorded the sorrows of Ireland and the crimes of its oppressors' (Brown, 1972, p. 46). In an article praising the idea of a 'Ballad History of Ireland', Davis, who had read Thierry, wrote: '... the first object of the work we project will be to make Irish History familiar to the minds, pleasant to the ears, dear to the passions and powerful over the taste and conduct of the Irish people in times to come' (Davis, 1914, p. 240). Davis never completed his projected 'Ballad History' but, nearly every week, he published a ballad in *The Nation* and his ballads and poems formed a substantial part of the collection *The Spirit of the Nation* which was published in 1843.

By adopting the ballad form Davis acquired a means of communicating, directly and regularly, with audiences of the same size as those who attended O'Connell's mass rallies. He used the opportunities the form presented to convey his conception of nationality, and to reinforce it with historical and contemporary illustrations. In line with his projected nationality a constant theme in the ballads is reconciliation between all of the various identifiable groups in contemporary Ireland. In 'Celts and Saxons', he wrote:

We hate the Saxon and the Dane
We hate the Norman men –
We cursed their greed for blood and gain
We curse them now again.
Yet start not Irish-born man
If you're to Ireland true
We heed not blood, nor creed, nor class –
We have no curse for you.

What matter that at different shrines
We pray unto one God?
What matter that at different times
Your fathers won this sod?
In fortune and in name we're bound
By stronger links than steel;
And neither can be safe nor sound
But in each other's weal. (Davis, n.d., pp. 354-5)

Duffy, Davis's collaborator, biographer and eulogist, suggested that the main purpose of 'Young Ireland', the small group of which Davis was the leading light, was to win over the Protestant middle class to repeal (Duffy, 1881, p. 229, p. 278). This aim was overt in the series of letters which Davis published anonymously in *The Nation* in 1842-3 under the general title 'Letters of a Protestant on Repeal' in which he sought to dissolve the common Protestant arguments against Repeal. As Duffy said: 'prejudice [i.e. Protestant prejudice] cannot be taken by assault. But a nature like Davis's was a focus of the social and intellectual forces by which it may be sapped and mined' (Duffy, 1881, p. 279). Davis's arguments were addressed to Protestants but equally he attempted to mediate between Catholics and Protestants and to show the former that the peaceful achievement of Repeal *required* Protestant participation. 'The real interest of the vast majority of the Irish Protestants', he wrote, 'is (like that of the vast majority of the Irish Roman Catholics) to have Ireland governed by and for its inhabitants and by and for them alone ... it is the obvious duty of those desiring nationality to try to convey this truth to the minds of the Protestants.' His argument was that: 'If you would liberate Ireland, and keep it free, you must have Protestant help – if you would win the Protestants, you must address their reason, their interests, their hope and their pride.' And to this end 'everything which offends even the prejudices of the Protestants – everything which identifies Repeal and Roman Catholicity as meaning two parts of the same thing, must disguise their true interests from the Protestants and must excite their feelings against the restoration of a native government' (Davis, 1842b, p. 153).

This theme received a ballad treatment in 'The Orange and Green Will Carry the Day' where he argued that England was the only beneficiary of sectarianism. Visualizing the result of an Orange/Green alliance he wrote:

English deceit can rule us no more;
Bigots and knaves are scattered like spray –
Deep was the oath the Orangemen swore,
'Orange and Green must carry the day!'

Orange! Orange!
Bless the Orange!
Tories and Whigs grew pale with dismay
When from the North
Burst the cry forth,
'Orange and Green will carry the day!'
No surrender!
No Pretender!
Never to falter and never betray –
With an Amen
We swear it again,
ORANGE AND GREEN SHALL CARRY THE DAY. (Davis, n.d., p. 358)

Reconciliation between 'Orange' and 'Green' was a constant theme of Davis's editorial and poetic writings together with the crimes of the landlords, as he sought to distance 'ordinary' Protestants from the landed Ascendancy. In 'A Scene in the South', Davis described finding the site of a ruined peasant's cabin where an old man tells him of the occupants:

'A loving old couple, and tho' somewhat poor,
'Their children had leisure to play;
'And the piper, and stranger, and beggar were sure
'To bless them in going away;
'But the typhus came, and the agent too –
'Ah! need I name the worst of the two?

'Their cot was unroofed, yet they strove to hide
'In its walls till the fever was passed;
'Their crime was found out, and the cold ditch side
'Was their hospital at last;
'Slowly they went to poor house and grave,
'But the Lord they bent to their souls will save.

...

'God of justice!' I sighed, send your spirit down
'On these lords so cruel and so proud,
And soften their hearts and relax their frown,
'Or else,' I cried aloud –
'Vouchsafe thy strength to the peasant's hand
'To drive them at length from off the land!' (Davis, 1869, pp. 197-8)

As this ballad shows, Davis's attitude to the landlords was unreservedly hostile. Saving a Pauline conversion of the Ascendancy class, its overthrow by the peasants was inevitable. Rather than primarily addressing the Protestants in this, and similar poems and ballads, however, he sought, as in the 'Letters of a Protestant on Repeal', to convince the

Catholics that, for the sake of Repeal, it is they who must accommodate to the Protestants.

Davis's notion of nationality, which permeates all his poetic and lyrical writings, was complex and dependent on a number of prerequisites, in particular the removal of the landlords and sectarian reconciliation. But without waiting for these conditions to be satisfied, Davis demanded his audiences' emotional commitment to a 'nation' which was transcendent, immanent and anthropomorphic:

> A nation's voice, a nation's voice –
> It is a solemn thing!
> It bids the bondage-sick rejoice –
> 'Tis stronger than a king... (Davis, 1869, p. 175)

As perhaps the single most widely known piece written by Davis asserts: 'my dear country shall be made / A NATION ONCE AGAIN' (p. 94).

Davis's programme placed large demands on the Catholic supporters of Repeal, for in calling for special treatment for Protestants within the Repeal Association he was asking Catholics to subordinate their own interests in order to conciliate those who controlled virtually all the land and capital of Ireland (Hill, 1975, p. 393; Hill, 1980; Robert Dudley Edwards, 1947; Clarke, 1942). Davis's project met with opposition even within the editorial staff of *The Nation*, with consequent sharp inconsistencies in the journal's editorial practice. In May 1842, while Davis exhorted *Nation* readers to 'Cultivate the love of your brethren – of your brethren in orange and blue [the political identification colours of Protestants] ... let no patriot Protestant come or go uncheered' (Davis, 1842a, p. 488), on the same page and directly following this advice appeared a long exposé of the excesses of Protestant proselytizers at Ventry, County Kerry: 'These so-called "religious" societies, whose practical operation is to excite the bigoted anti-Catholic landlords to persecute their Catholic tenantry for conscience sake; to induce the starving, the miserable, and the destitute, to practise an external conformity with Protestantism for the sake of whatever they can get from the distributors of pious bribes; and finally to mar the union of all Irishmen for national purposes, by scattering amongst them religious dissension' (O'Neill Daunt, 1842). Making formal obeisance to Davis's theories, the writer nonetheless attacked the proselytising societies and in particular the practice of using converts to 'reveal' the depravity of the priesthood and the Catholic religion (Hempton, 1980).

The author of these comments was O'Connell's close associate, D.J.

O'Neill Daunt, who had been included on the editorial board of *The Nation* to give it a solid appearance to Repealers (Duffy, 1881, p. 48). The similarities in approach and language between O'Neill Daunt's position and those of the Dublin Tories are remarkable, and if we accept them as representative of the temper of political discourse for the period we can measure the large distance between that practice and what Davis was trying to establish as a mediating position. Indeed, a refutation of 'indifferentism' in the same article illustrates one of the ways in which, without formally disavowing Davis and *The Nation*, O'Connell and his followers sought to undercut their legitimacy: 'We beg leave ... to protest against the supposition that there lurks in our [*The Nation*'s] liberal policy one iota of *indifferentism* (sic). On the contrary, if religion be worth having at all it is worth living for and if necessary dying for' (O'Neill Daunt, 1842). By denying 'liberalism's' compatibility with the relegation of religion to the private conscience, O'Neill Daunt reinforced the binary opposition of the sects and ruthlessly undermined a substantial element of Davis's programme.

The dependence of Repealers and Tories on maintaining their stereotypes of 'otherness', which functioned to produce cultural identification, is both acknowledged and reproduced in *The Nation* itself. Davis's position threatened to undermine both forms of 'otherness' and to substitute a new form, mobilizing anglophobia and anti-landlordism. For Repealers, however, the potential disadvantages of this novel departure were considerable. O'Connell may have been eager to attract support from Protestants, but not at the price of neutralizing the bond of 'sentimental affection' between himself – intellectual, landlord, wealthy barrister – and the 'people-nation' (Gramsci, 1971, p. 418) which Catholicism produced. For O'Connell, the Catholics of Ireland were synonymous with the Irish people (McDowell, 1952, pp. 124-5).

From 1842 to 1845 there was an unequal struggle between Davis and O'Connell on the nature of the basis of Irish nationality. Davis put forward residence and volition as criteria, buttressed by evocations of Irish historical experience, chosen to emphasize the possibilities of cross-sectarian co-operation or the identification of colonizers with the colonized, and encomiums on the Irish language, Irish talents and future potential. But religion, the area into which Davis could not venture, was freely traversed by O'Connell in his public speeches and through his close relationship with the Catholic Clergy. A decisive confrontation between Davis and O'Connell came in 1845, some months before Davis's sudden death from scarlatina; the ground of contention an Irish Colleges

Bill to found three secular colleges to meet demands for expanded higher education. Davis and *The Nation* enthusiastically supported the main principles of the Bill with reservations on detail designed to accommodate both Catholic and Protestant objections. The Catholic Bishops issued a statement which Davis and Duffy read as compatible with *The Nation*'s approach (Hill, 1975, p. 384). O'Connell, however, and his chief aide, his son John, denounced the Colleges as 'Godless', and in a debate within the Repeal Association, Davis, rising to respond to attacks on the Bill, made a fatal error of judgement which O'Connell père pounced upon. In Duffy's account of the incident Davis's discomfiture and O'Connell's jubilation at his challenger's slip are unmistakeable:

> I have not – Davis said on rising – more than a few words to say in reply to the useful, judicious and spirited speech of my old college friend, my Catholic friend, my very Catholic friend, Mr. Conway.
> Mr. O'Connell: It is no crime to be a Catholic, I hope?
> Mr. Davis: No, surely no for –
> Mr. O'Connell: The sneer with which you used the word would lead to the inference.
> Mr. Davis: No! sir, no! My best friends, my nearest friends, my truest friends are Catholics.
> (Duffy, 1881, p. 702)

O'Connell's exploitation of Davis's momentary jibe at the desire to make all considerations subordinate to the demands of Catholicism exposed the practical impossibility of Davisite nationality surviving in a cultural terrain dominated by the binary structures of Tory and Catholic stereotypes; not least because in seeking to displace one it simultaneously threatened the other. Memmi has written of the 'colonizer who refuses' that 'Despite his attempts to take part in the politics of the colony, he will be constantly out of step in his language and his actions. He might hesitate or reject a demand of the colonized the significance of which he will not immediately grasp. The lack of perception will seem to confirm his indifference.... Being oppressed as a group, the colonized must necessarily adopt a national and ethnic form of liberation from which he [the colonizer who refuses] cannot but be excluded' (Memmi, 1974, p. 42 and p. 39). Memmi's description of a generic problem for the 'colonizer who refuses' is clearly applicable to Davis's situation and also points to the reasons why collaboration between the 'colonizer who refuses' and the colonized may fail. Davis's projected nationality though inclusive was not necessarily expansive, for even after deserting the landlords it would have tended to preserve the status, integrity, and power of a dominant minority over the majority of the 'people-nation' and would have been, therefore, a particularly effective type of transformism because of its insertion within the national-popular movement.

Both Ferguson's and Davis's attempts to elaborate positions offering the possibility of Protestant participation (and preferably leadership) of a people-nation were unsuccessful. That Ferguson's project for the appropriation of the past should have failed when couched in such uncompromisingly sectarian terms is unsurprising, but his procedure of translating and critically sequestering the past offered much potential for development. Bardic texts from the pre-Christian era, which could be presented to readers as descriptions of a society based firmly on rank, could be evoked as exemplars of the naturalness of aristocracy and its roots in the Irish past; as O'Grady, Yeats and others were to demonstrate, writers who frankly acknowledged their debts to Ferguson. Davis's project, which in contrast to Ferguson's was firmly based on lauding the popular as opposed to the aristocratic, proved equally unsuccessful as a means of promoting a cross-class, cross-sectarian people-nation. But Davis's approach – the celebration of popular virtues and values, excoriation of the landlords as the promoters of sectarian hostility, presentation of 'England' as the supporter of 'landlordism', and not least the establishment of political ballads as the prime element of national-popular culture, set the parameters for future popular politics. In the fifty years after his death, Davis's ballads, essays and speeches were so constantly reprinted that they assumed the status of a strategic formation in their own right. Reprinted because of their accessibility to readers, and their emotive qualities, Davis's writings continued to disseminate the ideas upon which he had hoped to construct a new nationalism, and in particular the concept of inter-sectarian co-operation for which he personally became an emblem. But in the succeeding generations, those who accessed this strategic formation did so in the main from a strategic location defined by increasingly narrow material and cultural interests within the people-nation, utilizing Davis's writings and career as proof of the perverseness of those 'other' Protestants who clung to the Union, where Davis had embraced the people-nation.

3

An essentially feminine race

In the years 1845-51 'at least 800,000 people, about 10 per cent of the population died from hunger and disease' and between 1845 and 1855 approximately 200,000 emigrated (Lee, 1973, p. 1, p. 6). This sudden drop in population was not reversed in subsequent decades and a demographic decline set in, the product of a complex series of economic, social and cultural accommodations with material circumstances. Research has shown that the Famine had an uneven social impact, affecting most the landless labourers and their families who, as their numbers declined, ceased to exert the degree of influence that they had wielded before the Famine. In political terms, it has been convincingly argued that a simplification of rural social relations ensued upon the labourers' decline which made possible the communal solidarity of the tenant farmers, despite gradations of wealth, which enabled them to mobilize successfully in the 1870s and 1880s against the landlords (Fitzpatrick, 1980).

These profound social changes had their cultural counterpart in the means increasingly used by the tenants after the Famine to consolidate and extend landholdings and to transmit family wealth from generation to generation. C.M. Arensberg's and S.T. Kimball's study of 1930s County Clare farming families described the practices which the farmers used to prevent fragmentation of the family holding (Arensberg and Kimball, 1968). These practices, which Arensberg and Kimball termed 'familism', were directed towards enabling the father to select his heir from amongst his sons and to pass on the farm during his lifetime. Familism consisted of a number of procedures to control access to marriage, including the imposition and perpetuation of strict codes of behaviour between men and women, general endorsement of celibacy outside marriage and postponement of marriage in farmers' families until the chosen heir was allowed by the father to take possession of the farm. Recent studies have concluded that something very much like familism and the mode of property transfer that it made possible, stem inheritance, can be traced back to before the Famine (Fitzpatrick, 1983) when, however, it operated only amongst those who had material possessions worth transmitting to the next generation. Consequently, sudden changes in post-famine social behaviour: the spread of matchmaking as a preliminary to marriage; pressure on 'surplus' sons and daughters to emigrate; pressure on them to observe strict chastity and not, through following their own desires, to risk the transmission of the farm under unfavourable circumstances through a *mésalliance*, were the products of the impact of the Famine in making the tenant farmers, rather than the agricultural labourers, the most numerous class in Ireland in the later nineteenth century and after. As a result, the characteristics of the people-nation which both Davis and O'Connell had sought to constitute and address before the Famine, could be more precisely defined after it as the culture of the Irish tenant farmers, including the practices constituting familism, became, more-or-less rapidly, the core of what later nineteenth-century writers such as Charles J. Kickham and Canon Sheehan identified as that of the Irish *tout-court*.

After the Famine, contemporary observers surveyed the ruined cabins of the dead and departed of the Famine years, the deserted potato gardens of the labourers, and the apparent retreat from Repeal to parish-pump politics (Hoppen, 1979), and concluded that, tragedy though it had been, the Famine had solved a long-standing problem of rural over-population. In a debate in the House of Lords in 1859 the Earl of Desart declared that 'any man who had witnessed the condition of Ireland in 1849, and should revisit it after this lapse of ten years would scarcely recognize the country so much had its condition improved' (McCord, 1970, p. 41). This period of comparative political tranquility ended abruptly with the Fenian campaigns of the mid-1860s, when the issue of the long-term future of Anglo-Irish relations came under the scrutiny of a man who has been claimed as the foremost organic intellectual of the mid-Victorian bourgeoisie – Matthew Arnold (Storey, 1985).

Arnold's position on Anglo-Irish relations was an important but subsidiary component in the preparation of the mid-Victorian English bourgeoisie to underpin their material pre-eminence with cultural pre-eminence for which, he judged, they were poorly prepared. In essays such as 'The Function of Criticism at the Present Time' (1864) (Arnold, 1962, pp. 258-85) and 'Culture and Anarchy' (1867) (Arnold, 1965, pp. 87-256), Arnold sought to show to his fellow bourgeois – the 'Philistines' – that, without modification, their philosophy might suffice to challenge the political superiority of the aristocracy – the 'Barbarians' – but would equally empower the masses – the 'Populace' – in their struggle for political power. His formula 'force till right is ready' which, in English domestic affairs, meant the deployment of main force or coercion while hegemony was prepared, was also advocated as an approach in Anglo-Irish relations (Arnold, 1962, pp. 265-6; Baldick, 1983, pp. 18-58). Here, the deployment of main force was to precede and secure the conditions for the eventual willing acceptance of England's cultural pre-eminence which, in turn, would lead to England's hegemony in succession to its coercion. Arnold began seriously to consider the cultural relations of the English and the Celts – and particularly the Irish – after reading Renan's 'Poésie des Races Celtiques' in 1860 (Renan, 1897), and his conclusions were published in the form of lectures and serial articles in the *Cornhill Magazine* in 1866, later collected as 'On the Study of Celtic Literature', their timeliness increased by the outbreak of Fenian bombing activity in the Autumn of 1865 which Arnold took as a warning of the price to be paid if the Irish were not induced to accept their (subsidiary) place within the United Kingdom (Arnold, 1973, pp. 291-395).

Arnold's arguments, founded on Renan's, drew upon contemporary philology, ethnology and anthropology, to establish language as a racial identifier and the prime determinant of culture (Curtis, 1968, Chapter V). The basis of this argument originated in the works of the eighteenth-century philosopher Herder who had argued, not only that language was the prime determinant of identity, but that all cultures were incommensurable and could not be reduced to points on some scale of historical or aesthetic development (Berlin, 1980). The task of the scholar from this viewpoint was to recognize, describe, and appreciate the distinctive features of national character. This idea exercised a continuing appeal for early nineteenth-century nationalists; Thomas Davis, for example, argued that the 'language which grows up with a people, is conformed to their organs, descriptive of their climate, constitution and manners, mingled inseparably with their history and their soil, fitted beyond any other language to express their prevalent thoughts in the most natural way. To impose another language on such a people is to send their history adrift among the accidents of translation ... To lose your native tongue and learn that of an alien is the worst badge of conquest – it is the chain on the soul' (Davis, 1843a; 1914, pp. 97-9).

Herder's linguistic-cultural pluralism informed Davis's understanding of the cultural dimension of identity, but by the 1840s the works of Fichte, Hegel, the Brothers Grimm, and Goethe had developed the concept of language as a differentiating principle along lines radically opposed in their implications to Herder's by substituting hierarchy for incommensurability (Fryer, 1964, pp. 53-74). This shift was an effect of philology which not merely demarcated nations, but applied criteria of relative value to their languages and cultures (Said, 1985b, p. 131; MacDougall 1982, pp. 119-21). Languages were classsified into broad groupings – Indo-European, Semitic, Mongolian – and then sub-classified within those groupings. Most European languages fell within the Indo-European grouping and were further classified by principles of integrity and purity – the extent to which languages had or had not been influenced by other languages, principally Latin. This supplied a scale of relative vitality and cultural significance and on this basis the most vigorous and 'important' languages in the Indo-European family were the Teutonic languages – German, the Scandinavian languages, Dutch and, of course, English. As the elaboration of this concept proceeded, the pre-eminence of Teutonism was confirmed, the subsidiary status of Celtism produced.

As Edward Said noted, there 'is an unmistakeable air of power about the philologist ... what was philology on the one hand if not a science of all humanity [but also] a harsh divider of men into superior and inferior races?' (Said, 1985b, p. 133). For Renan, the mid-nineteenth century discourse of philology supplied his strategic formation, the corpus of texts which empowered and supported his judgements. His strategic location, his 'position in a text with regard to the material he writes about' (Said, 1985b, p. 20) was, in relation to the Semitic people he studied, that of an Indo-European who had *produced* the Semitic and for whom the Semitic was 'the symbol of European (and consequently his) dominion over the Orient' (p. 141). When, however, Renan wrote of the 'Poésie des Races Celtiques' his strategic location was as a Celt vis-à-vis the Teutons, the linguistic group which, so its philological proponents argued, represented the pinnacle of the Indo-European or Aryan peoples.

Renan's essay is significant because of its influence, via Matthew Arnold, on Irish writers and intellectuals of the later nineteenth century. They, like Renan, were confronted by philological discourses which assigned primacy in terms of linguistic and cultural value to the Teutonic languages. Renan's equivocal achievement was not to displace the Teutonic with the Celtic languages but, through a general elaboration of the philological discourse, to advance the notion of the Teuton as the energetic, brutal warrior complemented by the Celt, the producer of civility and culture. 'This ancient race', Renan wrote of the Celts, 'living ... its own life in some obscure islands and peninsulas in the West ... still faithful to its own tongue, to its own memories, to its own genius ... is in possession of a literature which, in the Middle Ages, exercised an immense influence, changed the current of European civilization and imposed its poetical motives on nearly the whole of Christendom' (Renan, 1897, p. 2). Contrasting the 'imaginative compositions' of Teuton and Celt, Renan defined those of the former as marked with 'all the horror of disgusting and blood-embued barbarism, the disinterested taste ... for destruction and death', whereas the Celts exhibited not only 'a profound sense of justice, but also a great capacity for devotion, an exquisite loyalty' (pp. 14-5). Renan's Celts were emotional and melancholic: 'If at times ... [the Celtic Race] ... seems to be cheerful a tear is not slow to glisten behind its smile' (p. 7). This line of argument supports Renan's general thesis that nations were composites of several races in which the characteristics of the individual races were mutually complementary, the rôle of the Celts being to supply the creative aspect of the (French) nation's cultural ensemble. This rôle was guaranteed when Renan invoked the categories of sexuality to underpin his arguments: 'If it be permitted us to assign sex to nations as to individuals we should have to say without hesitance that the Celtic race ... is an essentially feminine race' (p. 8). Thus the Celts were inscribed as the creative principle in the mutually interdependent Indo-European family, their centrality guaranteed by the needs of the 'masculine' Teutons.

As Renan's arguments in 'Poésie des Races Celtiques' were products of his strategic location so were Arnold's in 'On the Study of Celtic Literature'. But although drawing on substantially the same strategic formation, Arnold's arguments were advanced from a very different strategic location. Whereas Renan was himself a Celt, Arnold was a member of a Teutonic race and the arguments put forward within the essay were deployed by Arnold for the purpose of developing a bourgeois hegemony, and safeguarding the public order of the British Isles.

Arnold's opinion was that the language of the Celts in Wales and Ireland was 'the badge of the beaten race' (Arnold, 1962, p. 293), and the decline of the languages itself desirable, because the 'fusion of all the inhabitants of these islands into one homogeneous English-speaking whole ... the swallowing up of separate provincial nationalities, is a consummation to which the natural course of things irresistably tends' (p. 296). Reminding his readers that force could be employed for 'there is nothing to hinder us from effacing the last poor material remains of that Celtic power which once was everywhere' (p. 298), he argued that it was 'not in the outward and visible world of material life that the Celtic genius of Wales and Ireland can at this day hope to count for much' but that nonetheless the English should attend to Celtic culture because of its potential as an antidote to the less desirable qualities of Englishness: 'Out of the steady humdrum habit of the creeping Saxon, as the Celt calls him ... has come, no doubt, Philistinism' (p. 348). Philistinism, therefore, was a negative aspect of Anglo-Saxon steadiness, but one mitigated by other elements in the (English) national character *including the Celtic*. Maintaining that the true strength of the English derived from their blending in one race the positive aspects of Teuton and Celt, he argued that the full potential of such a hybrid could not be achieved without self-knowledge:

> so long as this mixed nature of our constitution possesses us we are blindly and ignorantly rolled about by the forces of our culture; ... so soon as we have clearly discerned what they are and begun to apply them to a law of measure, control and guidance they may be made to work for our good ... Then we may use German faithfulness to Nature to give us science and to free us from insolence and self-will; we may use the Celtic quickness of perception to give us delicacy and to free us from hardness and Philistinism; we may use the Latin decisiveness to give us strenuous clear method and free us from fumbling and idling. (p. 383)

To get his fellow Englishmen to accept the Celtic element in their own nature, rather than to reject out of hand the possibility of any affinity between Celt and Anglo-Saxon, Arnold reminded the English that they and the Celts were members of the Indo-European linguistic family, and set out in the greater part of the essay to establish Celtism's (Arnold's term) qualities in order to show their usefulness as complements to the other qualities *of the English*. By way of contrast, and to prevent these Celtic virtues being appropriated to form the basis of a separate Celtic power, Arnold argued that, in the Celts themselves, even the positive qualities of Celtism could not redeem their position. Recognizing the political dimensions of the cultural, Arnold put a politically independent future for the Celts beyond the bounds of possibility, for 'the skillful and resolute application of means to ends which is needed both to make progress in material civilisation and also to form powerful states is just what the Celt has least turn for ... as in material civilisation he has been ineffectual, so has the Celt been ineffectual in politics' (pp. 345-6).

In describing and producing the 'Celt', Arnold, drawing on Renan, projected a discourse which has been termed 'Celticism' (Curtis, 1968, Chapter IX), which had a major influence on the cultural productions of the Irish from the 1860s onwards. Edward Said's statement of the relations of power inscribed in the discourse of Orientalism are equally applicable to Celticism: 'Orientalism [Celticism] depends for its strategy on ... flexible positional superiority, which puts the Westerner [Englishman] in a whole series of possible relationships with the Orient [Ireland] without ever losing him the upper hand' (Said, 1985b, p. 7). In the discourse of Celticism the positional superiority of the English was guaranteed by the strategic formations of philology and anthropology which both inscribed the Irish as members of a second-order race in relation to the first-order Teutons, represented by the English. The products of anthropology – cephalic measurements, facial angles, indexes of nigrescence, which at their wilder extremities spawned the notion of the Irish as a race of covert blacks, became increasingly popular in the 1860s and particularly so after the emergence of Fenianism (Curtis, 1971, Chapter I; 1968, pp. 71-2 and 136-7). But anthropological discourses which simianized the Celt merely brutalized and, in so doing, justified treatment fit for brutes – coercion, the short-hand term for the suspension of *habeas corpus* and the passing of special crimes acts. Moreover, iconographic productions, such as those of *Punch* analysed by L.P. Curtis Jnr, in *Apes and Angels*, produced, in their turn, polar opposites as responses from the Irish. Simianization placed the English in only one possible relationship with the Irish – domination (Curtis, 1971). Celticism, in contrast, offered a whole range of positions, which in their more positive responses could be represented as highly complementary. Arnold's contribution to elaborating this discourse was recognized nearly forty years ago by John Kelleher when he stated that 'the lectures ... [on Celtic Literature became] ... a contemporary classic of criticism, and in another generation had become the accepted doctrine, not only on Celtic Literature, but on the literature of the Celtic Revival' (Kelleher, 1950, p. 197).

Arnold produced a Celt whose foremost characteristic was emotion, where 'the Celtic genius, sentiment as its main basis, with the love of beauty, charm, spirituality for its excellence, [had] ineffectualness and self-will for its deficit' (Arnold, 1962, p. 311). Throughout 'On the Study of Celtic Literature' this theme allowed the ingress of those judgements which, having established the Celt as '*always ready to react against the despotism of fact* (sic)' (p. 344), 'ineffectual in politics' (p. 346), and 'sensual' (p. 345), concluded, like Renan, that 'no doubt the sensibility of the Celtic nature, its nervous exaltation, have something feminine in them, and the Celt is peculiarly disposed to feel the spell of the feminine idiosyncrasy; he has an affinity to it; he is not far from its secret' (p. 347). Hence, in mapping the strategic formation which underpinned Celticism, to the positivism of philology, ethnology and anthropology must be added the positivism of that science of sexuality which produced a femininity for the nineteenth-century bourgeois woman which underwrote her ineffectualness, whether by medicalization and the reduction of woman to the status of a womb, or through the celebration of her disabling femininity, itself arising from the same source (Foucault, 1984, Part IV).

As a significant by-product of the preservation of English bourgeois hegemony, therefore, Arnold produced a procedure for the cultural and political incorporation of the Celts which flattered them into accepting a subsidiary position for themselves vis-à-vis the English. Recognition by the English of the qualities of the Celts' cultural products is seen by Arnold as a 'healing measure' in Anglo-Irish relations on the cultural plane, an accommodatory gesture to reconcile the Celts to their subordinate political and cultural status (Arnold, 1973, p. 282). Arnold's significance lies in his elaboration of the architectonic, to use his own term (Arnold, 1962, p. 345); the systematic basis of the strategic formation which informed both the creative and critical works of the Revival of the 1890s in which mutually supportive discourses of gender, race and politics advantageously preserved the Englishman's 'upper hand' in relations with the Irish.

In his investigations of the English imperial relationship with India Ashis Nandy has shown how power, deployed through discourse, narrowed and reshaped the possibilities of sexuality in a colonial people (in this case India's Hindus) by emphasizing an aggressive, warrior-like masculinity and a submissive, passive femininity as the 'normal' forms of gender. He has discussed how the projection of these norms in gender relations induced Hindu separatists, in order to demonstrate their race's virtue through shows of masculinity, to confront their colonizers militarily – to their own disadvantage. This concept enables Nandy's analysis of the ways in which Gandhi's campaigns reversed the 'normal' relations of dominance and subservience of the 'feminine' colonized to the 'masculine' colonizer, making the suffering victim triumph over the violent aggressor. In Ireland, the implications of linking femininity as a racial trait with subservience were sufficiently recognized for nationalist writers to respond by emphasizing the manly and masculine aspects of the Irish character and by locating the metropolis as the source of the 'effeminate follies' and 'masher habits' that were creeping into Irish life (Croke, 1884). In some writers, however, awareness of the negative connotations of femininity was so well developed that they employed it themselves to castigate the political and organizational ineffectualness of their audiences. As the journalist D.P. Moran wrote in 1899: 'On all sides one sees only too much evidence that the people are secretly content to be a conquered race, though they have not the honesty to admit it.... There is nothing masculine in the character; and when the men do fall into line with green banners and shout themselves hoarse, is it not rather a feminine screech, a delirious burst of defiance on a background of sluggishness and despair?' (Moran, 1905, p. 6). The 'disadvantages ... of the national disposition' (p. 13) defined by Celticism – femininity, emotionalism, material and political incapacity – were not regarded as such, however, by some Irish intellectuals, for whom the establishment of transcendental linguistic and racial categories supplied a mode of access to the past and present of the Celtic-Irish which showed considerable developmental promise for the construction of new relationships and the revalidation of old ones.

The flexible positional superiority that the discourse of Celticism conferred on the English, extended also to the Anglo-Irish, for Celticism offered them a range of possible responses to the cultural and political products of the Nationalists. In response to any particular text, critical commentary could either extol the Celtic merits of the piece, its sensitivity, its feeling for nature, its emotional or æthereal qualities, its 'otherworldliness'; aspects which emphasized the delicacy of feeling of the Celts but which at the same time reminded readers of their ineffectualness in material things. Alternatively, the critic could describe how the overdevelopment of the emotional led to bathos or sensualism at the expense of failures in technique. More negatively, critics, whether cultural or political, could always draw upon the meshing of discourses of Celticism and sexuality to remind readers of the Celts' emotional and mental instability - 'the tear behind the smile'. Thus, for the Anglo-Irish, Celticism offered the position of Ireland's resident Teutons, mentors who could safeguard the Celts from the unfettered play of their own nature. If the Irish appealed to their pre-colonial history to construct an identity, as Davis had done prior to the deployment of Celticism, the Anglo-Irish could also draw upon the historical dimension within Celticism which celebrated the virtues of the tribal society. In this permutation Celticism enabled the elision of the contemporary leaders of the people-nation, the Catholic bourgeoisie, by offering a reprise of an idealized Gaelic tribal society, based on identifying the warrior chiefs with the Anglo-Irish and the Chiefs' followers with the peasants, denying the Catholic bourgeoisie a rôle. The concept of an alliance of aristocrat and peasant, though attractive, was in practice politically impossible because of the contemporary opposition of the interests of the putative peasants, the tenant farmers, and the aristocratic warrior chiefs. While the 'emotional' dimension of Celticism was mobilized by Mathew Arnold in the 1860s, the next decade saw the clear articulation of the 'warrior' inflection of the discourse; a dimension which, while having an indelible effect on the subsequent Revival, was to prove both potent and problematic.

'Nationalism', as Ernest Gellner observed, 'usually conquers in the name of a putative folk culture. Its symbolism is drawn from the healthy, pristine, vigorous life of the peasants' (Gellner, 1983, p. 57). The problem which the contemporary peasant life posed for those of the Anglo-Irish intellectual élite who wished to re-vitalize their class's fading political fortunes by allying it with an emergent Irish nation was that peasant reality was one of destitution, Ireland having become 'a vast congested rural slum' (MacLochlainn, 1977, p. 31). In a political climate informed by the sentiments of James Fintan Lalor that: 'It is a mere question between a people and a class – a people of eight million and a class of eight thousand. They or we must quit this island ... they or we are doomed' (Lalor, 1947, pp. 62-3), it was difficult in the extreme for members of that class to invoke peasant life without raising the spectre of their class's perceived responsibility for that condition. Appropriation of the past then became the strategic means by which to preserve Ascendancy integrity while also accessing the power base which 'the people' could provide. But the past was hardly less problematic than the present, for as Ferguson had found in his confrontation with Hardiman's translations, the poetry could be read as political allegories whose central concern was the advocation of an Irishness which had no part for the descendents of the colonizer. As Stopford Brooke saw so clearly in 1893, the Irish literature written after the English invasions was 'nationalist as well as national. It was forced to conceive Ireland as a whole and as set over against England', whereas that written in 'the earliest and noble part' of the literature was national but not nationalist, so providing a place where 'we can forget our quarrels of party, and quarrels of religion' (Brooke, 1893, pp. 11-2). The same observation could equally well have been made by Standish O'Grady, the 'father' of the Literary Revival, who, two decades earlier, had acted on a similar insight.

O'Grady published his *Bardic History of Ireland Vol. 1* in 1879 - the very year in which Michael Davitt founded the Land League, an organization dedicated, as one of the League's founders stated, '[to] the tearing out, root and branch, of the class that caused the disease' (Brown, 1972, p. 254). Although O'Grady's explicit engagement with politics dates from the publication of *The Crisis in Ireland* in 1892 - the same crisis which had exercised the *Dublin University Magazine* in the 1830s - it is in O'Grady's historical and literary studies that one finds the intellectual underpinning, and reinforcement, of his political ideals. In the words of E.A. Boyd: 'there is no doubt that the author of the Bardic History owed his belief in the destiny of the Irish aristocracy to the contageous grandeur of the narratives of that ancient order which he had evoked with the intuitive sympathy of genius' (Boyd, 1916). Through his work on Irish history and legend O'Grady sought to demonstrate that the roots of his class were bedded in the fabric of Ireland, and that any Land League ambitions to tear them out would lead to the collapse, not simply of that class, but Ireland itself.

Boyd's comments point to the subjective involvement of O'Grady with his material, and although O'Grady was to acknowledge in 1879 that 'the blaze of bardic light' had blinded him to the fact that 'a literature so noble, and dealing with events so remote, must have originated mainly or altogether in the imagination' (O'Grady, 1879, p. 32), his urge towards academic rigour never dispelled his belief that: 'A noble moral tone pervades the whole. Courage, affection, and truth are native to all who live in this world' (p. 43). The partial retraction of the basis of his 1878 study never seriously undercut its romantic and aristocratic vision of Irish history; a vision which informs the cultural-political activities of subsequent decades.

In his *History of Ireland: The Heroic Period Vol. 1* (1878) O'Grady asked the fundamental question facing one embarking on a study of pre-history: 'Why not pass on at once to credible history?' (O'Grady, 1878, p. 22), and supplied an answer which informed the subsequent Literary Revival, and in which his recognition of the political potential of 'history' was explicitly revealed. 'The legends', he argued, 'represent the imagination of the country; they are that kind of history which a nation desires to possess ... They ... have a value far beyond the tale of actual events and duly recorded facts' (p. 22). Having so freed himself from 'the vulgarity of actual things' (p. 22), O'Grady conjured up an image of a heroic Ireland where warriors 'superhuman in size and beauty' gathered around their chiefs and kings in a world of 'torcs of gold', 'white linen tunics', and 'loose brattas of crimson silk' (p. 21). As Alf MacLochlainn observed in relation to both the nineteenth-century Celticists and their heirs in the Revival: 'These intellectual movements somehow ignore the eight million peasants and their real, vivid, and concrete way of life ... which owed nothing at all to the chieftains of the Gaelic order who were dead and gone two hundred years and more' (MacLochlainn, 1977, p. 31).

The point of O'Grady's idealization of pre-history and avoidance of present realities is clarified by reference to his study of Elizabethan Ireland where, in denying the views of the historian J.A. Froude, he asserted: 'Mr. Froude's picture of the upright, God-fearing, and civilized Englishman contending against a flood of Celtic barbarism, is doubly untrue' (O'Grady, 1896, p. xxx). Far from being barbarous, the Irish soldiers of the Elizabethan armies, 'drawn from a warrior caste, were ... engaged in the work which they loved, indeed, the only work for which they were fitted' (p. lvi). The warrior nation had then survived unbroken through to the period which saw its tragic, but necessary submission to England but, as O'Grady was only too well aware, the aristocracy who had led this people had now flown, leaving only the Anglo-Irish to take up their abandoned responsibilities. It was O'Grady's mission, as it had been Ferguson's, to make them see that their future survival depended on their seizing the moment, and he made his readers only too aware of how desperate their situation actually was: 'The political and social horizon to-day in Ireland is, at least for one class, and for the friends and sympathisers of that class, overcast and gloomy in the extreme. Yet dark and stormy as the outlook is now, it will be yet darker and stormier' (O'Grady, 1882, p. 3). To dispel the storm clouds was O'Grady's mission and his stories of ancient Ireland could become thinly veiled allegories of the contemporary situation.

In the Chapter entitled 'A Pioneer' in *History of Ireland: The Heroic Period Vol. I* O'Grady tells of the arrival of Laeg at the home of a noble where he intends to rest his horse and repair his war chariot. The lord, however, is not such by birth but by effort and purchase of property, and his refusal to proffer hospitality unless he receive 'a goodly pledge' (O'Grady, 1882, p. 249), is responded to by Laeg in terms which clearly articulate O'Grady's own pre-Yeatsian warning to the Ascendancy and Ireland of the consequences of abandoning power to 'paudeen'; the modern and materialistic: 'An evil time, indeed, will it be for the Gaeil if the ollavs and their wisdom concur to plant among us such shrubs of deadly poison as thyself, O vile and avaricious stranger, without gratitude or nobleness or love for aught save thy miserable accumulation of sorry pelf' (pp. 249-50).

While warning the Ascendancy of the consequences of idleness and the need for action O'Grady also had the equally clear perception that all was too little and too late: 'We had the opportunity, and we let it pass' (O'Grady, 1882, p. 10). Opposed alike to the German importation of socialism and 'the wolf of democracy' (O'Grady, 1882, p. 29), he also savaged those members of the Ascendancy – virtually the whole class as he saw it – who had betrayed their social responsibility and, in effect, impelled the people to increasingly violent means by which to achieve their aims. The way in which O'Grady expressed this point is significant, for it introduces his concept of social relations within the nation, both as it is and as he would – ideally – wish it to evolve.

'Society', argued O'Grady, 'is as a matter of fact based still on orders, classes, and degrees' and 'the modern Irishman, in spite of all his political rhodomontade, does very deeply respect rank and birth' (O'Grady, 1886, pp. 271-2). Such is this natural and innate respect – the continuation of the tradition of loyalty to the warrior chief – that it had offered the Ascendancy the means by which to avoid the coming conflagration, for the people had invested landowners with 'an imaginary strength', indeed 'In the general mind their [the landlords'] rights stood then firm and unremovable, like the mountain-chains of our country' (O'Grady, 1882, p. 9). The power invested in the Ascendancy had been such that: 'the Irish nation once lay like soft wax ready to take any impression and conform to any moulding upon which you [the Ascendancy] determined' (O'Grady, 1886, p. 226). The revelations of the Financial Relations Commission of 1897 concerning the massive and unbalanced contribution of Ireland to the Exchequer of the Empire gave O'Grady the opportunity to further his argument that: '[the] Ascendancy ... are the rightful natural leaders, defenders, and champions of this People who cannot furnish forth such from their own ranks' (O'Grady, 1897, p. 173). Here, he felt, was a cause which could unite a divided island and, crucially, re-instate the Ascendancy in the position which they had all but abdicated. Although somewhat coded, O'Grady's enthusiasm for the future was a declaration of the re-birth of the ancient Irish nation: 'Something is struggling to birth now, to-day in Ireland, whose gestation needed two thousand years of historic time. If this be not the birth of that mighty one foretold of yore by the prophets of our race, it is the first leap of the infant in the womb. Greater things than millions are concerned in this new Irish movement' (O'Grady, 1897, p. 173). These historically informed references to issues greater than concerns of mere materialism lie at the very heart of O'Grady's cultural-political programme although, as he could not be aware, that whose birth he aided with his heroic images of Ireland's warrior past would have no place for those for whom he evoked those glories.

In clear desperation at the ignorance and apathy of his own class, yet still strong in the belief that individuals within that class could put down roots to the betterment both of themselves and Ireland, he argued for little less than a return to the society recorded in his histories. To the concept of the 'Tory Democratic' advanced by Lord Randolph Churchill as a means of halting the advancement of democracy by allying the landowners with the workers – a reconstituted feudalism – O'Grady added the reminders that this was the original, and better, Irish way. If the problems of the Ascendancy were caused by the fact that 'they would not become frankly and loyally Irish' (O'Grady, 1886, p. 247), then they must become so by emulating their aristocratic models in the histories. As he argued in the most explicit terms: 'in this Irish history ... lay for you the key of safety had you but known it' (O'Grady, 1886, p. 238) and, in case his readers found this remark too cryptic, he went on: 'For I tell you again and again that all Irish history is on your side, every page redolent of captaincy and soldiership, of strong rule, and of allegiance and loyalty to the death' (O'Grady, 1886, p. 252). The models offered to the Ascendancy were the 'Doric states of old Greece [where] the ruling military class dined together' (O'Grady, 1886, p. 273), and that of 'The feudal landlord [who] dined with his people and saw his ale go round, in days before men had learned to prate about Liberty and Equality' (O'Grady, 1886, pp. 272-3). Only by binding men to them in a conscious re-creation of such examples would members of the Ascendancy save themselves and Ireland, and O'Grady argued his case in terms which pre-echo Gramsci's concept of transformist hegemony: 'The party must proceed step by step, and the first step – the essential preliminary of all others – is not aristocratic or oligarchic, but democratic, popular and national', for the primary objective is 'Not alone to hold society together, but to bind and compact it into a vital whole' (O'Grady, 1886, pp. 131-2). This symbiotic relationship between class and country was fundamental to O'Grady's programme in which was foreshadowed that fusion of an idealized vision of warrior Ireland with an explicit anti-democratic and anti-materialist stance which, with varying degrees of emphasis, was to colour so much of the work of the writers of the Revival.

England is personified as a 'mad Titan raging amid his huge industries' (O'Grady, 1918, p. 321) and, as with Ferguson, the home of a pernicious movement towards republicanism which, inevitably, will usher in the worship of Mammon. Both of these 'English' features – industrialism and materialism – are inimical to the essence of Ireland and so must be resisted, as what will be destroyed by such radical imports is the elaborate social structure erected by O'Grady on the basis of a landowning

Ascendancy and an indigenous people innately loyal to their chieftains. In order to combat these threats, he argued that the leaders of republican Ireland were embarked on a course of action which would inevitably destroy the very land for which they professed such love. To push the Ascendancy out of a position of prestige and influence was to condemn Ireland to the squalor of a state 'gross and materialised' (O'Grady, 1882, p. 51), for such a class, 'the costly product of centuries, containing elements of moral, personal, intellectual wealth, which this nation will yet sorely need' (O'Grady, 1882, p. 52), cannot be re-created once condemned to the footnotes of history.

The elaboration of Ferguson's model of the nation is clear, but whereas Ferguson could only envisage a people-nation converted to the Ascendancy's Protestantism, O'Grady implicitly, and on occasions quite explicitly, suggested an essential Irishness which, in pre-dating Christianity, side-stepped the contentious issue of Catholicism which formed such a formidable obstacle to the Ascendancy's sympathetic identification with the people-nation. In his essay 'An Irish Sunrise' he recorded his conversations with an elderly Irish shepherd who, when commenting on the weather, always rounded off his observations with 'thank God': 'Now Brady did not get this religious feeling towards Nature from his professed religion, which is hostile to it. Our ancient literature is steeped in that feeling' (O'Grady, 1918, p. 332). Not only is Brady to be seen as wearing Catholicism as a thin veneer over an innate pantheistic Irishness, but he, as 'a primitive Irish peasant', is 'not yet quite corrupted by civilisation' (p. 332). With such an observation O'Grady provided the final item on the agenda of the Revival; the Irish were not truly Catholic, rather they were a pagan warrior people and, since their headlong rush towards republicanism was destined to destroy their heritage, they must be protected from themselves by the Ascendancy heirs to the kingdom of ancient, aristocratic Ireland: 'the best class we have, and so far better than the rest that there is none fit to mention as the next best' (O'Grady, 1886, p. 216).

By the end of the 1880s the various permutations and interpretations of the Celtic character were mobilized; but always to the advantage of the English colonial power or the Ascendancy garrison. But the last decades of the century also saw the emergence of a counter-hegemony articulated by organic intellectuals of the people-nation, themselves often aided, for a variety of frequently strategic reasons, by members of an Anglo-Irish intellectual élite. With the concept of the cultural and linguistic 'De-Anglicization' of Ireland the cultural/political polemics of the century entered a new phase. Although conventionally referred to as the Irish Literary Revival or Renaissance, it was, in essence, a decisive engagement with an agenda whose items had been inscribed in the course of the.nineteenth century 'war of position' as English and Anglo-Irish intellectuals attempted to avert 'The Coming Crisis'.

4

What do we hope to make of Ireland?

In 1923 Yeats asserted that: 'The modern literature of Ireland, and indeed all that stir of thought which prepared for the Anglo-Irish war, began when Parnell fell from power in 1891. A disillusioned and embittered Ireland turned from parliamentary politics; an event was conceived; and the race began, as I think, to be troubled by that event's long gestation' (Yeats, 1955, p. 559). In ascribing a historical and cultural solidarity to this period Yeats not only located the cultural as central to the recently, and bitterly, concluded Anglo-Irish struggle but, in speaking of 'the modern literature of Ireland' glossed over and bound together in retrospective unity a range of factions and parties which were in many cases still in contention in 1924. In contrast to this unified Yeatsian Revival, 1890s commentators and subsequent historians and critics have pointed out that far from unity, the intellectuals of 1890s Ireland were locked in what D.P. Moran styled 'A Battle of Two Civilizations' (Lyons, 1971 pp. 224-46; 1982, pp. 27-55; Boyce, 1982, pp. 228-58; Watson, 1979, p. 19). Hence, the Revival may more appropriately be seen as the culminating episode in a cultural struggle for the leadership and articulation of the people-nation, which reached a decisive turning point signalled by '*The Playboy* Riots' in January 1907, rather than a unified movement which was the precursor to the Easter Rising of 1916. The key to a historically informed reading of the cultural products of this period is an understanding of the forces at play in that cultural struggle, a first step towards which is the further specification of certain important features of that people-nation for whose leadership the factions contended.

The demographic changes which simplified the class structure of rural Ireland did not spontaneously promote political solidarity. Among the tenant farmers, gradations of wealth produced differences in perspective on social and political issues, while further differences of interest separated the tenant farmers from the shopkeepers, who first emerged as an influential class in rural Ireland in the post-Famine years. Nor should all

Irish landlords be dismissed from account as either absentees or indifferent to their localities' interests, for landlord and land agent influence was vigorously, and frequently successfully, exerted in the counties and the boroughs from the 1850s until after the 1870s (Hoppen, 1977; 1979, p. 214; Vaughan, 1984). Hence, the diminution of the agricultural labourer class which made the tenant farmers *as a whole* the most numerous social class did not of itself make possible a shift from particularist to national politics or give the tenant farmers a united voice in national politics. Such developments only occurred under the stimulus of agricultural depression and with the benefit of an exceptional tri-partite leadership combining the Irish Parliamentary Party, agrarian social radicals, and Irish-Americans. Reassessments of the actuality of the Land League campaigns only emphasize that what bound together this alliance was some exceptional form of communal solidarity but, as Gramsci pointed out, 'a human mass does not "distinguish" itself, does not become independent in its own right without, in the widest sense organising itself; and there is no organisation without intellectuals' (Gramsci, 1971, pp. 334-5). While Vaughan rightly emphasizes the fragmentation and consequent disorganization of rural Ireland, his belief that the leadership of a few major figures, such as Parnell and Davitt, was the key to Land League successes is inadequate as an explanation (Vaughan, 1984, p. 35). To be effective, the Land League had to depend for its operation on the rapid emergence of local organizers to translate the directions of the leadership into action. Moreover, for those grass-roots organizers to bring a whole host of individuals with potentially conflicting material interests to couple the prospect of their own material advancement to that of others, and to the distant prospect of achieving a Home Rule Parliament in Dublin, required a high level of mutual agreement and understanding.

In recognizing this as a vital issue, Sam Clark has argued that 'boycotting' indicated the extent to which Land League organization 'was firmly grounded in the stable structure of social relationships in agrarian communities.... The interdependence necessary to make a tactic of this kind effective can exist only amongst a people who are bound together by strong communal and/or associational ties' (Clark, 1979, p. 312). While Clark seeks such 'strong communal and/or associational ties' in the straightforward instances of interdependency which he cites, such communal solidarity should be more widely viewed as manifestations of those shared common assumptions, practices and beliefs which also underpinned familism. For familism to operate it was essential that the codes of belief and behaviour upon which it depended, particularly the regulation of sexuality, and unquestioned patriarchal authority guaranteed by the Church's sanctions and underpinning stem inheritance, should be accepted both by the family and the whole community. Only widespread acceptance could make it possible to perpetuate a system which demanded so much of individuals (Arensberg and Kimball, 1968, pp. 200-5).

Consequently, in locating how familism was discursively regulated it is possible to arrive at a clearer understanding of the strategic formation of discourses which could empower certain forms of political and cultural activity. Familism and Catholicism constituted two of the three parts of a strategic formation of discourses to which all those who would lead and articulate the people-nation had to respond. For while familism might not seem either necessary or appropriate in the towns and cities of later nineteenth century Ireland its presence was there to be discerned. As migrants from the countryside flocked to the city in the 1890s and 1900s these new Dubliners whose very presence in the city was testimony to the operation of familism, together with their priests, themselves largely drawn from the tenant farmer class, perpetuated the codes of the countryside in Dublin and other towns and cities (Daly, 1981; 1982; Lee, 1978; MacMahon, 1981). Hence familism and Catholicism comprised discourses which were uniformly available to all non-Protestant Irishmen and women; discourses which were underpinned by the third component of this strategic formation – discourses of sexuality.

Michel Foucault has suggested that discourses of sexuality have been significant deployments and interventions of power within the day-to-day life of individuals. He has stated that, in every society, relations of sex give rise to 'deployment of alliance': 'a system of marriage, of fixation and development of kinship ties, of transmission of names and possessions' (Foucault, 1984, p. 106). Contrasting this deployment of alliance with the later, but interconnected, 'deployment of sexuality', he has suggested that the deployment of alliance is linked to the maintenance of social stability which it maintains through rules and prohibitions which define the licit and the illicit. Consequently, the deployment of alliance enjoys a privileged link with the law. The deployment of sexuality, however, does not operate through rules and prohibitions, but through multiplying the ways in which intimate areas of human experience may be opened up for examination, discussion and discursive regulation. Thus, while the deployment of alliance sets bounds on what can be spoken of, the deployment of sexuality, by recognizing no bounds, infinitely extends the scope of power and control at the individual level. Foucault states that sexuality has been deployed through the family, overlaying the extant deployment of alliance, and that the family unit does not act to expel sexuality but serves as its focus and anchor.

Within familism, it might appear that the deployment of alliance, with its rules and prohibitions of 'the commerce allowed or forbidden (adultery, extramarital relations with a person prohibited by blood or statute, the legitimate character of the act of sexual congress)' (p. 107) predominated to the exclusion of the deployment of sexuality, but such was not the case. As Arensberg's and Kimball's materials show, familism, as a deployment of alliance, was so demanding of individuals that sexuality had to be subordinated to alliance through elaborate and rigorous discursive regulation. While those few who did get married had large families, emigration 'offered compensation for non-inheritors of land; celibacy among non-inheritors signified the powerful linkage between marriage and succession to property and high fertility generated competition among potential inheritors and so bolstered the bargaining power of landholders' (Fitzpatrick, 1983, p. 369). Amongst the tenant farmers, sex was a subsidiary to a more important, material, transaction – the passage of farms and dowries from generation to generation. For example, even where extra-marital pregnancies or elopements took place, Arensberg and Kimball stated that the small farmers could not comprehend that these might be driven by desire. Such attempts to frustrate familism were explained as caused by the male culprits' 'greed for land and dowries' leading them to deliberately impregnate the girls. Indeed, 'Sex without familism seemed beyond the country peoples' imagination' (Arensberg and Kimball, 1968, p. 203). In the context of the discourse of sexuality their conclusion is striking: 'They [the small farmers] equate any departure from the accepted norm as a sin, a lack of religion. They bring the whole weight of all their sanctions and values to bear upon it' (p. 203).

The validity of these observations is confirmed by studies which indicate the enormous energy devoted to regulating the forms in which sexuality could make ingress into familism (Connolly, 1982, p. 214-18). When the survival of the tenant farmer class was dependent on familism, and when familism was in turn dependent on the proscription of sexual activity outside marriage, the entry of sexuality with its concern with 'the sensations of the body, the quality of pleasures, and the nature of impressions, however tenuous or imperceptible these may be' (Foucault, 1984, p.106), presented a fundamental problem. Since Ireland was at this time an open market for cheap English literature – the gothic shockers and penny dreadfuls which returning seasonal migrants brought with them into even the most isolated areas – the grounds for Archbishop Croke's condemnations of England's 'vicious literature' (Croke, 1884), and J.M. O'Reilly's castigations of her 'trashy ... novels and periodicals' (O'Reilly, p. 5), are easy to understand. What must be emphasized, however, is that condemnations of such material were themselves contributions to a growing deployment of sexuality, but one in which 'sex was equated for all practical purposes with sin' (Lee, 1978, p. 40). Hence, defence of familism in order to perpetuate the tenant farmers required intense co-operation between priests and laity as they struggled to counter the effects of discourses of sexuality produced in the metropolis and limit the potential disruption of unregulated desire. Consequently, for Irish authors to raise these issues in their works was to threaten the foundations of familism and the class it made possible. While moral purity was a high priority for the clergy on ethical and spiritual grounds it was hardly less so for the laity, for both ethical and material reasons, so that the success of the Catholic Church 'in instilling strict standards of sexual morality was largely fortuitous, depending less on the influence of the preacher than on the general acceptability of his message' (Connolly, 1982, p. 214). It is to the internal regulating codes of an expanding system of familism that one should look, therefore, to explain Irish Catholics' emphasis on sexual restraint rather than the suggested importation of Jansenism which contemporary inquisitions failed to uncover (Corish, 1979). Nonetheless, to reassess the Catholic Church's influence in one aspect hardly diminishes its overall significance, particularly since in the later nineteenth century what has been termed a 'devotional revolution' took place, which both intensified the capacity of the Catholic Church in Ireland to speak to the Catholic laity, and produced a uniformity of practice which embraced Catholics throughout the island.

Emmet Larkin has argued that during the supremacy of Cardinal Paul Cullen (Archbishop of Armagh and Apostolic Delegate, 1849-52, Archbishop of Dublin 1852-, Cardinal, 1866-1878) (Larkin, 1984) this 'devotional revolution' entailed for the clergy increased standards in administration, scrupulous adherence to the doctrinal positions of the papacy, and ready acceptance of the instructions of superiors, particularly the Cardinal Archbishop. Anything that smacked of irregularity or departed from the practices and procedures approved by Rome was rooted out (Corish, 1979). Simultaneously, this re-invigorated clergy extended to the laity as a whole an active and all-encompassing form of religious practice. A large number of new and imposing churches was constructed for the laity to worship in, religious societies were widely established to encourage individual devotion, and new forms of worship as ancillaries to the Mass were introduced. Attendance at Sunday Mass and at confession became practically universal (Connolly, 1982, p. 54). By the time of Cullen's death in 1878 he had placed his stamp firmly on Catholic Church in Ireland, which subsequently followed the trajectory he had impelled it along.

By the end of the nineteenth century, Catholicism – the long-term and fundamental constituent of the identity of the people-nation – had been institutionally reformed and re-invigorated. The direct and indirect influence of the Catholic Church was thereby increased through intensified contact between priests and people, while simultaneously tremendous opportunities for communication and the evocation of solidarity were produced for those who would – or could – grasp them. By the closing decades of the nineteenth century the Catholic Church and Catholicism, which both Ferguson and O'Grady had located as obstacles to the production of Anglo-Irish hegemony, were central, as the partners and guarantors of familism and the educator of the people-nation, to the strategic formation to which the writers of the 1890s and 1900s needed to refer if they were to forge a sentimental connection with the people-nation. George Sigerson asserted in an address to the first meeting of the Irish National Literary Society in 1892 that 'wealth of thought is a country's treasure, literature is its articulate voice' (Sigerson, 1894, p. 60), which only raised starkly, at the opening of the Revival, the matter of whose thought would be spoken and who, in that speech, empowered.

A common feature of nineteenth-century Anglo-Irish definitions of national identity and consequent national needs was the need of the imagined nation to be governed by the class from which the writers offered their less-than-disinterested analyses. After the death of Parnell many additional opinions emanated from within the people-nation itself, which at certain points overlapped with those of the Anglo-Irish to form a complementary phalanx in which 'Irishness' was increasingly defined against an English 'other'. As innate Irish virtues came to be defined against English vices, however, the question was, increasingly, to what extent an excluding identity could include an element (the Anglo-Irish) which itself conceived of 'the nation' as comprised of superior and subaltern castes. 'The fundamental question was.... What do we hope to make of Ireland?' argued Sir Charles Gavan Duffy in 1892 (Duffy, 1894, p. 19), and the history of the following decades is that of fiercely contradictory answers to that question and of often desperate attempts to become the definers of the thoughts expressed by the nation's 'articulate voice'.

As a variety of answers to Duffy's question were put forward throughout the 1890s a dominant issue emerged: the impact of 'literary garbage', destroying the Irish, a people whose qualities were those of 'purity, piety, and simplicity' (Duffy, 1894, pp. 12-3). The source of the 'garbage', as of a 'debasing social system' founded on mines and factories, was England, defined not simply as the denier of Ireland's right to self-determination but as the destroyer of the national identity which had survived centuries of oppression only to abandon itself to oblivion in a willing and wholesale Anglicization. In what initially appears to be a reprise of Davis's 1840s arguments, Duffy envisaged a race which would marry 'the fine qualities of the Celtic family' with 'the sterner strength of the North' and the discipline of the 'Norman genius of Munster'. As a one-time Young Irelander, whose activities had culminated in decades of Australian exile, Duffy was a living link with Davis's concept of an inclusivist nation whose ideal was an agrarian society of peasant farmers 'not needing or desiring great wealth, but enjoying free, simple lives' more in harmony with the nature of the people than those social systems producing 'the stricken legions who serve the steam engine and the water-wheel' (Duffy, 1894, pp. 19-20). Such an idyllic evocation of an Irish essence, which is being corrupted by the aping of English fashion, games, music, and periodicals, is the hallmark of the most significant of these many rallying calls of the 1890s, Douglas Hyde's 'The Necessity of De-Anglicising Ireland', an address delivered to the Irish National Literary Society in November 1892. The striking feature of the piece, however, is not so much the extent to which it reiterates Duffy's arguments, presented to the same society in the June of that year, but the tensions which emerge, not simply between Hyde and Duffy, but within the argument of Hyde himself; to de-Anglicize Ireland was an objective whose implications had almost to be denied at the very moment that it was proclaimed.

Duffy had offered an image of a race in which Ulsterman and Norman could be brought into the Celtic family. Hyde, while opening and closing his address with the declaration that 'De-Anglicisation' was an issue not simply for nationalists, but also for Unionists who wished 'to see the Irish nation produce its best' (Hyde, 1894, p. 161), went on to assert the essence of that nation in terms which were explicitly exclusive: 'we must strive to cultivate everything that is most racial, most smacking of the soil, most Gaelic, most Irish, because in spite of the little admixture of Saxon blood in the north-east corner, this island *is* and will *ever* remain Celtic at the core [emphasis in original]' (p. 159). To escape from the contradiction of wishing for an Irish nation formed on exclusive Irish lines, while simultaneously seeking to include those whom this definition of Irishness would otherwise have excluded, Hyde argued for cultural essentialism. Unable as a Protestant to utilize Catholicism, which had defined the Irish across the centuries, Hyde turned to the Gaelic language in an attempt to erect a concept of the nation distinctly Irish, yet capable of incorporating the Anglo-Irish, who clearly would have had every reason to welcome the entrée into security offered by the image of a nation defining itself in terms of the past and seeing modernity as a threat to its ancestral integrity. A further definition of what, to Anglo-Irish intellectuals, would be an acceptable concept of a culturally defined nation may be found in Yeats's 'The Irish National Literary Society' (November 1892), effectively the founding manifesto of the association, which, in its third person reference to himself as 'The Celt', shows the extent to which Yeats adopted not only that persona, but also the concept of the nation which was implied by that term.

Ireland, Yeats argued, had fallen away from grace as it 'grinds all things into pounds and shillings' and neglects to search for 'the imaginative and spiritual food to be got out of great literature' (Yeats, 1980, p. 17, 18). As the nation thus sells its birthright for material gain the issue becomes the need to join literature with 'the great passion of patriotism' to redeem both and bring the people 'to care once more for the things of the mind' (p. 18). Yeats, unlike Hyde or Duffy, avoided all overt reference to racial divisions, suggesting that this literary enterprise would transcend political factions and create a sense of national unity for which the only adequate description is spiritual. This re-vitalization of the concept of cultural nationalism aspired to deny contemporary division through the creation of a transcendental Irish essence: 'amidst the clash of party against party we have tried to put forward a nationality that is above party, and amid the oncoming roar of a general election we have tried to assert those everlasting principles of love of truth and love of country that speak to men in solitude and in the silence of the night' (p. 19). The metaphysical suggestion of the solitude and silence of the night merges with the use of 'country', in its topographical rather than national connotation, to evoke an Ireland whose truth is defined by fidelity to 'the great traditions of the past', a suitably vague phrase suggesting that alteration is anathema to an Ireland whose historic and social reality is made material in the spear heads and golden collars of the New Museum. Yeats claimed a 'pure' nationality that was above party; the reality of his claims, the possibilty of such a phenomenon, was the issue which was to exercise writers for the rest of the decade and beyond.

Malcolm Brown has suggested that such an objective was fraudulent from the outset. 'Nonpolitical poets', he maintains, 'do not form societies; they abhor societies ... with Yeats, as with Hyde, the question that lingered was: What kind of politics is it?' (Brown, 1972, p.356). Conor Cruise O'Brien has argued that before 1900 Yeats's cultural politics were 'popular and active', but after 1900, became 'aristocratic and archaising' (O'Brien, 1965, p. 222), a move which Peter Kuch has identified with a shift in Yeats's poetry and criticism from Celticism before 1900, to a subsequent concentration on the peasant and the aristocrat (Kuch, 1986, p. 140). In reality, however, Yeats's writing and practice were unified throughout the period from the 1880s to 1907 in an attempt to enable the fusion of the Anglo-Irish with the people-nation. The shift from Celticism pre-1900 to peasant/aristocrat post-1900 represents, therefore, a shift from accessing one stategic formation, that which had originated with Renan and Arnold, to a strategic formation having something in common with O'Grady's preoccupations, an approach which attempted to appropriate the figure of 'the peasant', already centrally important in the writings of the Gaelic League and kindred organizations, in order to weld it to the aristocrat as part of a harmonious social idealization. For Yeats, Thomas Davis's strategy of non-sectarian pluralist unity, although deferred to publicly by all elements of the people-nation and their would-be leaders, offered nothing. Despite Yeats's early Davisite poems (Yeats, 1957, pp. 709-15; pp. 737-8), the model was by that time too well defined, its audiences' expectations too pragmatic, for him to be able to develop it independently. Moreover, the return of Sir Charles Gavan Duffy to Irish cultural politics in the 1890s denied Yeats access to a space in those politics that he might otherwise have occupied. Duffy's take-over of the 'New Library of Ireland', which Yeats had projected, directed the poet towards other modes of access to the people-nation and initially towards a concentration on Celticism (Yeats, 1986, p. 310 et. seq.; Kuch, 1986, p. 24). But the continuity of Yeats's strategic location throughout the period from the 1880s to 1907, is sharply revealed in the forms of his projected 'nationality above party'. While in practice this unity could only be achieved by dissolving the barriers between the Anglo-Irish and the people-nation, that in turn was dependent upon the re-making of either the Anglo-Irish or the people-nation. Yeats's strategic location is sharply revealed in that, rather than seeking to re-make the Anglo-Irish, the people-nation was the object of his endeavours, as he sought in his pre-1900 writings to re-fashion them as 'Celts', and in his post-1900 writings as noble peasants.

Celticism offered Yeats an opportunity for such a re-making, but to be successful Celticism itself had to be purged of any tendency to reference the philological and ethnic roots of the Celt, whose identity had to be sought in more nebulous terms. If, following Arnold, the true marks of the Celt were to be found in emotion, natural magic, love of colour, quickness of perception and spirituality, rather than the Irish language, such intangible criteria could be deployed to make Celts of Yeats and his Anglo-Irish contemporaries. From his early epic 'The Wanderings of Oisin' (Yeats, 1957, pp. 1-63), throughout the poems of *Crossways* (1889), *The Rose* (1893), and *The Wind Among The Reeds* (1899), the Arnoldian criteria are constantly developed. In early poetry and criticism colour, time, and mythology are dominant. In 'The Wanderings of Oisin' descriptive passages are awash with references to colour and nature. Colours are used to evoke moods with a repetitiveness that appears almost didactic. Oisin's and Niamh's first meeting is by a 'dove-grey' sea. Niamh herself is 'pearl-pale' and the presentiment of eventual doom is conveyed at the moment of meeting by the colour of her lips 'like a sunset ... / A stormy sunset on doomed ships' (Yeats, 1957, p. 3). References to periods of time are dominated by evening, night, and early dawn. Oisin's reminiscent comments to St Patrick are of 'a hundred years / At evening on the glimmering sands' (p. 23). Similarly, these are the criteria mobilized by Yeats to analyse Katharine Tynan's poem 'The Ballad of Courcey of Kinsale'. Having praised her energy he added: 'you have sacrafised [sic] all things to colour.... Your best work – and no woman poet of the time has done better – is always where you express your own affectionate nature or your religious feeling, either directly or indirectly in some legend; your worst – that which stands in your way with the best readers – where you allow your sense of colour to run away with you and make you merely a poet of the picturesque' (Yeats, 1986, p. 119).

As Yeats's esoteric knowledge grew throughout the 1880s and 1890s the straightforward descriptive criteria of colour, place, and time, were overlaid by a proliferating symbolism drawn eclectically from philosophy, Theosophy and ritual magic. The result was a decline in emphasis on colour and time in his poetry, and increased emphasis on melancholy and spirituality. Reviewing his collection *The Celtic Twilight* in 1900, Dora M. Jones wrote: 'his [Yeats's] verse has the thrilling melancholy of a violin ... the mystical power of the hour 'twixt gloaming and the mirk, when the elemental spirits have power and the hills and trees seem to brood with half conscious life as they grow dark against the sky' (Jones, 1900, pp. 62-3), an impression of the tone of Yeats's Celticist poetry confirmed by poems from the later 1890s in which the abstruse symbolic references to trees, animals and locations, are so gnomic that even their author conceded the necessity for explanatory notes (Yeats, 1957, p. 800). Where references to nature in the poems of the 1880s were usually representative and, if symbolic, referred to well-known elements of Irish mythology, by the early 1890s 'the holy tree' growing in his lover's heart refers to the Sephirotic tree of the Kabbalah (Yeats, 1957, p. 134), whilst the centrality of the rose symbol within the eponymous collection published in 1893 testified to Yeats's increased use of occult symbols as a complement to Celticism. For while the rose had been a poetic symbol of Ireland for some time, in Yeats's writing it stood also as the central symbol of rosicrucianism, so that when in the poem 'The Rose' the two are coupled as in the final lines: 'I would, before my time to go / Sing of Old Eire and the ancient ways: / Red Rose, proud Rose, sad Rose of all my days' (p. 100), the intention to draw nationalism, Celticism and occultism together is made manifest. Yeats's purpose in this was to employ esoteric symbolism as a direct communion with his fellow countrymen and women via Celtic 'otherworldliness', by-passing the influence of Catholicism by reaching what he supposed to be a more fundamental level of their spirituality (Kuch, 1986, p. 20).

The reception accorded to Yeats's play *The Countess Cathleen*, and D.P. Moran's charge that the ' "Celtic note" ... [was] one of the most glaring frauds that the credulous Irish people ever swallowed' (Moran, 1905, p. 22), testify to Yeats's success in using 'Celtic' sprituality as a mode of access to the people-nation. The advice of Yeats's Fenian mentor, John O'Leary, that in Ireland 'a man must have upon his side the Church or the Fenians, and you will never have the Church' (Yeats, 1955, p. 209), was correct in its assessment of the centrality of Catholicism, albeit over-optimistic about the capacity of Fenianism to act as a counter. Nonetheless, throughout the 1890s the concepts of Celtic anti-materialism and spirituality continued to inform Yeats's poetry, prose, drama, and polemics. Initially directed at England, as Yeats encountered increasing hostility to his ideas within nationalist Ireland he discovered elements there, too, inimical to the Celt's spiritual essence. In 1899 Yeats warned the Irish writers of his day that the models of popular art that they had turned to – Scott, Longfellow, Campbell – were in fact the products of materialist England and Scotland's 'counting-house'. Copied in Ireland by the writers of a 'new Class', 'without breeding and ancestry', this new (Catholic bourgeois) class's 'new art' had interposed itself between the 'hut and the castle and the hut and the cloister' (Yeats, 1961, pp. 10-11). Dismissing the idea that there was no common ground on which the art of the people and of the 'coteries', or intellectuals, could meet, he argued that both 'are alike strange and obscure' and that what was alien to both people and intellectuals was the 'new art', the spuriously named 'popular poetry' whose 'manifest logic, [and] clear rhetoric' was unlike true 'popular poetry' which, like that of the coteries, 'glimmer[ed] with thoughts and images whose "ancestors were stout and wise," "a nigh to Paradise" "ere yet men knew the gift of corn" ' (p.8). Yeats extended similar condemnations to the clergy, arguing that they had embraced materialism and that the cause of true spirituality had now devolved upon 'the arts' which were 'about to take upon their shoulders the burdens that have fallen from the shoulders of the priests, and to lead us back upon our journeys by filling our thoughts with the essences of things, and not with things' (Yeats, 1961, p. 193).

Such barely adequate responses to increasingly well directed critiques of his cultural politics exposed the shifting foundations of Yeats's attempt to develop sentimental connections between the Anglo-Irish and the people-nation, and in a debate with AE (George Russell) and John Eglinton in the *Dublin Daily Express* in late summer 1898, Yeats was publicly forced to confront the prospects and practical possibility, as others saw it, of his demand for a literature that would link with patriotism and produce a mutual ennobling in a love of country that was above party. As Eglinton recognized in his article 'What Should be the Subject of a National Drama?', the choice of subject matter for a national drama 'might serve as a test of what nationality really amounts to in Ireland'. Alert to the propensity of the revivalists to seek their subject matter in folk-lore and legends, he asked if anything other than *belles-lettres* was likely to be produced by such determined pre-occupation with the past, in preference to the realities of the present and swiftly responded in the negative. 'Ireland', he declared, 'must exchange the patriotism which looks back for the patriotism which looks forward.... In short, we need to realise in Ireland that a national drama or literature must spring from a native interest in life and its problems and a strong capacity for life among the people' (Eglinton, 1899, pp. 9, 12, 13).

Yeats replied to Eglinton that it was precisely by looking to the past that the poet served the present; through his association of Irish landscape with Irish legend he made Ireland 'a holy land to her own people' (p. 19).

Eglinton's riposte was precise and opposed: 'The poet looks too much away from himself and his age, does not feel the facts of life enough, but seeks in art an escape from them. Consequently, the art he achieves cannot be the expression of the age and himself – cannot be representative or national' (p. 27). While Eglinton prosaically stated that Yeats could not be speaking for the people, Yeats resorted to otherworldliness, asserting that poetry should be divorced from the contemporary and, far from seeking to become a criticism of life, should concern itself with the revelation of a hidden life of beauty. As he argued in the conclusion of 'National Drama and Contemporary Life', it is by passionate service to the aesthetic ideal of beauty that harmony is produced, and 'all criticism that forgets these things is mischievious, and doubly mischievious in a country of unsettled opinion' (pp. 36, 37). AE's contribution to the debate was to declare that Irish nationality was beginning to be felt 'less as a political movement than as a spiritual force' (p. 83). The objective of a national literature should be 'to create the Ireland in the heart' for, in Ireland, as once in the Egypt and Greece of antiquity, there were writers who had as their objective the creation of 'a soul for their people' (p. 81). AE's spiritual extremism here fused with the anti-materialist bias of Hyde as he proclaimed that the modern age was riven with 'psychic maladies', that the cosmopolitan spirit was obliterating distinctions, and only in Ireland 'are [we] not yet sick with this sickness' (p. 80). For AE, the creation of an Irish nationality was a spiritual crusade predicated upon separatism and difference, for 'If nationality is to justify itself it must be because the country which preserves its individuality does so with the profound conviction that its peculiar ideal is nobler than that which the cosmopolitan spirit suggests' (p. 82).

Yeats's contribution to this debate, marked the high point of his Celticism. Subsequently the influence of Nietzsche, Synge, and Lady Gregory, combined with Yeats's experience of the theatre to turn him away from Celticism, but there were other influences also at work in making its attractiveness wane. The writers of the Irish-Ireland movement were not slow to offer their appreciations of Celticism. D.P. Moran was only one of many who criticized Yeats's attempts to redirect Irish energies away from politics to metaphysical speculations; the preserve, one might add, of those for whom social reality was, on the whole, eminently acceptable. Political necessity, argued a *United Ireland* review in 1895, demanded that: 'While the struggle for our national rights goes on politics is indispensable' (Hall, 1980, p. 45). This did not mean, however, that in rejecting the lure of Celtic faeryland the nationalist movement was advocating an engagement with Irish actuality after the model proposed by Eglinton, rather it saw the example of Thomas Davis as that to be emulated in which actuality was idealized to the point where the Irish people, and above all the Irish peasant, became the threatened repositories of virtue in a land besieged by Saxon materialism.

Thus, while Anglo-Irish and Irish-Irish polemic frequently overlapped on the matter of materialism versus anti-materialism, albeit for conflicting strategic reasons, the conflicting concepts which both held of the pure peasant as the quintessence of the nation acted to crystallize their differences. For Anglo-Irish writers the value of the image of the peasant lay, with some significant variations, in the physical vitalism which could be attributed to the avoidance of the debilitating vices of modernity. For nationalist intellectuals of the people-nation, however, the essential literary function of the peasant was to show forth an image of the Irish in which avoidance of the English vices was achieved through acceptance of the rigid moral guidelines of Irish Catholicism as enforced by the priest. The duality of priest and peasant as the cornerstone of the nation became the crucial test of a writer's position within the cultural politics of the Literary Revival. To question the relationship became heresy, and to advocate any path to freedom in which individual desire took precedence over a political movement which was underpinned by the priesthood was to risk being condemned as dangerously cosmopolitan. While on the one hand, therefore, Catholicism became a fundamental tenet of the political movement of the people-nation in its move towards national self-determination, it simultaneously became for many writers the cause of an even more profound enslavement than that of Union with England – the enslavement of the self. Paradoxically, both groupings argued for their vision as encapsulating the Irish essence, but for one that essence lay in the peasant to the extent that the movement of centuries had failed to eliminate an innate paganism, albeit one which frequently necessitated the maintenance of the complementary corollary of a 'warrior' aristocracy. For the other, however, it lay in the extent to which the contemporary reality of peasant Ireland was founded on a purity buttressed by the priesthood. In the 1900s, the outcome of the struggle to capture the concept of 'the peasant', in order to mobilize it as a sentimental connection between the various contending groups of intellectuals and the people-nation, gave a particular form of definition and concretization to that people-nation. A significant step in deciding which of these two concepts would prevail was marked by the reception of Yeats's *The Countess Cathleen* in 1899.

The controversy over the play began with F. Hugh O'Donnell's pamphlet 'Souls For Gold' (O'Donnell, 1972; Hogan and Kilroy, 1975, pp. 31-2). O'Donnell had seen an early text of the play published in Yeats's *Poems* (1895) in which one of the peasants kicks a shrine of the Virgin Mary to pieces (Yeats, 1966, p.31, l.182e). His condemnation of the 1899 play was issued before the actual production and Yeats's collaborator, Edward Martyn, had already prevailed upon him to delete the offending passage before the play opened. Nevertheless, the performance of a *tableau vivant* version of the play at the Vice-Regal Lodge in January 1899 indicated to some an Ascendancy/Dublin Castle connection, an opinion underwritten by the resonances of a drama set in a famine, in which souls are being bartered for gold and food, and in which the landlord saves the lives and the souls of the peasants. In picking up the incident of the shrine, and in reciting the tale of 'the demented female, Countess Cathleen, who exhibits her affection for the soul-selling and soup-buying Irish people by selling her own soul to supply them with more gold and soup, and is rewarded for her blasphemous apostacy by Mr. W.B. Yeats, dramatist and theologian, by being straightway transmigrated to heaven' (O'Donnell, 1972), O'Donnell gave enough details to satisfy many of his readers that Yeats's play was politically and theologically suspect. Such was the impression of Cardinal Archbishop Logue who (with an appropriate reservation because he had not read it) condemned the play on the basis of O'Donnell's pamphlet, and was later to write to the *Daily Nation* on 10 May 1899 to say that 'an Irish Catholic audience which could patiently sit out such a play must have sadly degenerated, both in religion and patriotism' (Hogan and Kilroy, 1975, p. 43).

Contemporary accounts suggest that antagonism to the play amongst the audience was confined to a small, well-behaved minority. But for the whole audience the play posed problems, not only of theology but comprehension. Yeats argued that 'what they had to do' in the Irish Literary Theatre 'was to spiritualise the patriotism and drama' (Hogan and Kilroy, 1975, pp. 50-1) of Ireland, and *The Countess Cathleen* was but a stage in this programme: 'The play is symbolic: the two demons ... are the world ... The Countess herself is a soul ... The symbols have other meanings, but they have this principal meaning'. (Yeats, 1954, p. 319). The power of the pure soul to transcend the snares of materialism is Yeats's preferred, occult and Celticist, reading but the text provides another possibility in that feudalism is vindicated through the actions of the Countess whose commitment to the peasants is seen as preferable to the deceits of the 'devils'; the Merchants from the East whose geographical location embraces both England and 'fallen' metropolitan Ireland. The conclusion of the encounter between Anglo-Irish and Catholic Nationalism was that Celticist spirituality, or its corollary, Ascendancy supremacy, was decisively worsted by institutional Catholicism while the play's esoteric symbolism failed to evoke appropriate responses from the audience. Moreover, Yeats was confirmed among the general public as a writer with heterodox opinions. In particular, O'Donnell's comments on Yeats's supposed slanders on Irish womanhood, referring to the exchange between 'A Woman' and the First Merchant in Act V (Yeats, 1966, p. 137), was to be taken up later by the *Freeman's Journal* in relation to *Diarmuid and Grania* when there was condemnation of 'the selection of such a sensual and immoral legend as Diarmuid and Grania for dramatic representation'. The complainant, a priest who had not seen the play, added that if 'rumour speaks truly, it was just as grossly represented as it dare be' (Hogan and Kilroy, 1975, p. 126). Thus Yeats learned that in contemporary Ireland some symbols and evocations had meanings which were unproblematically clear for his audiences – a point confirmed when he saw his other play, *Cathleen Ni Houlihan*, go on to become a nationalist classic.

Cathleen Ni Houlihan, first performed in April 1902, extolled the sacrifice of one of the people-nation for the sake of Ireland. In commenting that 'the full impact of the play can only be felt if the audience is aware of the great weight of patriotic associations behind Yeats's references to the French landings at Killala', A.S. Knowland emphasizes the shift in Yeats's practice (Knowland, 1983, p. 126). In turning from occultism and Celticism, pitching the conflict as one between invader and natives, and dramatizing the suppression of the desired marriage for the sake of the death-demanding nation, Yeats demonstrated a capacity to access radical republicanism, and history, not as interpreted by Ascendancy historians like W.E.H. Lecky, but by popular writers such as A.M. Sullivan in his *The Story of Ireland*. Such a strategic formation, however, permitted an Anglo-Irish writer only two strategic locations – in effect either approving or condemning the struggles of the people-nation, with all the limited scope for individual opinion that choosing to support the people-nation through Davisite models allowed. In *Cathleen Ni Houlihan*, Yeats chose to write a secular myth for the people-nation. Subsequently that very fact of production enabled him to draw on the prestige of 'the author of *Cathleen Ni Houlihan*' (as during '*The Playboy* Riots') to support a very different strategic location: one from which he was to criticize and condemn the Catholic bourgeois leaders of the people-nation.

Yeats's collaborator in the Irish Literary Theatre and with him the co-author of *Diarmuid and Grania*, the novelist and playwright George Moore, reflects in both content and composition of his short-story collection *The Untilled Field* the dilemma that he and other writers confronted in that moment. The stories in the collection were designed to provide new readers of Gaelic with matter on which to exercise their linguistic skills. Although Moore spoke no Gaelic he was committed to the concept of Ireland which he saw emerging and wrote the stories for translation and then publication in 1902. Each story in the collection published in English in 1903, however, was a constant reiteration of Moore's growing belief that since it was 'impossible to enjoy independence of body and soul in Ireland' (Moore, 1976, p. 349), the stories he had to write 'were drawing [him] away from Catholic Ireland' (p. 347). In the 1914 edition of *The Untilled Field*, Moore claimed an influence on Synge, and many critics have pointed to the parallel conception between *The Untilled Field* and Joyce's *Dubliners*. But that influence apart, what unites these writers is a demand for freedom which is personal and, above all, sexual; there could be no greater affront to the nationalist Ireland which Yeats had embraced, albeit temporarily, in *Cathleen Ni Houlihan*.

Throughout the collection Moore points to the priest as the self-righteous and self-interested moral arbiter of the community. Whether it is extending a meeting on poultry keeping to an hour beyond pub closing, arriving at cottages to condemn the drinking and dancing therein, or haranguing courting couples out walking in the lanes, the priest is presented as an all-pervasive force in peasant life. The full impact of this is demonstrated in two stories in which an exile returns, 'Home Sickness' and 'The Wild Goose', for there Moore is able to dramatize the clash between an impoverished actuality and a consciousness alerted to the vitality of a wider world. For, even though the exile of 'Home Sickness' finally determines to go back to the brutality of the Bowery bar in which his health has deteriorated, the 'modern restlessness and cold energy' of New Yorkers is preferred to the 'weakness and incompetence' of this 'primitive people clinging to religious authority' (Moore, 1914, p. 43). The 'pathetic ignorance' of the people and the 'bleak' country play their part in influencing his return, but above all 'It was the priest who came to forbid the dancing. Yes, it was the priest' (p.46). The point is reinforced in the speech of the returned exile in 'The Wild Goose' who, having entered into the fray of nationalist politics, argues that Ireland's energy was being sapped through an emigration of those who could not tolerate the 'joyless' life whose insidious influence was greater than any economic causes. Ned Carmady, the protagonist of the story, starts to feel that 'Ireland was wakening from the great sleep of Catholicism, and at the next parish it seemed as if the impossible were going to happen and that the Gael was going to be free' (p. 305). Carmady, however, commits the indiscretion of quoting John Mitchel and unleashes all the hostility of a church which sees the spirit of atheistic revolution in his words. Frustrated in his objectives he, like Moore himself, returns to exile in flight from 'A mean, ineffectual atmosphere of nuns and rosaries' (p. 310).

Despite the apparently anti-nationalist sentiments, what is noteworthy in the collection, as indeed in Synge and Joyce, is the view that Ireland is being betrayed by the heavy hand of clericalism. As the old James Bryden of 'Home Sickness' reflects back on his life from the vantage point of his own bar-room it is of his abandoned love and Ireland that he thinks: 'Margaret's soft eyes' and 'the green hillside, and the bog lake and the rushes about it, and the greater lake in the distance, and behind it the blue line of wandering hills' (p. 49). The Irish landscape evokes a similar positive response in Ned Carmady who thinks of 'the great pagans who had wandered over these hills before scapulars and rosaries were invented'. 'Will Usheen ever come again,' he wonders, and expresses his conclusion in his determination to leave (p. 310). A marriage destroyed, an idealist excluded, but above all a people repressed, is Moore's theme, a joyless life that is an insult to the natural beauty of the land and its ancient history. 'In Ireland men and women die without realising any of the qualities they bring into the world', Moore wrote in *Hail and Farewell* (Moore, 1976, p. 58), and it is AE's question to the nationalist movement that proved to be of paramount importance: 'But what use will her language be to Ireland if she is not granted the right to think?' (p. 343). The central issue for intellectuals who would forge a sentimental connection with the people-nation was the extent to which they would be able, or permitted, to extend or confront the limits set by the strategic formation which defined the integrity of the people-nation and made possible their cultural and material reproduction. This issue was to be most directly approached in drama – hence the genealogy of the Abbey Theatre and other theatre groups helps to define the course and progress of the contention for hegemony in early twentieth-century Ireland.

The stated intention of the Abbey Theatre group was to be 'outside all the political questions that divide us' (Lady Gregory, 1972, p. 20), and

J.M. Synge's letter to Maud Gonne in 1897 separating himself from her 'revolutionary and semi-military movement' (Synge, 1983, p. 46), the *Association Irlandaise*, coupled with Gonne's resignation from the Irish National Theatre Society over her opposition to his *The Shadow of the Glen*, could be taken as substantiating a divorce between a progressive revolutionary nationalism on the one hand, and an élitist aestheticism on the other, particularly as Synge's Anglo-Irish pedigree and cosmopolitan intellect set him far apart from any parochial Irish-Irish exclusivism. The reality, however, is suggested by Synge's comment in the same letter that he wished 'to work in [his] own way for the cause of Ireland' as he had his own 'theory of regeneration for Ireland' (p. 47). Such claims could be subsumed within the frequent general assertions of advancing Ireland through art of quality were it not for the furore surrounding Synge's work, a reaction caused by the fact that he dramatized the explicit belief that the revolution required, if not desired, by Ireland, was of the sensual – and frequently female – individual.

What was expected of nationalist drama is nowhere better revealed than in the productions of Maud Gonne's patriotic women's organization *Inghinidhe na hEireann* ('Daughters of Erin'), which included amateur dramatics in its activities (Ward, 1983, pp.40-87). The group had sponsored the first production of Yeats's *Cathleen Ni Houlihan* in which Maud Gonne had played the title rôle, and it is that play's advocacy of sacrificing individual desire for national advancement which characterizes the movement's other propagandist productions. Padraic Colum's *The Saxon Shillin'* had been found too contentious by the Fay's Irish National Dramatic Society because of its overt propagandizing in which a family's eviction is resisted by the son who, having once taken 'the Saxon Shillin' ' and joined the British army, comes to see that his loyalty is with the family in whose defence he dies. Produced by the children's dramatic class of *Inghinidhe na hEireann* in 1903, Colum's basic theme of rejecting British authority and asserting Irish rights to land and property, even at pain of individual loss, anticipates Maud Gonne's own *Dawn* which was published in *The United Irishman* in 1904. Gonne, like Colum, but with more consciously 'poetic' language, stresses the callous brutality of 'The Stranger' but goes further in ending not on the glorious sacrifice for Ireland, but on the dedication of the men to revolutionary action. The play's conclusion merits attention, for its emphasis on (re)-dedication of life to a Mother Ireland links it to Yeats's *Cathleen Ni Houlihan*, as Seamus, who had also taken the 'Saxon Shilling' declares: 'Mother, forgive me for Brideen's sake. Let me, too, die for you'; an act of individual and communal assertion through which 'Bride of the Sorrows' will be transformed into 'Bride of the Victories' (Hogan and Kilroy, 1970, p. 84). The notable feature is not so much the willing embrace of death for the nationalist cause, but the fact that death is chosen so as to transform Kathleen and Bride (The Mother of *Dawn*), namely Ireland herself, into a state of youth, beauty, and Freedom. The personification of Ireland as 'Woman' and 'Mother' necessitated that the purity of that image was maintained on all levels for, in order to maintain its mobilizing force, 'Woman' could only ever be an eternal essence beyond the physicality which suggested other, darker, demands and desires. Synge's 'theory of regeneration' lay in the acknowledgement, and even celebration, of female desire, a revolutionary concept which starkly revealed the contradictions and limitations not only in the nationalist camp, but also in the Abbey group itself.

Synge's *The Shadow of the Glen* is essentially a thematic prelude to the later, more complex, *The Playboy of the Western World* in its examination of life in a community in which sexual desire is subordinate to economic necessity. Nora has been driven into marriage with an older man through need, but on counting the cost of security bought at such a price concludes that she has been a fool. The grim environment of wind, rain and mist that she evokes functions as the dramatic externalization of a relationship which is just as bleak, for the 'death' of her husband is seen as an extension of the sterility of their life together: 'Maybe cold would be no sign of death with the like of him, for he was always cold, every day since I knew him, – and every night, stranger' (Synge, 1958, p. 4). Deprived of a warmth which she yearns for in explicitly sexual terms Nora, it is implied, has found satisfaction with the now dead Patch Darcy and intends to do so with Michael Dara, as desire revolts against a repression enforced by economic necessity. Although Nora is finally ejected by her husband for the infidelities of which he has become aware while masquerading as a corpse, the play's conclusion is no easy triumph for social normality. The community microcosm of Dan (the husband) and Michael Dara settle back into slothful security while Nora, fully aware of the harsh environment she must now face, goes with the Tramp in an assertion of her need for the vitality which neither her old husband nor the conformist Michael Dara can provide. Seamus Deane has argued against over-estimations of Synge's subversive intentions within an imperialist context on the grounds that the plays repress the brutal facts of 'famine, eviction, military oppression and landlordism' (Deane, 1985a, p. 59). While it is necessary to qualify the nature of Synge's revolt, his plays provide a critique of nationalist ideology while simultaneously advocating a liberation which was absolute to the extent that it was of the woman; idealized into impotence by the nationalists, and taken as the epitome of Celtic ineffectuality by the apologists of imperialism.

The response to *The Shadow of the Glen* revealed the profoundly disturbing nature of Synge's fully conscious critique of Irish actuality. 'Men and women in Ireland marry lacking love, and live mostly in a dull level of amity. Sometimes they do not – sometimes the woman lives in bitterness – sometimes she dies of a broken heart – but she does not go away with the tramp' declared Arthur Griffith; an assertion of Irish female morality which found dramatic form as *In a Real Wicklow Glen*, a one-act play published in *The United Irishman* in 1904 and of which Griffith himself may have been the author (Hogan and Kilroy, 1976). The environment is still harsh and lives are still ruled by an economic necessity which forces this Norah to reject a loved but poor suitor in favour of an elderly but wealthy husband. Distraught at his rejection the young man turns to drink and, ten years after the event – the time of the play – encounters Norah who pleads with him to give up the drink for her sake. When he turns 'with both arms out' and declares 'give us a kiss and I will' (p. 151), the reaction of this 'nationalist' Norah is exemplary; she rejects his advances as an insult to her married status and swears that never again will he see her face. The Old Woman of the play to whom the suitor has told his story consoles him with the suggestion that he should give up drink and concern himself with making money, so that when Norah's husband dies he will be financially attractive for, while 'It is hard to marry without love' as the Old Woman observes, there is no questioning the situation as an ever present economic necessity. Morality moulded by materialism is the message of the play, a pressure which operated not only on the level of maintaining the idealization of woman as symbol of Irish purity opposed to English corruption but, more fundamentally, underpinned the material production of the class which was the bedrock of the nationalist movement.

The nature of the nation was Synge's fundamental concern yet, while suggesting that the Irish essence was to be found in the life of the peasant, his view of that life led both to his vilification by the nationalists and, more recently, to a critical inference that his work is underpinned by an anachronistic vision of reality whose effect could even be reactionary. Synge's distance from what he disparaged as an 'unmodern, ideal, breesy [sic], springdayish, Cuchulainoid National Theatre' (Synge, 1983, p. 76) is readily apparent. As he expressed it in his poem 'The Passing of the Shee' he preferred the vitality of peasant drinkers and poachers, and what he had to say of poetry – that it must learn to be brutal again before it can be human – is both the source of his plays' dramatic potency and their interpretative problems (Synge, 1958, p. 229). The point is made succinctly in a letter which he wrote to Stephen MacKenna in 1905 on his return from the West of Ireland on which *The Manchester Guardian* had commissioned a series of articles: 'In a way it is all heartrending, in one place the people are starving but wonderfully attractive and charming and in another place where things are going well one has a rampant doubled-chinned vulgarity I haven't seen the like of' (Synge, 1983, p. 117). The debilitating effect of a materialism which Synge associated with Anglicization, suggests an Ascendancy preference for the halt of progress based on the self-interested argument that advancement into the twentieth century was inimical to Ireland. Synge's picture of the Aran Islands, his location for an undimmed edenic vitalism, is most frequently objected to as being 'an intellectual's idealisation' (Kelsall, 1975, p. 258), based on the morbid *fin de siècle* phase of European Romanticism. While the vestiges of Rousseau and Wordsworth can not be denied, the foregrounding of, particularly, sexual energy, furnished a profound critique, not only of the restrictive and moralistic materialism which underpinned the nationalist movement, but also of all repression which denied the individual a right to such self-expression. If Synge has a limitation in this respect it is not so much in his suppression of the details of colonization, but in the romantic-anarchistic conclusion to his major plays where liberation is of the individual beyond the bounds of society. In this respect *The Shadow of the Glen* is progressive in theme and reactionary in realization, only in *The Playboy of the Western World* does Synge partially transcend this limitation with the result that the play is still capable of generating shock-waves in its audience.

Dedication to the nationalist cause involved commitment also to a complex matrix of supportive interpellations which constituted a unified ideological discourse (Laclau, 1977). The potential for disruption of the nationalist moment, however, allowed no deviation from the totality of that matrix whose cement was Catholicism – the very proof of Ireland's purity and the sanctity of the nationalist cause. As in the case of Yeats's *The Countess Cathleen*, to transgress those values was to risk being vilified as one who denigrated Ireland and, by implication, supported her continued subjection. Yeats learned the lesson and ceased to speak of that of which he did not know. *Cathleen Ni Houlihan* earned Yeats a place in the nationalist pantheon; simultaneously, however, it earned him the disapproval of the man who was to stand for a nationality in which liberation could only be inclusive and absolute. As James Joyce wrote to his publisher in May 1906: 'I have taken the first step towards the spiritual liberation of my country' (Joyce, 1975, p. 88), and since the country was conceived of as a composite of individuals, then national liberation was essentially, and primarily, a liberation of the self. *Dubliners*, the subject of Joyce's letter, is his first testimony to the need for, and the nature of, Irish liberation.

In the original version of the opening story 'The Sisters', published in George Russell's *Irish Homestead* in August 1904, the first line foregrounded the colonial connection in the form of the priest's address in 'Great Britain Street'. But Joyce's guerilla campaign, although striking against the imperial power through his infiltration of its literature, is directed primarily against that priestly paralysis which is associated throughout *Dubliners* with absence, immobility, functionlessness: the priest of 'Araby' whose reading of *The Memoirs of Vidocq* suggests a suspect taste for the yellow leaved literature of decadence is dead, his rusty bicycle pump a posthumous memorial to a priestly life which, Joyce implies, is always one of denial – of self and others; the priest of 'Eveline' whose yellowing photograph located by the broken harmonium is to be read as confirmation of an insidious paralysis. These trace lines of paralysis emanate outwards from the first story, 'The Sisters', whose paralysed priest becomes the focal point for the collection as a whole for, as Joyce noted in a letter of May 1906, the sequence of stories was to deal with the subject of Irish paralysis under four of its aspects: 'childhood, adolescence, maturity, and public life' (Joyce, 1975, p. 83). The stories then deal with what may be termed the birth of consciousness as the multi-faceted collective protagonist is interpellated into a society whose full reality can only be comprehended, in terms of its causal networks, when the reader, along with the final emanation of the protagonist in Gabriel Conroy, comes to perceive what Ireland has lost must be regained if paralysis is not to become the permanent state of the fledgling nation.

In this context the opening repetition of colour adjectives from the description of the clothing and facial features of the priest in 'The Sisters' to that of the 'queer old josser' in 'An Encounter' merits attention, creating as it does the essence of this fallen world into which youthful passion emerges, briefly flickers and fading, dies. The priest's 'green faded' garments and his 'blackened' handkerchief, his grey face with 'big discoloured teeth', find their stylistic echoes in the 'greenish-black' suit and 'ashen-grey' moustache of the man with his 'yellow' teeth. The masochistic diatribe which follows on from the man's masturbation, in which the prospect of whipping any boy guilty of having a sweetheart is described as being delivered 'as if he were unfolding some elaborate mystery', is advanced as a secular/sexual rite of denial which parallels that of the priest in 'The Sisters' who, through his 'great wish' for the future ordination of the boy, had initiated him into the 'complex and mysterious' institutions of the Church. The response of the boy to the news of the priest's death is remarkable in this context of priestly celibacy and insanity and the Church's production of a perverted adult sexuality based on denial rather than celebration of the flesh: 'I walked away slowly along the sunny side of the street, reading all the theatrical advertisements in the shop-windows as I went. I found it strange that neither I nor the day seemed in a mourning mood and I felt even annoyed at discovering in myself a sensation of freedom as if I had been freed from something by his death' (Joyce, 1977a, pp. 10-11). The sensation of freedom, however, is only fleeting and the sequence of *Dubliners* charts the manifestations of its absence as successive stories conclude on epiphanies of bleakness. Joyce's description of the collection as a step towards the spiritual liberation of Ireland appears simply perverse until the final epiphany, that of Gabriel Conroy in 'The Dead', recaptures, if not the sensation of freedom experienced by the boy in 'The Sisters', at least the awareness of the need for the presence of that on which freedom is predicated.

The concluding paragraphs of 'The Dead' contain what is essentially the epiphany of the collection as a whole. As Gabriel contemplates his wife's sorrowing memory of her dead lover he achieves a recognition of his, and Ireland's situation, which justifies Joyce's confident assertion 'that you [Grant Richards, his publisher] will retard the course of civilization in Ireland by preventing the Irish people from having one good look at themselves in my nicely polished looking-glass' (Joyce, 1975, p. 90). In the face of mortality 'Better pass boldly into that other world, in the full glory of some passion, than fade and wither dismally with age' concludes Gabriel, and although 'He had never felt like that himself towards any woman ... he knew that such a feeling must be love' (Joyce, 1977a, p. 200). The passion of the dead Michael Furey comes to represent an essentially Irish vitality as signified in his association with the west and 'the dark mutinous Shannon waves', which stands in contradistinction to the earlier avoidance of Ireland practised by Gabriel in his preference for trips to continental Europe over pilgrimages to the Aran Islands. 'I'm sick of my own country, sick of it', Gabriel had declared to the nationalist Miss Ivors, but his rejection – and subsequent acceptance – can only be comprehended, along with Joyce's total *oeuvre*, within the context of the latter's rejection of political and literary misrepresentations of Irish need and Irish actuality.

F.S.L. Lyons has argued that the paradox of Joyce's image of Dublin as a city of paralysis at the very moment of the Literary Revival is explained by the fact that, since the Revival was largely the work of the Anglo-Irish, rather than the Catholic bourgeoisie of Joyce's background who fuelled the more explicitly political Gaelic Revival, then the two views are essentially the products of divergent experiences of history (Lyons, 1970). What is so striking about Joyce, however, is the extent to which he rejected both Revivals for what he perceived as the desertion of the high ideals of their own rhetoric. The promise of the Irish Literary Theatre to give Dublin the best of European culture was abandoned, Joyce argued in 1901, in the decision to stage Douglas Hyde's *The Twisting of the Rope* and Yeats's and George Moore's *Diarmuid and Grania*. This was a betrayal of their 'protest against ... sterility and falsehood' and a 'surrender to the trolls', those nationalists whose only aesthetic consideration was whether a work conformed to their predetermined concept of Irish art (Joyce, 1964, pp. 69, 71). The very parochialism of the concept of Irish art was anathema to Joyce, especially as the focal point of the Revivalists was an ancient Ireland of which he dismissively concluded: 'Its death chant has been sung, and on its grave stone has been set the seal' (p. 173). What Joyce implicitly advocated in his rejection of the Revival's dual impulse towards parochialism and the past was a modern and European concept of Ireland, but it is quintessentially Irish when it is most cosmopolitan and most modern when it rejoins the Revivalists in the rejection of the materialism.

The Ireland of both nationalist and Literary Revivals captured by Joyce in his stories of public life is squalid and mercenary; a land of neither aristocrats nor peasants, but members of a self-interested and shabby petit-bourgeoisie who, whether canvassing for a nationalist candidate in 'Ivy Day in the Committee Room' or seeking to capitalize on the advantages of having a daughter named Kathleen in 'The Mother', are only interested in 'four pound eight into her hand', or what one of the canvassers calls 'the spondulics'. Joyce's image is of an Ireland in which material self-interest permeates society from the canvassers and concert accompanists to the political candidate who, although a nationalist, will still welcome Edward VII because of the influx of capital such a visit would bring to the city in which he is a 'big ratepayer' with 'extensive house property in the city and three places of business' (Joyce, 1977a,

p. 120). Much recent criticism has been directed to establishing the political credentials of Joyce, but it would be an over-statement to see such observations on the nationalist candidate as indicating anything approaching a Marxian critique of capitalism. Joyce's orientation is indeed political, but it is more of a lament than a programme. As 'Old Jack raked the cinders together with a piece of cardboard' at the opening of 'Ivy Day in the Committee Room' he establishes the expectation of the same re-vitalizing flames evoked in the elegy to Parnell with which Mr Hynes concludes the story. But what the whole stands testimony to is the absence of any principles, Phoenix flames, or passion for anything beyond money or drink. The day dawns in *Dubliners* with the pallid shaft of grey light in 'After the Race' which serves only to illuminate all that has been lost on the personal as well as on the political and public level.

'Ivy Day in the Committee Room' and 'The Dead' are the two critical stories as the former establishes the cause of the condition while the latter posits a potential correction. If the death of Parnell has led to a dissolution of nationalist principles into a seedy grubbing in the till of the imperial power, then Joyce neither proposed, nor perceived, the possibility of any 'passionate' nationalist alternative to which he could pledge his allegiance. He was not unaware of the nationalist revival in both its military and literary forms, but as he indicated in his two semi-autobiographical works, the apprentice piece *Stephen Hero* and the more fully realized *Portrait of the Artist as a Young Man*, the former was perceived as a rebellion with hurleysticks waiting for the inevitable informer (Joyce, 1960, p. 201), while the products of the latter were themselves a betrayal of literary quality in their 'tawdry lines, futile change of number, [and] the waddling approach of Hughes's "Ideal" ' (Joyce, 1977b, p. 77). The fact that Joyce had once taken Gaelic lessons from Patrick Pearse reinforces the intended parallels between Pearse and the Mr Hughes of *Stephen Hero*, and gives an extra resonance to the dispute between Stephen and Hughes as to the nature and function of art in Ireland. The attack launched by Hughes on Stephen expresses the fundamental issue which was to stalk the no-man's land between the nationalist and Literary Revivals: 'a man that was of all countries was of no country – you must first have a nation before you could have art' declared Hughes, and if Ireland was to have art 'let it be moral art, art that elevated, above all, national art' (p. 95). On this matter as on the rejection of materialism as a political principle Joyce was at one with Yeats in holding to the values of art above propaganda, but unlike him he could not subscribe to the idealistic vision of ancient Ireland propagated by that 'mumming company' with whom Yeats whinged 'With gold-embroidered Celtic fringes' (Joyce, 1964, p. 150). 'Not this', declares Stephen in *Portrait of the Artist*, 'Not at all', as he evokes the Yeatsian ideal of 'the loveliness that has long faded from the world' (Joyce, 1960, p. 251). Joyce perceived the need for a radical change in Irish society but saw that this should be no return to the Celtic hearthstone and even less a nationalist revolution based on what he described in 1906 as 'the old pap of racial hatred'. Joyce, like Stephen, saw more merit in aspiring to 'the loveliness that has not yet come into the world' and his sympathies, as O'Casey's, were with 'the starving rabblement' on whom 'Caesar' and 'Christ' waxed fat. But, in what is clearly a position derived from the secular revolutions of Europe, Joyce could rail against the fact that 'The Roman not the Sassenach, was the tyrant of the islanders' (Joyce, 1977b, p. 52), and demand a liberation of the self in which commitment to the abstract principle of art fused with a commitment to the vital life of which that art was the expression. When Gabriel Conroy epiphanized that passion was the principle to which one should be committed, he prepared the way for Stephen Dedalus's declaration that he would fly the nets of nationality, language and religion in a refusal to submit himself to 'the old sow that eats her farrow' (Joyce, 1960, p. 203). The paradox of this comparison lies in the fact that Gabriel's passion is perceived to be essentially Irish, while Stephen's self-realization is founded upon a rejection of that very nation and its claims. The reality, however, was that Joyce was holding to the principle of liberation of self and nation through loyalty to individual truth rather than in obeisance to short-term nationalist shibboleths. The absence of a generous Furey is Joyce's lament and the source of his protagonist's declaration that it is only in the smithy of the free soul that one can create the conscience of the race.

In a lecture delivered in Trieste in April 1907 Joyce declared that it was time for Ireland to have done with failure: 'If she is truly capable of reviving, let her awake, or let her cover up her head and lie down decently in the grave for ever' (Joyce, 1964, p. 174). The reality of the Revival had already been revealed in the January of that same year, but in a form which confirmed Joyce in his choice of exile and locked the Anglo-Irish into their final redoubt of a literature which rapidly became a critique of a movement from which their marginalization became increasingly apparent. The occasion was the première of Synge's *The Playboy of the Western World*, an event which, more than any other, demonstrated the extent of the polarisation which existed between nationalist and Literary Revivals and, more crucially, where power now resided.

While Joyce stressed an Irish passion which he saw as having died with the western Michael Furey – the fictionalized and personal expression of the loss that Parnell represented on the political plane – the location of his works in Dublin represents a significant orientation of Ireland towards the modern urban experience and away from the reductive obsession with the peasant which dominated contemporary literary expression. The peasant referred in Joyce's work is decidedly less than the ideal of either Gaelic or Anglo-Irish Revivals. Living a life described by Stephen Hero as taken up with 'the calculation of coppers, the weekly debauch and the weekly piety' (Joyce, 1977b, p. 53), the peasant, he suggests, has earned a reputation for chastity simply because masturbation is a private vice. Such iconoclastic visions of Irish actuality found subtler and more complex expression in *Portrait of the Artist as a Young Man* where the child Stephen's desire to sleep in the warm dark of a peasant cottage is translated into the young man's image of the peasant woman as a shadowy seductress. Stephen's expressed fear of 'the red rimmed horny [eyed]' peasant with whom he must struggle is tempered by his concern for this oppressed people who, both rural and urban, 'entrust their wills and minds to others that they may ensure for themselves a life of spiritual paralysis' (Joyce, 1977b, p. 132).

Such views are untypical of the writing of the period, for whether portrayed as image of pagan vitality or Catholic morality the figure of the peasant continued to dominate the literary terrain, and the struggle for control of the connotations of the peasant marks distinctly the divergent views of the Ireland desired by the conflicting factions. In his *Life Story of an Old Rebel* John Denvir provided a fascinating insight into the popular nationalist fare provided by a theatre group entitled the 'Emerald Minstrels' which reinforced the idealization of the peasant experience and contributed to the climate of expectations for the treatment of that subject. The ideological antecedents of the troupe were Young Ireland and *The Nation* and their dedication to the cultivation of Irish culture and 'above all Irish Nationality' reveals the continuing potency of aspects of the Davisite imagery nowhere more clearly than in the set for their productions. Denvir's record of *Terence's Fireside: or The Irish Peasant at Home*, which purported to be an evening of typical peasant entertainment, details 'a drop set representing the Lower Lake of Killarney. When it was raised it disclosed the interior of the living room of a comfortable Irish homestead, with the large projecting open chimney, the turf fire on the hearth, and the usual pious and patriotic pictures prior to such an interior - Terence's Fireside' (Denvir, 1972, p. 120). That such idealized expectations were the base from which divergent images were tried and found wanting is clear from the case of *The Shadow of the Glen*. An even more striking example of the 'peasant quality' by which contemporary Irish drama was judged is Douglas Hyude's *Casadh an tSugáin* (*The Twisting of the Rope*). Written and performed in Gaelic to a scenario provided by Yeats, translated into English by Lady Gregory, it was staged in 1901 by members of the Gaelic League Amateur Dramatic Society with Hyde in the principal rôle; its relationship to nationalist culture of the period could not be more central.

The play is set in a farm house in Munster and concerns the efforts of the rural community to protect Oona from the attentions of the outsider Hanrahan whose fascinating strangeness threatens to entice her away from Sheamus her intended. The parallels with Synge's *The Playboy of the Western World* are clear, but here the community reveals itself to be intelligent and resourceful, working together to exclude Hanrahan and leaving the final word to Sheamus's assertion of settled communal values rather than the Syngean lament at the loss of individual vitality: 'Isn't it a fine thing for a man to be listening to the storm outside, and himself quiet and easy beside the fire?' (Hyde, 1974, p. 148). The audience expectations of the play were high, particularly since it was seen as signalling a genuine re-vitalization of Gaelic culture and, in the words of the *Freeman's Journal* of 22 October 1901, 'Every Gaelic Leaguer ... everyone interested in the old tongue who could elbow his way into the theatre was there last night, and the enthusiasm was tremendous'. Reports of audience response emphasize this ecstatic reception as songs and shouts in Irish rang out in encouragement throughout the evening. As Synge, who reported on the production for a French journal, observed: 'the soul of a nation had entered the theatre'. Stephen Gwynn, having experienced this production in the course of which 'there was a magnetism in the air', concluded that 'One began to realise what the Gaelic League was doing' (Hogan and Kilroy, 1975, pp. 113-14). What was being successfully dramatized was 'the same spontaneously lived ideology', (Althusser, 1979, pp. 150-1) shared by stage and auditorium, in which 'the spectators' quest for identity' (Pavis, 1982, p. 89) was being satisfied in such a way as to produce an aesthetic/ideological matrix of expectations which could only permit unquestioning confirmation of the absolute nature of nationalist claims for Irish peasant ideality. The 'riotous' reactions to Synge's *The Playboy of the Western World* can only be understood within such a context.

The disturbances which surrounded the première at the Abbey

Theatre in January 1907 have been chronicled in Robert Kilroy's *The Playboy Riots*. The expressions of outrage are conventionally assumed to have been triggered by the reference to 'shift', suggesting indecorous behaviour by Irish womanhood and so affronting nationalist sensibilities. The crucial point in *The Playboy*, however, is that the self-realization necessary as a prelude to liberation is realized only through the killing of the Father. The situation dramatized by Synge in which Old Mahon attempts to arrange Christie's marriage as a means of consolidating his own security is a powerful expression of the actuality of the patriarchal power vested in familism. To benefit, as does Christie, from shattering the hold of the Father and choose his own partner is to advocate, by example, a rejection of the whole economic basis of the fundamental class of the nationalist movement, and was reacted to accordingly. But the ramifications of this action go even further, extending to the fundamentals of nationalism amd the people-nation as a comparison of Christie and Shawn Keogh demonstrates.

Shawn is the arrested alter-ego of Christie, a presence which serves to remind the audience of the extent of Christie's psychological growth. As Christie's development consequent upon his 'killing' his Father becomes clear, Shawn's cry that he is 'afeard of Father Reilly' becomes an acknowledgement of the repressive power of the other restrictive agency in peasant life; Christie's liberation from the power of the patriarch becoming a model for liberation from that of the priest. The fact that Pegeen Mike responds to Christie and rejects Shawn, only further adds to the undermining of nationalist values, and although her assertion of community in the final act superficially accords with the rejection of the disruptive influence first essayed in Hyde's *The Twisting of the Rope*, the play contains even more power to disturb in its keening conclusion. Pegeen laments the loss of Christie and violently and decisively demands that Shawn quit her sight in what is both a reprise of the theme of *The Shadow of the Glen* and simultaneously its extension. While the earlier play dramatized the turbulence of, particularly, female desire, that potent power to disturb was finally projected beyond the community. Although Christie, as model of self-realization, also exits into an undefined elsewhere, the play's final expression of female anguish at the loss of a vitality which accorded with need, presents audiences with an image of frustration and regret at the denial of desire, which is all the more disturbing for remaining to trouble a community which assumes it can settle back into its customary inactivity and obeisance to established authority. That the dramatization of liberation through violence allows Synge's play to be read as anti-imperialist is but one of its interests, that it dramatized the Irish woman as driven by desire for a man who had liberated himself by striking down the figure of the Father was, for contemporary audiences, an issue which, perhaps paradoxically, set Synge and the Abbey Theatre irrevocably on the margins of the move towards self-determination. As Patrick Pearse commented on the play and its reception in the editorial of the Gaelic League organ *An Claideamh Soluis* on 9 February 1907: 'for Anglo-Irish drama – it is the beginning of the end'.

In the decade that followed *The Playboy* the reality of Moran's assertion that 'The Gael must be the element that absorbs' unfolded (Moran, 1905, p. 37). With Joyce self-exiled, Synge terminally ill, and Yeats ever more explicit in his advocacy of 'aristocratic' values, the voices of creative criticism were silenced. The move to 1916 was to be fuelled by fundamentalist principles.

5

The work of years overturned?

The fragmentation of Parnell's parliamentary following, which many contemporaries and critics have seen as providing a space for 'the Literary Revival', came to an untidy resolution at the end of the old century. A kind of unity was patched up amongst the parliamentarians through a combination of external pressure from the Church – which required their input into Westminster debates on education – and their own fear of permanent eclipse. Reuniting within a new shell organization, the United Irish League (the U.I.L.), the parliamentarians reasserted their erstwhile domination of the political landscape so that 'around the turn of the century most people in Ireland expected Home Rule to be achieved peacefully and by parliamentary means' (O'Brien, 1985, p. 27). A corollary of the regrouping of the parliamentarians was their reassertion of the supremacy of the political vis-à-vis the cultural, a position typical of the years before the fall of Parnell. Whereas Parnell, however, had only had to contend with the cultural content of journals which rehashed the themes and materials of *The Nation*, in the interval between Parnell's fall and the reuniting of his followers, the development of a multitude of literary, debating, and theatrical societies contributed new dimensions and concepts of Irishness to the struggle for independence.

Consequently, from 1900 to the outbreak of the First World War there took place a 'rhetorical competition – involving the glorification of past insurrections etc. – ... [which] was mainly about pushing out people whom you expected to leave anyway, and about being able to take the credit and the power' (p. 27). For Gramsci, such a competition characterized the manoeuvrings of groups seeking to construct, develop, and interpret an ideological position capable of binding together and leading an alliance of classes and class fractions, for 'a social group can, and indeed must, already exercise "leadership" before winning governmental power' (Gramsci, 1971, p. 57). What complicated the early twentieth-century struggles for hegemony in Ireland, however, was the colonial dimension for, as F.S.L. Lyons has stated: 'The dominant culture was the English culture – other cultures had no option but to relate closely to [it]'

(Lyons, 1982, p. 17). Would-be challengers of the U.I.L., therefore, had to elaborate a critique of its policies that was effective, not merely in relation to U.I.L. positions, but to those of the metropolitan power. One form of discourse through which engagement with the metropolitan power was invited – on terms which advantaged the metropolitan vis-à-vis colonial culture – was Celticism. A political counterpart was parliamentarism which, as Ralph Miliband has argued, operates under a similarly disabling set of rules, structurally benefiting the dominant group by constraining would-be challengers to confine the sphere of 'legitimate' political action to parliamentary activity (Miliband, 1973). Acceptance of the rules of either, or both, of these discourses supplied those who conformed to them with a means of securing positions of relative supremacy within Ireland, but at the cost of subscribing to metropolitan-produced rules which simultaneously disabled the would-be leaders of the colonized in their relations with the dominant – metropolitan – culture. The realities of such a situation were penetratingly seized upon by D.P. Moran when he wrote: 'Irishmen ... [are] ... in competition with Englishmen in every sphere of social and intellectual activity, in a competition where England has fixed the marks, the subjects and had the sole making of the rules of the game' (Moran, 1905, p. 22).

Recognition of the ways in which Irish attempts to respond to metropolitan material, cultural, and political dominance were deformed by pressures transmitted by 'the rules of the game', could lead to the position adopted by the Irish Republican Brotherhood, where only physical force could be seen as likely to produce independence on terms acceptable to the colonized people. Most early twentieth-century Irish writers, however, aware of the overwhelming superiority of the Imperial power, rejected such a course out of hand. Moran reminded his readers in 1899 of the crushing defeat that had befallen Spain in its recent war with the United States and predicted a similar outcome to any attempted Irish insurrection. Moreover, Catholic theology and ethics placed limits on the circumstances in which it was justified to oppose a sovereign power. Even a 'just war' should not be undertaken in hopeless circumstances, for to participate in such an exploit could be seen as tantamount to suicide. Such teachings bolstered the supremacy of parliamentarism in relation to other would-be leaders of the people-nation by placing a premium on constitutionality. Effectively this meant that, despite recognition of the disabilities of the parliamentarians' position, fully exposed by the Liberal's massive parliamentary majority after 1906, which made Irish voting strength at Westminster useless for the purposes of winning independence, the construction of alternative strategic locations was an immensely difficult enterprise. The practical limitations on such an attempt are well illustrated by the struggles of Moran, Griffith, Connolly, and Pearse to offer alternatives to parliamentarism after 1900. Further, the absence of flexible positional superiority which characterizes the strategic location of Pearse after 1914, re-emphasizes the limited scope that existed for inverting and redirecting, through their rules, the discourses which empowered imperial dominance.

What distinguished the various attempts at constructing strategic locations in this period was less the subtle differences in the concept of Irishness that each advanced (for virtually all challengers to the U.I.L. 'the Gael', and the Gaelic League's positions on language and history, were shared points of departure), than variations in approach to the problem posed by the dominance of the parliamentarians. Moran, Griffith, Pearse, and even the marxian socialist Connolly, all regarded the basis of Irishness as 'the Gael' who, in contradistinction to the Celt, was masculine and antagonistic to the Anglo-Saxon, 'the Gall'. But whereas Griffith's Gael, following closely the position of the Gaelic League, was primarily a linguistic and historic construct, only incidentally Catholic, Moran's Gael was pre-eminently Catholic. As he reminded readers of *The Leader* in August 1901, 'the Irish nation is *de facto* a Catholic nation' (Boyce, 1982, p. 243), a position which, allied to his triumphalism, resulted in a strategic location which produced a hard-line, exclusive position. Explicitly directed towards the Catholic majority, however, Moran's arguments yielded no practical, political or cultural returns. As early as 1900, rejecting the relevance of contemporary parliamentarism to the achievement of 'real' independence, Moran argued for concentration on the language movement: 'A distinct language is the great weapon by which we can ward off undue foreign influence and keep ourselves surrounded by a racy Irish atmosphere' (Moran, 1905, p. 25). His policy, therefore, was to advocate the insulation of the Irish from the contagion of Anglo-Saxonism: 'the English-speaking race, in the meshes of which we are interwoven by a thousand material and immaterial ties, is making the pace and we must either stand up to it – which I fear we cannot; isolate ourselves from its influence – which we largely can do; or else get trodden on and swallowed up – which it appears to me, is, if we keep on as we are going, inevitable' (p. 12).

Recognizing the duration and difficulty of the course he was advocating, Moran argued that the people must be broadly re-converted to Irish speakers, while in the interim their attachment to the metropolitan culture, and its supporters in Ireland, must be undermined by 'an active vigilant and merciless propaganda in the English language. Anglicisation must be fought all along the line on every day of the week' (p. 81). Week after week, in his journal *The Leader*, Moran criticized the parliamentarians and their hypocritical talk of nationality, along with big business and those who willingly accepted metropolitan standards and mores. Moran's critical technique was crude but satisfying: his targets were characterized through epithets which stigmatized them as not truly Irish. Parliamentarians were 'sulky West Britons', indicating that despite their canting references to Irishness they had accepted (but with a bad grace) the manners of their opponents; big business was identified by its interests (liquor manufacturers and traders were 'Mr Bung'); Protestants were 'sourfaces', while apers of metropolitan ways were 'West Britons' if they were of the upper classes and 'shoneens' (little squires) if of the farming classes. J.J. Horgan asserted that Moran had an immense contemporary influence (Horgan, 1948, p. 111), but however valid that point might be, Moran remained on the sidelines of contemporary politics as an acid observer; his ability to contribute to contemporary politics more directly undermined by a diagnosis of Ireland's situation which left the political field open to those who could attempt more positive combinations of cultural and political activity – such as Griffith, Connolly, and Pearse.

In initially framing his ideas on culture, politics and nationality, Arthur Griffith was heavily dependent upon the writings of his friend and political mentor, William Rooney. While the language used in their surveys of the situation of Ireland and the Irish in 1900 bears a superficial resemblance to Moran's, their joint approach to politics and culture (which Griffith was to continue to develop after Rooney's death in 1901) was substantially different. Like Moran, Griffith and Rooney advocated the cultural positions of the Gaelic League with enthusiasm and conceived of Irishness in terms of the Gael. But Griffith's and Rooney's Gael was less exclusive than Moran's, and while Griffith anticipated that Catholics would predominate in a Home Rule Ireland, he did not shrink from trying to construct a political position which would enable him to gather support from many different quarters. Griffith recognized in the support the parliamentarians could command an obstacle which any would-be supplanter would have to overcome. But having vigorously opposed parliamentary nationalism in the 1900 general election, Griffith subsequently moderated his position, advocating instead a policy of participation in parliamentary elections on a pledge of withdrawal from Westminster if elected, with the aim of constituting an Irish assembly in Dublin which would become a *de facto* Irish Legislature. Griffith sought to produce a position easily distinguishable from that of the U.I.L., capable of sustaining a critique of their policy and practice but which, unlike Moran's position, would enable him to compete with them for a mass following. This policy was spelled out in articles in Griffith's journal *The United Irishman* republished as *The Resurrection of Hungary* in 1904 and *The Sinn Féin Policy* in 1905 and, according to Griffith, was modelled on the policies which won the Magyars substantial autonomy.

This approach had obvious advantages in relation to Moran's purist isolationism. Griffith argued that his was a tried policy which would achieve the substance of independence while leaving links with the British monarchy intact to appease Anglo-Irish and Ulster sensitivities. Perhaps more importantly, it allowed electoral competition with the U.I.L. while preserving a radical nationalist standpoint. In Griffith's strategy, electoral participation offered the opportunity to progress towards a struggle for legislative independence with the Imperial power, with the advantage of a popular mandate which might avoid the necessity for insurrection.

Griffith's and Rooney's political eclecticism had its counterpart in the cultural field. Where Moran scathingly dismissed any possibility that there could be an Irish literature in English (Moran, 1905, p. 43), Rooney had argued that Davis, Mitchel, Kickham and others 'have not perhaps given us distinctly National literature, but they have given us a Nationalist one'. And whereas Moran would have limited the scope of Irish writing in English to 'merciless' criticism, Griffith and Rooney were prepared to recognize that, since 'two millions of our population can never hope to be able to appreciate a Gaelic literature', it would be unwise to deprive non-Irish speakers of some substitute for the products of the dominant culture (Rooney, 1909, pp. 66-7).Where Moran took a frankly confessional approach to issues, Griffith's commitment to economic development, his willingness to envisage some form of working relations with Unionists and Protestants, the nature of his political strategy, and the absence in his writing and practice of deference to the clergy, exposed him to accusations of indifferentism and of actively threatening a social and moral order of which the Catholic Church strongly approved.

The Catholic clergy as a body was deeply hostile to any talk of economic development which might bring to the faithful in the Irish countryside what was viewed as the moral pollution of current urban life. Amid general agreement, the Rev. Thomas Macken told the Maynooth Union in 1903: 'No lover of Ireland – no genuine Irishman – can contemplate without feelings akin to horror an industrial Ireland with centres of manufacture such as are to be found in ... England ... it is emphatically not the ideal to strive for.... If we are to look abroad for examples it is to be hoped that Ireland will develop after the lines of Belgium or Denmark rather than on the lines of those countries where the land is deserted, and where the toiling millions are congregated in large cities and towns, and [lead] lives of moral and physical degradation' (Miller, 1973, p. 73). By criticizing the consequences for individuals of continuing to subordinate Irish economic potential to metropolitan interests – evident in contemporary high emigration rates – Griffith's remedy of rural economic development and protectionism threatened both the pastoral economy and its cultural foundation of familism. Contacts with Unionists exposed him to charges of an absence of the correct degree of fervour in condemning landlordism, while the policy of abstentionism, which was the hallmark of Sinn Féin, left him vulnerable to charges from the Hierarchy that a vote for Sinn Féin would leave vital Catholic interests, particularly in educational matters, undefended.

These differences over issues of principle account for much of the barely-masked hostility of the Hierarchy and many of the clergy to Sinn Féin. The apparent conflict between Griffith's position in 1899, when he ardently supported Yeats's stand against clerical hostility to *The Countess Cathleen*, and his attacks on Synge's plays *The Shadow of the Glen* and *The Playboy of the Western World* merely demonstrating that, in the absence of deference to the clergy, soundness on faith and morals had to be proved all the more strongly in other ways. In contrast to Griffith and Sinn Féin, the U.I.L.'s policies, in particular, its willingness to advocate the interests of the Catholic Church in Ireland, Great Britain and the Empire, its support of the tenant farmers before and after land-reform, and its support for the perpetuation and development of existing forms of economic activity, ensured that its links with the people-nation were based on widely-shared sentiments. Despite occasional minor rifts, that particular form of sentimental connection was practically endorsed and actively reproduced by the Catholic Church. Necessarily then, such a combination of material, ideological, and cultural interests posed tremendous problems for would-be challengers to the U.I.L.'s political hegemony. In these circumstances, the poor showing of Griffith's followers in national elections is easy to understand, while their marginally better performance in local elections, particularly in urban areas, only emphasized their overall weakness amongst the rural majority.

Before the First World War Griffith and his followers remained confined to the margin of Irish politics. But if Griffith operated on the margins others, such as the tiny band of Irish socialists, whose popular leader was Jim Larkin and whose leading polemicist was James Connolly, operated on the margin of the margin. In Ireland, the Catholic Church mounted pre-emptive strikes on the potential threat of socialism to such effect that Connolly was reduced to making fundamental concessions to the ideological dominance of Catholicism. In developing what Bernard Ransom calls a 'hibernicised' form of marxism, Connolly abandoned frontal opposition to the Church and all forms of nationalism for attempts at compromise, maintaining that clerical condemnations of socialism, such as in the papal encyclical *Rerum Novarum* (1893), were mere accommodations forced on the Papacy by its need for the assistance of secular capitalism and not a mark of immutable antagonism (Ransom, 1980, pp. 6-39). More significant, however, as a pointer to the power and influence of the Catholic Church and nationalism in Connolly's thought, are the modifications that he attempted to make to basic materialist formulations in the interests of attempting an ideological penetration of this apparent monolith.

Writing in the Irish socialists' organ *Forward*, some months before the great Dublin lock-out of 1913, Connolly took up Marx's fundamental statement that '[the] proletarian movement is the ... movement of the immense majority, in the interests of the immense majority' (Marx, 1977, p. 230), and redefined it for contemporary Irish conditions. 'Just as the socialist knows that the working class, being the lowest in the social system, cannot emancipate itself without emancipating all other classes', he wrote, '*so the Irish Catholic has realised that he, being the most oppressed and disfranchised, could not win any modicum of political freedom or social recognition for himself without winning it for all others in Ireland* [our emphasis]' (Ransom, 1980, p. 24). In defining a proletarian by sect, rather than position in relation to the categories mode of production/relations of production, Connolly deviated from current marxian orthodoxy but, more importantly, gave a practical illustration of the operation of hegemony. The compulsion that would-be competitors for leadership of the people-nation were under to conform to certain unyielding requirements – Catholicism, familism and parliamentarism – ensured that just as in metropolitan-colonial relations the rules of discourse favoured the colonial power, within the people-nation the rules of discourse ensured the dominance of the parliamentarians of the U.I.L.

Connolly's attempts to align socialism and Catholicism were augmented by his supportive gestures towards the members of the Gaelic

League. In particular, in *Labour in Irish History*, he sought to produce a perspective in which, in keeping with the Gaelic League's enthusiasm, the ancient Gaels were seen as socially co-operative, holding property communally with democratically elected chiefs – a society ideal in its time and only gradually destroyed by the Norman invaders. By mobilizing history, Connolly attempted the production of a precedent for an advocated position. Some of Connolly's contemporaries in the Irish labour movement, however, disdained to attempt such carefully constructed engagements with the people-nation, favouring instead frontal attacks on their leaders. Jim Larkin, O'Casey's hero and leader of the Irish Transport and General Workers' Union in which Connolly was the foremost organizer, was one such. His bid to extend trades union organization for the unskilled to Dublin's workers, was brutally repressed by the Dublin employers (with the Catholic Church's active support) in the course of the long months of the Dublin Lock-Out (August 1913 - March 1914). That experience convinced Connolly that his approach, rather than Larkin's, was more likely to bear fruit. When Larkin went into self-exile in 1914 Connolly took his place as leader of the I.T.G.W.U. Subsequently, the result of Connolly's continuing willingness to seek accommodation with other groups marginalized by the U.I.L.'s dominance was to be seen on the streets of Dublin at Easter 1916 when he led the I.T.G.W.U.'s militia, the Irish Citizen Army, into the Rising.

The hegemony of the U.I.L. which in its marginalization of so many declared itself as transformist, affected all writers and thinkers in contemporary Ireland. When Conor Cruise O'Brien's observes that after 1900: 'the poet [Yeats] ... now turned aside from Irish politics ... his nationalism now became aristocratic and archaizing ... he was releasing a part of his personality he had been forced to suppress during the years of political activity', his judgement is that this was the resurgence of Yeats's 'Protestant' self, which nationalist politics had forced him to deny, allowing the conclusion that: 'By 1900, with the reunification of the Irish party and the burying of the Parnellite hatchet – which was an anti-clerical hatchet – the clergy had recovered most of their former authority, and life among nationalists must have become proportionately depressing for Protestants' (O'Brien, 1965, pp. 222-3). Changes in Yeats's writing after 1900 are thus accounted for by reference to the incompatibility of resurgent Catholicism and Protestantism, but in concentrating on Yeats, O'Brien's explanation ignores the fact that Protestants were only one of a number of other groups, such as Sinn Féin, currently being marginalized in Ireland. Yeats's experience of this process of marginalization commenced with his bruising encounters with those who, in his judgement, demanded that plays 'make no discoveries in human nature, but repeat the opinions of the audience' (Yeats, 1962, p. 136), and in retreat, he more fully articulated views and positions which had been implicit in much of his work from the 1890s. He had written to Alice Milligan in September 1894: 'She [Ireland] will never be greatly better until she governs herself but she will be greatly worse unless there arise protesting spirits' (Yeats, 1986, p. 399). The limits to exploration and innovation which Yeats lamented were the same limits which confined Griffiths and Moran, as the latter noted when in 1900 he commented that to 'ask a question or make an independent remark is an outrage upon the sacred cause of Irish nationality' (Moran, 1905, p. 69). But a shared experience of limitation did not mean that Griffith and Moran were any more hospitable to each others or to Yeats's opinions than they were to the parliamentarians'; indeed, the hostility that Moran and Griffith manifested towards each other and to Yeats and his protégés was part and parcel of the general struggle between the editors of *The Leader* and *The United Irishman* both for readers and relative political superiority in a terrain dominated by the parliamentarians. In this struggle for influence one of the key weapons that each employed was castigation of others for failure to show a 'proper' regard for the sensitivities to be associated with the 'national' ideal. This was one of the elements which made the press campaign which greeted *The Playboy of the Western World* so intense.

The disputes over the legitimacy of the term 'national' when used in association with the plays of Synge, culminating in '*The Playboy* Riots' of January 1907, 'rang down the curtain so far as I [Yeats] was concerned on what was called "The Celtic Movement". An "Irish Movement" took its place' (Yeats, 1962, p. 72). This supplanting 'Irish Movement', the preserve of 'a new class ... without exceptional men' made up of 'shopkeepers [and] clerks' (Yeats, 1961, pp. 259-60) and dominated, it is implied, by Sinn Féin and the Gaelic League, was one from which Yeats was temperamentally, socially, and intellectually isolated. His sense of an ending was heightened by the death of his mentor John O'Leary in March 1907 which marked, for Yeats, the end of 'the romantic conception of Irish Nationality' on which the literature, art and criticism of the Revival had been founded. The essay 'Poetry and Tradition' (August 1907), stimulated by the double sequence of blows which the early months of 1907 gave to the ideal Ireland for which he had laboured, is a key expression of the purpose which the poet now saw he had to fulfil, since 'Ireland's great moment had passed' (Yeats, 1961, p. 260). The artists, the 'Artificers of the Great Moment', could now only function by being 'protesting individual voices' (p. 161). Opposition to the new class then became an explicit feature of Yeats's work after 1907, albeit only as an ever more explicit expression of earlier attitudes – as a comparison of two plays, *On Baile's Strand* (1903) and *The Green Helmet* (1910), makes clear.

The central issue of *On Baile's Strand* is King Conchubar's desire for an ordered society, an objective which is deemed incompatible with Cuchulain's insistence on absolute independence. When Cuchulain, against his better judgement, swears allegiance to Conchubar he is doomed to destruction as his oath of loyalty results in his successfully championing the king against a challenger who is revealed to have been Cuchulain's only son. Maddened by grief at his loss Cuchulain attacks the waves, whose every crest symbolizes Conchubar's crown, in a wild expression of self-destructive lamentation. If Conchubar, 'a solid bourgeois citizen', 'stands for reason's click-clack' (Donoghue, 1971, p. 102), then the opposition of the independent Cuchulain, endorsed by the destruction consequent upon his succumbing to bourgeois order, is that of aristocrat/artist – the true Celt. The resonance of this individual-aristocratic disdain for bourgeois order is extended into a rejection of bourgeois morality when, as Declan Kiberd observes, he dismisses the 'tame living ... [and] ... seductive comforts of family life' which Conchubar's peace has brought to the nation, preferring the fierce vitality of Aoife's 'wild body' (Kiberd, 1986, p. 107). In this first play of the Cuchulain sequence, the condemnation of parsimonious order is part of that general desire of Yeats to ennoble Ireland by leading her 'to hate with the passion of hatred what Morris and Ruskin hated' (Yeats, 1961, p. 248). As an objective of romantic-nationalism it was also compatible with that of a more purely political-nationalism since England was the source of malignity for both. Faced with the new realism of shopkeepers and clerks, however, Yeats's conception of Cuchulain became even more overtly a dramatization of the 'protesting individual voice'.

Superficially, *The Green Helmet* is a contradiction of the thesis of *On Baile's Strand*, in that Cuchulain offers up his life in order to save the country from the destruction threatened by the mythical Red Man. This is not to be read, however, as a surrender to bourgeois order and demands for the suppression of the individual to the needs of the state. The motivation of Cuchulain is self-gratification and expression in which he is fully realized at the very moment that his action also, and even incidentally, liberates the people from oppression. In Yeats's conception of the rôle that the artist now had to play the action of Cuchulain takes on a precise meaning, in that the many will only benefit according to the extent that the individual remains capable of acts of self-expression rather than becoming the victim of social conformity. The belief that Ireland needed the heroic individual is central to Yeats's conception, just as he was equally convinced that it was precisely that quality which was lacking in the emergent nation. The double sense of the necessity and its negation permeates his work as he sees the class of virtues Ireland needs as not only marginalized, but even threatened with extinction. Cuchulain's evocation of himself as 'the great barnacle-goose' in *The Green Helmet*, prepares for his sense of his reincarnation as a bird conveyed in *The Death of Cuchulain*, and the images of swans which, in the poems of the 1920s, convey the doomed dignity of an Ascendancy whose final hour has come.

The Green Helmet offers a critique of the implications of particular forms of relations between the individual and society and, as in the drama, so in Yeats's poetry of this period whose principle theme is most clearly suggested by the title of the short collection released in 1913, *Poems Written in Discouragement* (Yeats, 1957, pp. 287-93). Despite critical esteem, self-confidence and awareness of his technical abilities, the distraction of 'the seeming needs of my fool-driven land', 'a woman's face' (p. 267) and 'plays / That have to be set up in fifty different ways' (p. 260), together with awareness that 'the Door of Death is near' (p. 298), combined to make his best achievements seem 'but a post the passing dogs defile' (p. 321). *The Playboy of the Western World* proved to be a climacteric in the relations between the Abbey and its audiences. After January 1907 the Abbey Theatre directorate made no policy decision to 'repeat the opinions of the audience' but neither did they openly confront them. There was some element of mockery of Douglas Hyde in 'At the Abbey Theatre', but the question Yeats posed was a serious one: the relations between the intellectual and the people-nation:

> Is there a bridle for this Proteus
> That turns and changes like his draughty seas?
> Or is there none, most popular of men,
> But when they mock us, that we mock again? (p. 265)

The poetry written after 1907 represents both a response to the reception of *The Playboy of the Western World*, and a retreat from engagement with the people-nation to construct a critique of the ideological hegemony that bound them together. That critique had long been implicit within Yeats's politics and his aesthetic but, dating from his reading of Nietzsche in 1902, that critique became increasingly founded on Nietzsche, genealogy, and history. Nietzsche confirmed Yeats's belief that the codes which determine the behaviour and aesthetic standards of the leading individuals in a society are proper to them alone, having no relation to the codes by which 'democratic vulgarity' (Zwerdling, 1965, p. 20) guides its actions and appreciations. Increasingly aware of the enormous gap that existed between his expectations of a leading group and the reality of the leading groups in both metropolis and colony, Yeats devoted much effort from 1907 to 1915 to defining his ideal through the construction of an idealized aristocracy; Nietzschean heroic individuals possessed of the renaissance courtier's nonchalant omnicompetence (*sprezzatura*) that comprised 'The gifts that govern men' (Yeats, 1957, p. 264). These heroic figures were made concrete in Yeats's poetry through contemporary and near-contemporary figures such as Parnell, Maud Gonne, the Gregory family (Lady Gregory, Robert Gregory, Sir Hugh Lane) and John O'Leary. These constructs were not, however, solely nostalgic; in addition to serving as poetical devices they functioned as polemical weapons, whereby Yeats could expose the failings of the contemporary leaders of the people-nation. The gulf that separated his idealized models and the actuality of the leaders of people-nation was a constant reference in Yeats's poetry in these years as he energetically dedicated himself to attacking the leaders of 'the new class' exemplified by William Martin Murphy, Timothy Healy and the rest of 'the Sullivan gang' who had 'dragged' Parnell down.

The individual poems which constituted *Poems Written in Discouragement* were written as interventions in the controversy raised by the Lane bequest of impressionist paintings to the Dublin Municipal Art Gallery. Containing 'To a Wealthy Man who promised a Second Subscription to the Dublin Municipal Gallery if it were proved the People wanted Pictures', 'September 1913', 'Paudeen' and 'To A Shade', the collection expressed a vitriolic passion which, in addressing once more the central issue of *whose* ideological and aesthetic standards should prevail in contemporary Ireland, revealed the extent to which the poet, far from being – as in the 1890s and after – a shaping influence on debate, had been expressed from the people-nation and reduced to a voice on the sidelines. Where Celticism had allowed Yeats access to a species of sentimental connection with the people-nation through folk-lore and landscape, his new and profoundly anti-popular discourse furnished a critique of the leaders of the people-nation which saw their mediocrity defined by the very solidarity of outlook between them and the people-nation; a solidarity revealed, as it is mocked, in calling representative figures of both 'Paudeen' (Yeats, 1957, p. 289; p. 291). In these poems, criticism of the aesthetic shortcomings of the leaders of 'the new class', 'the fumbling wits, the obscure spite / Of our old Paudeen in his shop' (p. 291), led to despair that the outcome of the long nationalist struggle should be the triumph of those who:

> ... being come to sense,
> But fumble in a greasy till
> And add the halfpence to the pence
> And prayer to shivering prayer...
>
> 'Was it for this ... that all that blood was shed,
> For this Edward Fitzgerald died,
> And Robert Emmet and Wolfe Tone, ... ? ('September 1913', Yeats, 1957, p. 290)

It was the prospect of this new 'ascendancy' that in the years before 1916 drove Yeats to give voice to the despairing refrain 'Romantic Ireland's dead and gone' and it, and its leaders, 'with O'Leary in the grave' (p. 290).

Yeats's double marginalization in this period – from his social class because of his 'nationalism' and from the people-nation because of his anti-popular sentiments – placed increasing pressure on his sense of identity. The elaboration of a corporate Mask for the Ascendancy, which looked to the qualities of the courtier, had been one way of handling this problem, but pressure on Yeats's personal position intensified his need to establish a family lineage and heightened his sensitivity to his unmarried and childless state. The wounding attacks of George Moore on the lack of distinction of the Yeats's family ancestry, and particularly upon the validity of Yeats's claim to kinship with the great Butler dynasty of the ducal house of Ormonde, forced Yeats back to fundamentals in an attempt at self and social definition through asserting the longevity of the Yeats family's existence and its historical presence in Ireland. Part of the context, then, for 'Pardon Old Fathers' was the bitter quarrel with Moore, but in moving away from the indefensible position of claiming an Ormonde ancestry, Yeats was forced to shift to more genealogically justifiable ground which, in turn, led him to confront the reality that the Yeats's family fortunes had been founded upon trade, the very activity which in *The Countess Cathleen* had been the mark of the Devil, and which Yeats had taken as one of the defining characteristics of 'the new class' to which he was so opposed. The resolution to this problem lay in his assertion that 'Merchant and scholar ... have left me blood / That has not passed through any huckster's loin' (p. 269), so producing a dichotomy between honourable 'merchants', who were acceptable as ancestors, and dishonourable 'hucksters' or petty shop-keepers. The two are further differentiated by the references in the poem to: 'Soldiers that gave, whatever die was cast.... / Old Merchant skipper that leaped overboard / after a hat in Biscay Bay', examples of *sprezzatura* which confirmed the distance between 'merchant' and 'huckster' in the former's demonstration of 'the wasteful virtues'.

The shifts to which Yeats was put in order to sustain this new self-conception testify to his insecurity, further emphasized by the use of the word 'prove' in the concluding line of 'Pardon Old Fathers': 'I have no child, I have nothing but a book, / Nothing but that to prove your blood and mine' (p. 270). That Yeats should feel his identity could be stabilized by an appeal to the past was unremarkable, but that he should turn from a national to a dynastic identity and envisage the resolution to his personal crisis in the birth of a child, indicates the severity of his isolation, while 'the barren passion' for Maud Gonne, once a source of inspiration, now required exculpation. Moreover, Yeats was convinced that sexual potency and poetic ability were linked. Reflecting on the urgings of Lady Gregory that he should settle down and get married, uttered in the context of the break-up of an unsatisfactory and, on his part, purely physical relationship, he worried, lest the price of propitiating 'the devil that is between my thighs' (p. 299) through marriage with 'a comely lass' might be artistic immobilization: 'I'll grow respected at my ease, / And hear amid the garden's nightly peace, / ... / The wind blown clamour of the barnacle-geese' (p. 300).

Yeats's conviction that there was a relationship between sexuality and power extended also to political power. In an analysis of the contemporary situation recorded in his diary for 1907, and published under the graphic title 'Estrangement', he had observed that the petit-bourgeois who formed the nation's political class had suffered the intellectual equivalent of 'a certain surgical operation. Hence the shrillness of their voices' (Yeats, 1955, p. 486) While he criticized this sterility as that of 'eunuchs' in comparison to Don Juan in 'On those That Hated "The Playboy of the Western World" 1907' (Yeats, 1957, p. 294), discerning that over 'the last ten or twenty years', a 'perpetual drying out of the Irish mind' had occurred, he recognized that the consequence of this intellectual castration, and the diversion of the potency of sexuality into other channels, might have wider applications. In late 1910, he acknowledged that concentration on 'theatre business' and intellectual activity might also affect his own vitality: 'The fascination of what's difficult / Has dried the sap out of my veins, and rent / Spontaneous joy and natural content / Out of my heart' (p. 260). Thus, while sterility and impotence are the charges which Yeats directs at the 'new class', for they 'no longer love, for only life is loved' (Yeats, 1961, p. 314), there is a recognition of the interdependence of deployments of sexuality and power.

Images of Ascendancy 'Dons' reviled by the 'eunuchs' of the Irish middle class resonate throughout Yeats's work, encompassing the Parnell and Lane poems and the Cuchulain plays, but even more noteworthy is the analysis Yeats provides of the consequences of this willed celibacy. In 'J.M. Synge and the Ireland of his Time' Yeats recorded his response to '*The Playboy* Riots' which signalled 'the dissolution of a school of patriotism that held sway over my [Yeats's] youth' (p. 312), and contemplated the future actions of those who could revile a play of such vitality: 'After a while, in a land that has given itself to agitation overmuch, abstract thoughts are raised up between men's minds and Nature ... till minds, whose patriotism is perhaps great enough to carry them to the scaffold, cry down natural impulse with the morbid persistence of minds unsettled by some fixed idea' (p. 313). Here, Yeats pinpointed the impulse which fuelled the new 'Artificers of the Great Moment', the artist-intellectuals of the 1916 Rising, members of a generation whose minds, said Yeats, had become stone. In seeking to mobilize a people-nation cemented together by the discourses which constituted familism, these 'Artificers' succeeded, where Griffith, Connolly, and Moran, failed, by drawing upon Catholicism as their sentimental link with the people-nation.

Any would-be challenger to the dual dominance of the U.I.L. and the Church in these years was confronted by a series of potentially disabling choices of strategy – parliamentarism as against abstentionism or insurrection, sectarian exclusivity as against indifferentism or pluralism – and the experience of Moran shows that refusal to compete was the most disabling choice of all. In its mature form, from 1914, Pearse's response to this discursive regulation was a practice which embraced death-in-insurrection not as suicide, but as an equivalent of crucifixion in which, having foisted responsibility for the act of suppression on to the materially superior colonial power, the innocence of the 'victim' secures the 'resurrection' of the nation which the victim has symbolically become. The cultural products which this form of discourse enabled is exemplified in Joseph M. Plunkett's 'The Little Black Rose Shall Be Red At Last', one of a group of Plunkett's poems dedicated to Caitlín Ní Uallachain (Cathleen

Ni Houlihan), in which the consequences of that meshing of patriotism with the sexual is most strikingly revealed. The poet dedicates his life to the revivification of Ireland – the 'dark rose' – in explicitly sexual terms as the 'passionate flood' of the poet's blood 'spend(s) its strength' in making poet and 'dark rose' 'only one flesh' (Ryan, 1963, p. 201). While this poem is one of the most extreme instances of the return of the (sexually) repressed it is also paradigmatic in the sensuality of expression with which mortality is patriotically embraced. The extent to which the poet-insurgents were conscious of the psycho-sexual implications of their imagery is debatable, but that they were aware of the fundamental choices which they poetically advocated – and politically acted – is beyond contention. A central feature of their literature is the Romantic centrality of the self, a factor which along with the images of nature and death locates them in a wider European context, but with a vital distinguishing feature; the self, and particularly that of the intellectual, is only to be fully realized in a dedication of the individual life to the greater glory of the nation. Merely to reflect artistically on the nation's fate from the security of an ivory tower was, said Thomas MacDonagh, to earn the 'tyrant's fate' and his work, and that of Pearse, was an examination and ultimate vindication of the denial of self for national salvation.

MacDonagh's *Pagans*, a one act drawing-room drama of ideas, exposes the high degree of conscious choice exercised by the insurgents and also, most penetratingly, the only rôle perceived to be available to the patriotic intellectual. John Fitzmaurice, the protagonist, has resisted the temptations of two women, leaving his wife and fleeing from the possibility of an affair, in favour of what is essentially a Christ-like period of exile from Dublin. The play features his return with a resolve which he articulates at the conclusion:

> John: Frances, I shall do better than write. A man who is a mere author is nothing. If there is anything good in anything I have written, it is the potentiality of adventure in me – the power to do something better than write. My writings have only been the prelude to my other work ...
> I am going to live the things that I before imagined. (MacDonagh, 1980, p. 53)

The play was premièred at the amateur but highly cosmopolitan and intellectual Irish Theatre, where MacDonagh was managing director, in April 1915, exactly twelve months before the Rising in which he, too, lived what he had before imagined.

The clear sense that the literary work is both a public statement and a form of psycho-drama, in which individual uncertainties are resolved by the act of artistic exteriorization, is what separates the creative work of the insurgents from that of simple propaganda. As MacDonagh observed in his *Literature in Ireland* 'Propaganda has rarely produced a fine poem', rather the great literature of Ireland will be produced when the poet 'in great stress ... will feel his patriotism as if he alone felt it, and utter it unconscious of propaganda ... His poetry is a matter between himself and himself' (MacDonagh, 1916, p. 151). Such statements reveal that in many crucial respects the insurgents subscribed to aesthetic values which were not dissimilar to those of Yeats. MacDonagh was a serious and sensitive literary critic, fully aware of contemporary Anglo-Irish authors but, in the very moment of his recognition delineating that which enforced exclusion. An Anglo-Irish literature worthy of a special designation, he argued, 'could only come when English had become the language of the Irish people, mainly of Gaelic stock, and when the literature was from, by, of, to and for the Irish people' (p. viii). The Irish race, MacDonagh argued, was now mostly English speaking, but the life and ways of thought expressed were 'still individually Gaelic, spiritually, morally, socially' (p. 23), and in his definition of the essential characteristics of the Irish it is the note of agrarian idealization which is heard again. The 'true' Anglo-Irish literature could only be produced by 'the new English speakers of the country whose fathers or grandfathers spoke only Irish' (p. 24), for the Irish were 'an agricultural people, fresh from the natural home of man' (p. 23). The exclusion was absolute, for although others may claim patriotic feeling this 'patriotism of the Pale [was] a very different thing from the national feeling of the real Irish people' (p. 27). Clearly it could only be on the impossible attainment of the organic connection with the people of which Pearse wrote in the aptly titled 'The Rebel' that any 'colonists who refused' could be allied to the national cause: 'I am come of the seed of the people ... I am the flesh of the flesh of these lowly, I am bone of their bone ... And because I am of the people, I understand the people ... I speak to my people, and I speak in my people's name to the masters of my people' (Pearse, 1979, pp. 25-6).

That the 'sentimental connection' with the people which resonates throughout the work of the insurgents is based on Catholicism, is made explicit in their rejection of the Celtic mysticism which permeated the work of Anglo-Irish writers. Plunkett pithily expressed his view of Anglo-Irish mysticism in the title of an essay 'Obscurity and Poetry', and MacDonagh's play *Metempsychosis* (1912) ridiculed the notion of reincarnation which had been taken up by Yeats and AE after the work of Madam

Blavatsky. Even when Anglo-Irish writers returned to Irish materials and the Irish language they treated it, claimed MacDonagh, 'as W.S. Gilbert and such writers for comic purposes used to treat French' (MacDonagh, 1916, p. 49). Pearse, too, saw such raids on the ancient literature of Ireland as producing an essential misrepresentation. Although several critics have pointed to the pagan tradition behind the Rising as a realization of redemption through blood sacrifice, to stress the pagan roots of the concept is to locate the insurgents on a continuum which includes the pagan mysticism of Yeats *et al.*, a relationship which Pearse and MacDonagh rejected in the name of theological purity. While the pagan ritual of sacrifice resonates through the Rising, its potency lay in the ability of its architects to ground it in the Catholicism which was now the cement of the people-nation (Dalton, 1974; Williams, 1983).

The evidence for the assertion lies in the work of Pearse, whose concept of a 'Cuchulain baptised' emphasizes the conversion of paganism to the overall informing faith. Cuchulain becomes Christ, retaining his pagan heritage in that this crucifixion is for Ireland, but maintaining equally his Christian divinity in that the Irish are a chosen people whose resurrection is at hand. The resurrection of the chosen people is a common literary trope of both Anglo-Irish and Irish-Irish Revivals, but the significant distinction between them lies in the nature of the resolution of the works; resurrection as part of a living faith, or as an ideal which, in its infinite postponement, allows the literary expression of a redemptionist ideology while still inferring that its achievement is beyond the bounds of actuality. An examination of what F.S.L. Lyons has referred to as the 'Parnell Theme in Literature' clarifies this point, and reinforces understanding of the mobilizing nature of the insurgents' literary work.

As Lyons makes clear, not only did the myth of Parnell have a widespread influence in the decades after his death but 'it changed its character according to the needs of individuals who used it, and according to the exigencies of the situations with which they had to grapple' (Lyons, 1977, p. 69). As Lady Gregory's *The Deliverer*, performed at the Abbey Theatre in January 1911, illustrates, despite the extent to which Anglo-Irish writers espoused the nationalist cause, the dominant mood which they expressed through the Parnell theme was of fall, betrayal, and an uncertain future. While both the title, and the setting in Ancient Egypt, nationalistically evoke the idea of Moses leading the chosen people from bondage, the chosen people, whose diction marks them as Irish, reject their Deliverer and the play closes as questions as to the actuality of his death and the possibility of his resurrection are discussed in hesitant and regretful terms. The same theme informs Lennox Robinson's *Patriots* performed in the same theatre four months later, only here the one-time leader returns from a gaol sentence imposed for his patriotism to find that the interest of his erstwhile followers is in 'the Moving Pictures at the Town Hall' (Lennox Robinson, 1982, p. 53). This is an Ireland which is 'never going to fight again' (p. 56), where the Deliverer returns to the offer of employment as a clerk in a co-operative store, and although the preferred reading is of disdain for the betrayal of principles and admiration for the dedication of the distraught patriot – the play is dedicated 'To the James Nugents of History' – the ultimate effect, as with *The Deliverer*, is to suggest that revolt or resurrection will never come because of the cowardly materialism of 'the people'. The links with Yeats's disparaging poems on 'Paudeen' are clear but, in addition to the critique of the people, and the lament for the lost and aristocratic leader, these two plays suggest that the time for action is located in an abandoned past rather than in an emerging future.

Although written after the Rising it is Robinson's *The Lost Leader* (1918) which makes the point most explicitly for, although passion had re-entered politics, the voice of Lucius, who may be Parnell awakening from the sleep of intellectual and emotional exile, is raised in condemnation of the un-heroic qualities of contemporary Ireland. The question raised by the play is into what shape is Ireland to be moulded, to which Lucius/Parnell's reply is that 'no nation can live by bread alone, that a nation must be noble and beautiful before it can be free – spiritually' whereas the contemporary struggle for Home Rule has become 'merely the exchange of government by English shop-keepers for government by Irish gombeen-men' (Lennox Robinson, 1918, pp. 96-9). While such expressions of disillusion refer forward to the critiques emanating from Sean O'Faolain in the 1930s and 1940s, the Parnellite theme also refers back, to link with those pre-Rising works which also suggested the base nature of the people and the futility of leading them to any level higher than that catered for by 'the Moving Pictures'. Failure, it is implied, is the quintessential feature of Ireland but, far from being a cause for regret, it is seen as the guarantor of a spiritual purity uncorrupted by the compromises which success in the world would entail. In the opinion of Lady Gregory the Irish poet 'is in touch with a people whose heroes have been the failures ... who went out to a battle which was already lost' (Lady Gregory, 1900). The political consequences of such romantic melancholy have been summarized by Wayne E. Hall: 'to the writers, Parnell's avoidance of public action held out, however faintly, the promise of a halt to the changes in Irish society; but they also came to believe that the only response to such inevitable change was to avoid it, to withdraw from the processes of history ... they seek to retreat from, or even to annihilate their experiences of modern Ireland' (Hall, 1980, p. 36). Superficially there is implied regret for the loss of passion and principles, but in terms of dramatic effect the profoundly anti-revolutionary impact of these works is highlighted by comparison with work produced from within the people-nation during the same period.

One such play is *The Last Warriors of Coole: A Heroic Play in One Act* by Terence MacSwiney, the future Lord Mayor of Cork who died on hunger strike in 1920, produced in April 1910 by the Cork Dramatic Society which MacSwiney co-founded with Daniel Corkery. The play's treatment of the issues of defeat, resurrection and triumph is revealing of the deep psychological gulf which had opened up between the increasingly marginalized Anglo-Irish writers of nominally nationalist sympathies, and those intellectuals within the people-nation whose treatments of parallel themes were essentially triumphalist. Although an un-dramatic play, unsuccessful in its attempts to create a heroic diction in keeping with its pagan warrior setting, *The Last Warriors of Coole* is explicit in its dialogic references to the belief in the rewards which will be divinely delivered to those who practise uncompromising resistance. 'No land shall ever fail, / Where but a few for freedom stand' is the message of Lugh delivered to the resistants by Fionn who was 'born / To lead my people forth' (MacSwiney, 1984, p. 76). The fact that it is the faithful maintenance of 'the dream of the coming time' that has empowered the beleaguered warriors to resist until the moment when liberation becomes an actuality, stands as a warning to the oppressor to 'Beware the dreamer', for the nationalist thought can clearly empower the nationalist deed.

While MacSwiney's heroic parable mobilizes the mythic past as a model for action, MacDonagh's *When the Dawn is Come*, staged by the Abbey Theatre in October 1908, is set 'Fifty years hence, in Ireland in time of insurrection' (MacDonagh, 1908, p. 6), and while its sub-Shakespearian plot and diction contradict the implied modernity of the moment this play also ends in triumph for the forces of Ireland. The response of contemporary audiences to the work emphasizes the necessary distinction to be drawn between these nationalist works and those Anglo-Irish treatments of similar themes. It was praised as 'The first Sinn Féin drama' and the editor of the diary of school events for St Enda's, the school founded by Pearse, at which MacDonagh was a master, noted that 'We were present in a body at Mr. MacDonagh's *When the Dawn is Come*, at the Abbey theatre. Our youngest boys came home yearning for rifles' (Parks and Parks, 1967, pp. 102-4). Although the diarist of the Dublin theatrical scene, Joseph Holloway, expressed his bafflement at the play, his observation that the enthusiastic reception was the work of young Gaelic Leaguers goes to the central point of the work in that the insurrection is led by the intellectual who acts and, in fighting 'like one seeking death', brings triumph to Ireland even at the cost of his own life. The death may be that of the individual but, as MacDonagh wrote in 'Of A Poet Patriot', a short poem originally entitled 'To William Rooney', the resonances of that individual action will 'have echoes still / When the dawn is come' (Ryan, 1963, p. 112). This dramatization of the organic intellectual as spiritual and physical liberator of the people is one factor that links the works of MacDonagh and Pearse; the fact that the intellectual of *When the Dawn is Come* is also the leader of a Catholic people is a fact which resonates throughout their work, becoming in Pearse little less than a conscious imitation of Christ.

The poem 'A Mother Speaks', written by Pearse in prison and included by him in his farewell letter to his mother in which he urged her 'not to grieve for all this but to think of it as a sacrifice which God asked of me' (Ruth Dudley Edwards, 1979, p. 322), makes explicit self-identification with the crucifixion of Christ and, coupled with the post-execution posters on Dublin walls depicting Pearse in pietà position supported by Mother Erin, indicates how pervasive was the image of his self-willed immolation. Self-willed is the operative word, but such a choice was the result of highly conscious decisions in which sensual pleasure was suppressed with the resolution of an anchorite: 'Naked I saw thee / O beauty of beauty ... I blinded my eyes ... I closed my ears ... I smothered my desire ... And to this road before me / I turned my face ... To the deed that I see / And the death I shall die' (Pearse, 1979, p. 36). The poem is appropriately entitled 'Renunciation', and it is the sensual life which is renounced just as it is a sensual death which is embraced: 'A rann I made to my love / To the king of kings, ancient death' (p. 34). Such repression is what Yeats referred to as the act of making the heart like a stone with all the suggested rigidity and immobilty that phrase suggests, but it was also perfectly in keeping with the Christ-image in which worldly temptation was to be overcome in order to concentrate the mind on the struggle with which Pearse was above all concerned – 'To set bondsmen free' (p. 27). It is as a literal rehearsal of the act of liberation that his plays must be regarded.

While the poetry frequently expresses the act of decision-making, the plays have only the certainty of resolution due, in part, to the intended place of production and intended audience. Several major productions were mounted at St Enda's each year, and while the performances were open to the public with Yeats, Hyde, and O'Grady among the luminaries in attendance, it is essentially as acts of confirmation that they should be viewed. Of the eight dramatic works written by Pearse, all, with the possible exception of *The Singer*, were written for performance by the boys and masters of the school and an examination of *The King*, his first play as opposed to pageant, reveals Pearse's concept of drama as a ritual pre-enactment of an advocated action.

The play, first performed in June 1912, is set in an ancient monastery at a time when the nation is struggling against an oppressor who can not be defeated because the people are led by a sinful king. Only when a little child, Giolla Na Naomh ('the servant of the saints'), takes on the mantle of leadership is the enemy crushed but only and, it is inferred, necessarily, at the cost of the pure life. 'Freedom', pronounces the Abbot, 'is not purchased but with a great price' (p. 77). Only the dedication of the pure life can redeem the people, and although Pearse denied in 1913 that 'we have ever carried on anything like a political or revolutionary propaganda among our boys' (Ruth Dudley Edwards, 1979, p. 143), it is merely a semantic quibble made possible by Pearse's belief that his cause was raised above politics by the very purity of its objective. The objective of St. Enda's, Pearse wrote in 1912, 'was radical: it strikes at the root of anglicisation' (p. 188), and although de-anglicization of Ireland was equally a cultural and linguistic objective his observation at the time of the first St. Enda's pageant in March 1909 reveals the essentially military connotations of the term: 'They [the boys] will leave St. Enda's under the spell of their beloved hero' (p. 124). That hero, Cuchulain, was present in a strikingly visual sense in St Enda's as one of the original pictures in the school showed the arming of the young Cuchulain underneath which were blazoned his dedicatory words: 'I care not though I were to live but one day and one night provided my fame and my deeds live after me' (p. 117).

While such an ego-charged dedication to death is more in keeping with the Cuchulain of Yeats than that of Pearse, the way in which the deeds were to live on is the crucial distinction. For, as one of Pearse's poems declares in its title 'I am Ireland' (Pearse, 1979, p. 35), the death of the one would be followed by the resurrection of the 'risen people' (p. 26). That Pearse was seeking to be the sacrificial Christ, just as he inculcated the same spirit of sacrificial selflessness in his pupils, is most explicitly pre-figured in the closing lines of his last, and unperformed, play, *The Singer*, where it is the artist-intellectual who leads by, literally, Christian example:

> One man can free a people as one Man redeemed the world. I will take no pike, I will go into the battle with bare hands. I will stand up before the Gall as Christ hung naked before men on the tree! (Pearse, 1979, p. 125)

The stage directions read 'He moves through them, pulling off his clothes as he goes' (p. 125).

The Singer's exit to 'crucifixion' dramatically pre-figures Pearse's exit to his chosen Calvary, the more prosaic Dublin Post Office. But despite the apparent bathos of such a juxtaposition it is Pearse's question in 'The Fool' which merits attention: 'what if the dream come true? / What if the dream come true? and if millions unborn shall dwell / In the house that I shaped in my heart, the noble house of my thought?' (p. 24). The expectations aroused by the Singer's Christ-like diction and anticipation of death depend upon an ambiguity, for the Singer advocates no blasphemous resurrection for himself but rather, slipping from the fate of the individual to the fate of the people, asserts that it is they who will awake to eternity from the tomb. For the purposes of our examination of the cultural impact of the Easter Rising, the debate between historians and contemporaries on Pearse's intentions, and upon whether self-immolation was intended or caused by a botched plan, is irrelevant. Given the circumstances of the Rising, in the midst of an Imperial War, in which the Colonial power was stretched to the utmost, death either in the insurrection itself or by firing squad after was a near certainty, whether the Irish Volunteers throughout the country rose or not. Similarly, the ideological and emotional impact of the Rising was augmented, but not shaped, by the measured slowness with which the Imperial State carried out the executions of the leaders. What was important, however, was that the liturgical quality of the conduct of the leaders, particularly Pearse, made it possible for Pearse's followers to forge an immediate, and in some cases enduring, sentimental connection of feeling-passion, with the people-nation. Moreover, whereas the Catholic Church had actively condemned the conduct of previous insurrectionaries, such as the Fenians and the Young Irelanders, general clerical condemnation was made virtually impossible by Pearse's appropriation of religiosity, while the absolution which a Capuchin priest gave Pearse before his execution seemed to provide a clerical seal of approval for his actions (Ruth Dudley Edwards, pp. 320-1). In these circumstances the intellectual resources and apparatuses of the Church which hitherto had guaranteed the survival of parliamentarism became the channels through which Pearse's insurrectionary message was propagated. By recruiting the Church's intellectuals (however briefly and reluctantly) as supporters of the Easter Rising, Pearse disrupted the relationship between the old constellation of forces which had led the people-nation and made possible the emergence of an alternative.

Like other observers, Yeats received the news of the Rising with surprise and, as news of the deaths and executions filtered through the censor, distress. Yeats recognized how, in one sense, he had made a fundamental misjudgement in 'September 1913' when he had assumed that the age of heroism was past in Ireland. In one of his first responses to the Rising he wrote to Lady Gregory: 'I had no idea any public event could so deeply move me – and I am very despondent about the future. At the moment I feel that all the work of years has been overturned, all the bringing together of classes, all the freeing of Irish literature and criticism from politics' (Jeffares, 1968, p. 226). As an immediate response to the Rising the opinion that it represented the destruction of half a life's work was histrionic, inaccurate, but characteristic. 'All the work of years' had not been overturned by the Easter Rising and to suggest that it had been was little more than an attempt to assert a centrality of position which was wholly imaginary in current circumstances. The 'freeing of Irish literature and criticism from politics' was, if anything other than an empty phrase, a reference to Yeats's equivocal ambitions to determine standards and not an almost-achieved fact. But his recognition in the same letter 'that terrible beauty has been born *again* [our emphasis]', gave not only the refrain to 'Easter 1916' but marks here, as in the poem, an awareness that 'rebirth' necessarily meant that the older heroism, in which the Anglo-Irish had taken such a prominent part, was now superceded. The group which, in 'September 1913' Yeats had thought incapable of the romantic heroism of Tone, Fitzgerald or Emmet, had seized their tradition.

The two poems written on and in 1916 – 'Easter 1916' and 'Sixteen Dead Men' – although not published until 1920, constitute observations on the consequences of the Rising, as Yeats followed developments in which he could take little or no part. Given that Yeats was in England when the Easter Rising took place, and shared only acquaintanceship, rather than intimacy, with a few of the leaders, the personal quality of 'Easter 1916' is remarkable, in that the readers' access to the leaders of the Rising is mediated through their relationship with the poet: 'I have met them ....'. Similarly, the poet asserts through the power of naming ('number him in the song', 'murmur name on name'), powers of exclusion and prohibition from posterity and fame, which are attempts to recover from this unlooked-for situation some means of warding-off the almost immediate collapse of the position of the Anglo-Irish which he clearly foresaw as a near-inevitable outcome of the Rising (Yeats, 1957, pp. 393-4; Eagleton, 1971). In 'Easter 1916' Yeats explicitly recognized that the lower middle-class origins of the insurgents' leaders ('coming / From counter or desk among grey / Eighteenth-century houses' (p. 391), accentuated the precariousness of the Anglo-Irish situation. Now, to the existing threat to their position that Yeats traced to the Land Acts, and that he had made the subject of 'Upon a House Shaken by the Land Agitation' was to be added the threat posed to the estates and properties of the remnants of Ascendancy by the 'new class's' own interests. For, despite the Dublin location of the Rising, these 'hearts ... enchanted to a stone / ... trouble the living stream' (p. 393). A disruption, not of townscape or city river, but a countryside scene in which the figure of the rider, standing for the Anglo-Irish, joins other symbols of transcience to emphasize the unyielding fact that 'The stone's in the midst of all' (p. 393). The corollary of the potential power of the new class, seen in the Easter Rising, was the inevitability of the decline of the Anglo-Irish.

The assessment that the Rising, and more important, 'the hearts ... Enchanted to a stone' had irrevocably changed the political and all other circumstances of contemporary Ireland, is confirmed in 'Sixteen Dead Men' in which Yeats stated that the absolute of the insurrectionaries' deaths had ended 'talk of give and take', while in a further denial of conclusions reached in 'September 1913', he recognized the links forged by the Rising leaders with 'those new comrades they have found, / Lord Edward and Wolfe Tone' (p. 395). Easter 1916, in contrast to Emmet's, Fitzgerald's, and Tone's actions, had been led 'of, by, from and to' the people-nation. If the consequence was not the victory of the Gael, in Moran's sense of a victory for a cultural independence of identity, then arguably it represented one of the few ways in which would-be leaders of the people-nation could secure the disruption of the structures which marginalized them. The implications of the form of that disruption, in particular the production of a fundamental bistability in Catholicism in Ireland, whereby Christian submissiveness could be turned into a powerful weapon against the Imperial power, was to have considerable consequences in post-Colonial Ireland. More immediately, the form of the Easter Rising ensured that the price of inclusion in the people-nation – even for a colonizer who refused – was deracination: not Gaelicization, but acceptance in one form or another, of the supremacy of Catholicism.

6

Revolutions are what happen to wheels

David Fitzpatrick has suggested that if 'revolutions are what happen to wheels, then Ireland underwent a revolution between 1916 and 1922 ... social and political institutions were turned upside down, only to revert to full circle upon the establishment of the Irish Free State' (Fitzpatrick, 1977, p. 232). From 1917 to 1922 Sinn Féin was transformed from a party organization under the virtual sole direction of Arthur Griffith, to a unifying front organization in which a host of nationalists and radicals coalesced, usurping and extending the U.I.L.'s position as leader of the people-nation. United by a bond of feeling-passion, the result of Pearse's and others' short-lived seizure of the rules of discourse of Catholicism and parliamentarism, which had previously marginalized dissent, the inchoate emotions aroused by the executions of the insurgents engendered hatred, not only of the British Government, but also of the leaders of the U.I.L. for alleged 'collaboration' with the British. The widespread emotional response to the Easter Rising dragged parish-pump politicians from support for the U.I.L., and into endorsement of its rival, and in this moment Sinn Féin became briefly united with the people-nation in an expansive form of hegemony produced from unified opposition to continued British rule, distilled in 1918 in the threat to extend conscription to Ireland. This common feeling survived more-or-less to the end of the Anglo-Irish war in 1921, manifested in the subordination of sectional claims of women, political radicals, and organized labour to the struggle for independence (Fitzpatrick, 1975, p. 235; Munck, 1983; Ward, 1983, p. 248 ff.).

This unification embraced all political and social groups willing to accept independence as the supreme goal but, as Fitzpatrick has shown, the predominance in the new Sinn Féin of erstwhile supporters of the U.I.L.– shopkeepers, publicans, newspaper editors, national school teachers, and the Catholic clergy – meant that when these politically active intellectuals turned away from the U.I.L. to its new and emotionally charged supplanter, Sinn Féin acquired not only an enormous draft of provincial intellectuals and organizers to staff its campaigns and spread its easily-grasped slogans; the new recruits, schooled in the U.I.L., brought with them everything from that association except its leaders – techniques, language, supporters, but above all ideology (Fitzpatrick, 1977, Chapter 4; Laffan, 1971). After 1922 the cultural forces which were dominant in the new Free State, were the values of the farmers – familism and Catholicism.

The 'crisis of the [leading] group's hegemony' (Gramsci, 1971, pp. 210-11) which the Rising produced was resolved, therefore, by the wholesale replacement of 'men and programmes', but not by a shift in power, which continued to reside with the farmers who, 'despite their organisational weaknesses, by sheer weight of numbers, wealth and social status, directed the course of revolution as though by right' (Fitzpatrick, 1977, p. 279). This 'revolution-restoration' or 'passive revolution' as Gramsci termed it (Gramsci, 1971, pp. 58 f., 59 f.), resulted, therefore, in a political, but not a social, revolution. As early as 1917-1918 Sinn Féin intervened decisively in conflicts between larger farmers on the one hand, and smaller farmers and landless labourers on the other, to condemn the latter's attempts to seize and redistribute land, not only from landlords, but from the larger farmers. By suspending such actions in the name of national unity and subsequently outlawing them, Sinn Féin revealed what and whose interests were to be regarded as priorities in post-independence Ireland (Fitzpatrick, 1977, p. 156 ff.).

Subordination of sectional challenges to Sinn Féin hegemony was achieved on the whole through persuasion, but when the issue of the Anglo-Irish Treaty split Sinn Féin in 1921, once again protection of the interests of all those who stood to lose from the renewal of all-out war with the Crown forces became paramount. Main force was deployed ruthlesly against an *ad hoc* coalition of dissidents who refused to accept anything less than the Republic proclaimed in 1916, and who embraced, from a variety of standpoints, dislike of the prospect of a return to the *status quo ante*, along with emotional attachment to the memory of men and women killed in 1916 and after, and an inability to accept a rôle for the Crown in Irish affairs. The motives of many of the men and women who opposed the Treaty were honourable, but their opposition opened up the prospect of a continued struggle with the British, or a Civil War, and in these circumstances the Catholic Hierarchy threw all its weight behind the pro-treaty arguments, stating in *The Irish Catholic Directory* in April 1922: 'like the great bulk of the nation, we think the best and wisest course for Ireland is to accept the Treaty' (O'Callaghan, 1981, p. 12). The

Hierarchy had followed a pragmatic line after 1916, switching its support from the U.I.L to Sinn Féin, and from 1919 reacting to individual actions by both the Crown forces and the Irish Republican Army (I.R.A.) on their merits, gradually offering tacit endorsement of the I.R.A. as Crown reprisals became increasingly brutal and indiscriminate. Its own policies continued to be constrained by its ability 'to lead [its] people only in the direction in which they wanted to go' (Whyte, 1960), but Civil War, in prospect and then actuality, elicited the Hierarchy's forthright condemnation of the Republican cause whose supporters were 'parricides and not patriots', their actions 'scandalous and uncalculable criminality' (O'Callaghan, 1981, p. 17). Outnumbered, pursued by a security force which knew them intimately, lacking in majority popular support, and condemned by the Church, the defeat of the Republican forces nonetheless took eleven months (June 1922 to May 1923). But with the neutralization of that challenge the consolidation of the Irish Free State began.

Arthur Griffith, Treaty signatory and leader of the pro-Treaty majority within Sinn Féin, died in August 1922, ten days before the death of his colleague and the new State's 'strong man', Michael Collins, who had been the leading figure in the I.R.A. before the Treaty. Their successors in the 1920s followed conservative economic and social policies, their radicalism confined to the sphere of foreign affairs where they pushed to consolidate and then develop the freedoms of dominion status which the Treaty had conferred. Domestically, however, the persistence of pre-independence economic structures, and particularly the Free State's dependence upon the British market for export of its pastoral products, together with continuing reluctance to see industrial development as suited to Irish needs, ensured that both the material and cultural bases of familism continued to be reproduced. It is not surprising, therefore, that the needs of familism should be forcefully drawn to the attention of the new State's legislators. Thus, in 1925, the Free State legislature, the Dáil, sought to ensure that its prerogative right to permit divorce would not be exercised, while in 1928 the demands of a host of vigorous pressure groups were acceded to and censorship was introduced. What was characteristic of the accompanying debates and pamphleteering was a continuing disassociation of body and spirit, as campaigners sought to impose upon all Free State citizens an ethic which viewed the desires of the body as a menace to the prospect of eternal life; paradoxically, constant exhortations to chastity multiplied immeasurably the extent to which sexuality was talked about in contemporary Ireland.

As Margaret O'Callaghan has shown, the Hierarchy feared that an enduring legacy of the Anglo-Irish War and, particularly, the Civil War, would be the 'demoralisation especially of the young, whose minds are being poisoned by ... false notions on social morality' (O'Callaghan, 1983, p. 67). This threat justified on one level the Hierarchy's support for the government of the Free State and condemnation of the Anti-Treaty forces, on another level, seeing support for the I.R.A. as symptomatic of a universal moral malaise, it also justified renewed efforts to control access to literature, films, and participation in pastimes such as dancing, which might excite passion, and threaten that self-denial 'which is the nurse of all the manly virtues' (p. 72). Lenten Pastorals from the Hierarchy condemning 'evil literature', and reports and press statements from organizations such as the Catholic Truth Society and the Irish Vigilance Association, were given prominence in journals such as *The Leader* and *The Catholic Bulletin* which, in constantly talking of the ease with which the pure could be corrupted, sought to track sex down, to trace it through a 'discourse [of examination, confession, penance] that allowed it no obscurity, no respite' (Foucault, 1984, p. 20). These Pastorals exemplify Foucault's comments on such statements that they 'made the flesh the root of all evil'. Moreover, a consequence of the 'need' for discretion and reserve which dictated that 'sex must not be named imprudently, but its aspects its correlations, and its effects must be pursued down to their slenderest ramifications' (p. 19), was that statements became 'roundabout and vague' in deference to the dangerous topics of which they spoke, and hence increased in both number and circumlocutory length as discourse 'had to trace the meeting line of the body and the soul, following all its meanderings: beneath the surface of the sins it would lay bare the unbroken nervure of the flesh' (pp. 19-20). The very imprecision of the Hierarchy's 1925 condemnations of 'the spirit of worldliness that has spread into the lives of Catholics ... the overmastering desire for amusement ... the grave scandal of modern dances and fashions ... the dangers of evil literature and objectionable cinema films' served, therefore, both to condemn social events carrying a potential for impropriety, and to alert listeners to the ease with which their downfall could be encompassed (O'Callaghan, 1983, p. 73).

Organizations such as the Irish Vigilance Association, the Catholic Truth Society, *The Catholic Bulletin* and *The Leader* ceaselessly talked of sexuality in terms which defined it as debasing, mechanical, and bestial, in the process contributing to the passing of 'everything having to do with sex through the endless mill of speech' (Foucault, 1984, p. 21). In turn, such activity defined these organs and organizations as part of a deployment of power which defined the licit and the illicit and laid down 'law' as prohibition, such that 'the subject who is constituted as subject – who is "subjected" – is he who obeys'. Hence, the groups which lobbied the Free State Government on the need to place high tariffs on all imported publications, and to ban those deemed 'prurient and demoralizing', formed part of an apparatus of power which was itself 'incapable of doing anything, except to render what it dominates incapable of doing anything either, except for what this power allows it to do' (Foucault, 1984, pp. 84-5; Brown, 1985, pp. 70-2; Adams, 1968, Chapter 1). The equation of sex with sin, which Joseph Lee noted in an earlier period, became a central concern of the new State in the 1920s and 1930s, to the accompaniment of bitter condemnation by isolated voices. One of the loudest was that of Yeats.

It has become customary to regard Yeats's Senate speech of June 1925 on the issue of divorce as constituting a statement of self-identity: '*We* against whom you have done this thing are no petty people. *We* are one of the great stocks of Europe. *We* are the people of Burke; *we* are the people of Grattan; *we* are the people of Swift [our emphasis]' (Pearce, 1961, p. 99), as indeed it was in part, identifying the Anglo-Irish of the contemporary moment as the lineal descendants of the leaders of eighteenth-century Irish society. It was also taken at the time as indicating that the only – certainly the main – sufferers from a ban on divorce would be Protestants, a point that many of Yeats's fellow Protestants found deeply objectionable. But as Yeats was to make clear in writings on the subsequent Censorship Bill, he discerned in both these measures an attitude of mind which regarded the body and soul as distinct and separate, and accorded priority to the needs of the soul, to the eternal survival of which the body and its intemperate demands posed a recurrent threat.

The central clause in the Censorship Bill defined 'indecent' as 'calculated to excite sexual passions or to suggest or incite to sexual immorality or in any way to corrupt or deprave', while the Minister responsible was empowered to 'prohibit the sale or distribution of a book that is indecent or obscene or tends to inculcate principles contrary to public morality or is otherwise of such a character that the sale or distribution thereof is or tends to be injurious or detrimental to or subversive of public morality' (Adams, 1968, p. 47; Yeats, 1975, p. 481). In response to the sweeping powers of censorship thus granted, Yeats wrote several critiques of the positions of the pro-censorship lobby which turned on his support for what he stated to be the 'orthodox' Catholic dogma of Aquinas: 'that the soul is wholly present in the whole body and in all its parts' (Yeats, 1975, p. 478). Yeats's condemnation of the pro-censorship lobby turned, therefore, not only on freedom of expression, but also on what he perceived as a denial of the physical reality, needs, and drives of the body. In the 1927 poem 'Among School Children' this understanding informed a meditation on the implications of a religious devotion which demanded that 'the body is ... bruised to pleasure [the] soul' and exalted 'beauty born out of its own despair'. By opposing the images of mothers' dreams and hopes for their children with the hard, tangible shapes of marble or bronze on which nuns' reveries are centred, Yeats was able to establish the antagonism of the 'Presences' of which the marbles and bronzes are representative to the real interests of mankind and further, to assert that such antagonism proceeded from the attempt to separate body from soul (Yeats, 1957, pp. 443-6). In asking: 'chestnut tree, great-rooted blossomer, / Are you the leaf the blossom or the bole?', he highlighted the necessity to see the whole as the indissoluble sum of its parts while, in denying the possibility of knowing 'the dancer from the dance' (p. 446), Yeats affirmed what he was later to state more fully in the 1937 version of *A Vision*: 'contemplation and desire united into one, inhabit a world where every beloved image has bodily form, and every bodily form is loved' (Yeats, 1937, pp. 135-6).

Confronting a society in which sexuality was incessantly discussed in ways which reduced the sex act to its mechanical elements, Yeats increasingly registered his estrangement from contemporary Ireland. In the opening poem of *The Tower*, 'Sailing to Byzantium' (1928), the first word announces his sense of alienation in the change from 'This country' in an early draft to 'That country' in the published version (Jeffares, 1968, p. 254). Yeats's abhorrence of constant 'incitement to discourse', born of the need, in defence of familism, to 'hear [the regulation of sexuality] spoken of more and more' (Foucault, 1984, p. 18), led the poet to undercut what might otherwise be a symbol of renewal and hope – 'the young / In one another's arms' – by joining that coupling with the avian procreation of 'birds in the trees' and the cold-blooded rush to spawning of 'The salmon-falls, the mackerel-crowded seas' (Yeats, 1957, p. 407). Age diminishes the body until it is 'A tattered coat upon a stick', but as the body's powers decline the intellect must assume the burden which the body cannot bear 'and sing, and louder sing / For every tatter in its mortal dress'. Yeats is distanced from contemporary society, therefore, by the contrasts in their preoccupations; his with 'monuments of unageing intellect', theirs with the 'music' of a sensuality which denies the union of intellect and physique. To take refuge from sensuality in pure intellectualization is, Yeats recognized, no answer to this problem. Byzantium, the school of the intellect was, he wrote in September 1928, the source of a 'Platonizing theology' which had sustained a religion where saints with 'thought-tortured faces' and bodies which were 'but a framework to sustain the patterns and colours of their clothes', had renounced 'the body and all its works' (Yeats, 1975, p. 478). This vision of Byzantium as the locus of a philosophy which subordinated the body to a 'pitiless intellect' (p. 478) indicates the dilemma he recognized: the artificiality of oppositions of body and soul, and therefore the correctness of his denying that opposition, while he simultaneously yearned for personal release from the burdens of a 'heart ... sick with desire / And fastened to a dying animal' (Yeats, 1957, pp. 407-9). In such a situation the prospect of re-incorporation induced dread, not hope, so that if reincarnation there must be, reincarnation as an asexual automaton 'of hammered gold and gold enamelling' (p. 509) is to be preferred to the pain of existence in a body where subjectivity is the product of desire: death its only surcease.

The isolation which Yeats experienced and poetically articulated in the 1920s had been apparent from at least the end of the preceding decade. In 'A People's Theatre', a letter to Lady Gregory published in the *Irish Statesman* in the autumn of 1919, he stated his intention to create an exclusive theatre capable of generating 'a bond among chosen spirits, a mystery almost for leisured and lettered people' (Yeats, 1976, p. 192). The reason went far beyond the initial dissatisfaction with the Abbey Theatre and embraced that fear of the consequences of democracy anticipated by O'Grady: 'Ireland has suffered more than England from Democracy, for since the Wild Geese fled, who might have grown to be leaders in manners and taste she has had but political leaders' (p. 197). As the mutually exclusive use of the terms 'leaders in manners and taste' and 'political leaders' indicates, Yeats had lost none of his disdain for the leaders of the people-nation. In an Ireland impoverished by passionless 'intellectual hatred' (Yeats, 1957, p. 405) whose image was people 'withered old and skeletal-gaunt' (p. 475), and sundered by a war in which 'a drunken soldiery / Can leave the mother, murdered at her door, / To crawl in her own blood, and go scot-free' (p. 429), Yeats experienced both a personal and public malaise whose profundity is encapsulated in the title of Section VII of 'Meditations in Time of Civil War': 'I see Phantoms of Hatred and of the Heart's Fullness and of the Coming Emptiness'. Faced with images of collapse which had already been pre-figured in 'The Second Coming', Yeats could only turn away and question himself as to whether he could have played a more active rôle in politics: 'I turn away and shut the door, and on the stair / Wonder how many times I could have proved my worth / In something that all others understand or share' (p. 427).

Age and ill-health, along with political, and cultural isolation, raised Yeats's sense of marginalization to new heights as the 1920s progressed. At the end of the Anglo-Irish War his decision to establish his domicile in Ireland had taken concrete form in Thoor Ballylee, an ancient fastness in the neighbourhood of Coole Park which became a central image in his writing throughout the 1920s. Where Somerville and Ross, Lennox Robinson, and Elizabeth Bowen, used the Great Houses of the Anglo-Irish as metaphors to explore the social and cultural isolation of their inhabitants, Yeats's choice of a once-ruined fortress as both dwelling and symbol was even more suited to his sense of embattled determination not to surrender. Remarking on the similarities between his own situation and that of the Tower's first builder he wrote:

Two men have founded here. A man-at-arms
Gathered a score of horse and spent his days
In this tumultuous spot
Where through long wars and sudden night alarms
His dwindling score and he seemed castaways
Forgetting and forgot;
And I, that after me
My bodily heirs may find,
To exalt a lonely mind,
Befitting emblems of adversity. ('My House', Yeats, 1957, p. 420)

Written in 1923, the poem indicates a determination to resist and survive in new circumstances, but the notion of the poet's heirs' future as 'lonely', their condition 'adversity', indicates an awareness of marginalization which might reduce them to the condition of Thoor Ballylee's founder as 'castaways'. By the end of the decade the realities of exclusion bore even more strongly on Yeats, and in 'Coole Park, 1929' and 'Coole Park and Ballylee, 1931', he anticipated the final destruction of his ideal, the possibility of which he had envisaged in 'Upon a House Shaken by the Land Agitation' in 1910. The past tense expression of the image of 'His dwindling score and he *seemed* castaways' (p. 420), from houses which will soon be desolate 'When nettles wave upon a shapeless mound' (p. 489), is actualized in the present tense location of deracination and the past tense expression of now fled splendour: 'We *shift* about – all that great glory *spent* – / Like some poor Arab tribesman and his tent' (p. 491).

The final lines of 'Coole Park and Ballylee, 1931' close with bleak finality on both poem and, for Yeats, an historic period: 'But all is changed, that high horse riderless, / Though mounted in that saddle Homer rode / Where the swan drifts upon a darkening flood' (p. 492). The powerlessness of the Ascendancy is nowhere given more potent expression than in 'drifts': the once dominant class is now perceived as directionless in a State for which the image of 'the darkening flood' carried associations of an apocalyptic end.

In the first years of the Free State Yeats had hoped that this would not be the case. The Government had nominated him and a substantial number of Southern Unionists to the upper house, the Senate of the bicameral Oireachtas, where he had had high hopes that he, among others, would have influence. Writing to a friend in late 1922 he stated that 'We [i.e. the Senators] are a fairly distinguished body and should get much government into our hands' (O'Brien, 1965, p. 244). But as the 1920s passed, however, the number of occasions on which the Government intervened in defence of Catholic conservatism goaded him to fierce denunciations of its promotion of confessional interests. Yeats's political position during the 1920s and subsequently in the 1930s when he briefly embraced the Irish Fascist 'Blueshirt' movement, is unsurprising. Both his politics and his aesthetics were virulently anti-democratic, born of his belief that the rule of democracy was the harbinger of cultural collapse as his prophetic 'philosophy', set out in *A Vision*, sought to demonstrate.

Convinced that civilizations alternated between aristocracy and democracy, Yeats contrived a system based upon lunar cycles to explain the process of transition. Fusing together the insights of ritual magic and Nietzschean philosophy with esteem for aristocratic *sprezzatura*, Yeats argued that the contemporary moment was witnessing the beginning of the end of a 2,000 year conic cycle, or gyre, which had commenced with Christ's annunciation. While the Christian cycle had been preceded by an aristocratic, antithetical cycle, dominated by Greece, the annunciation of which had been Zeus' rape of Leda (Yeats, 1937, pp. 268-72), the Christian cycle had been primary or democratic in its essentials. Hence, the coming cycle would be antithetical or aristocratic, and as the democratic developed to its apotheosis, the new cycle was simultaneously being prepared: 'When the new era comes bringing its stream of irrational force it will, as did Christianity, find its philosophy impressed upon the minority who have, true to phase, turned away at the last gyre from the *Physical Primary*' (Yeats, 1978, p. 213).

A Vision supplied Yeats with a framework for poetry and politics which informed and heightened his sense of estrangement from the society of the contemporary Free State. The full intensity of his hostility was expressed in 1937 when Yeats, anticipating a counter-Renaissance which would redeem the ancient sanctities, looked out in despair at contemporary Dublin: 'When I stand upon O'Connell Bridge in the half-light and notice that discordant architecture, all those electric signs, where modern heterogeneity has taken physical form, a vague hatred comes up out of my own dark and I am certain that wherever in Europe there are minds strong enough to lead others the same hatred rises' (Yeats, 1976, p. 269). Moreover, in identifying the coming age as antithetical or aristocratic, the philosophy of *A Vision* encouraged Yeats to identify himself as one of 'the few', the precursors of the new cycle, and the Blueshirts as possibly preparing the way for a new order. The collapse of Blueshirtism in the face of De Valéra's resolute handling of its challenge did not bring Yeats's interest in Fascism to an end, as his final prose work *On the Boiler* shows (Yeats, 1939). It did, however, mark the end of his hopes for an Irish variant, while his frustration that poetic potency was matched to physical decline was expressed in one of his last poems, 'Are You Content?', a codicil to the apologia, 'Pardon Old Fathers', in which Yeats asked, 'Have I ... / Spoilt what old loins have sent? / Eyes spiritualised by death can judge, / I cannot, but I am not content' (Yeats, 1957, p. 604).

That late resurgence of the urge to comment on, and even participate in, the contemporary moment, found dramatic form in *Purgatory* (1938), a play whose setting before 'A ruined house ... a bare tree in the background' (Yeats, 1966, p. 1041), places its historic moment on the cusp between the collapse of the Great Houses and the onset of Beckettian bleakness. In an interview given in August 1938 Yeats clarified the historic and political specificity of the play: 'In my play, a spirit suffers because of its share, when alive, in the destruction of an honoured house; that destruction is taking place all over Ireland today. Sometimes it is the result of poverty, but more often because a new individualistic generation has lost interest in the ancient sanctities' (Jeffares and Knowland, 1975, p. 275). As Donald Torchiana has elucidated, the informing structure of time behind *Purgatory* is Yeats's conception of history as outlined in his commentary on 'A Parnellite at Parnell's Funeral'; a basic four period division marked by the flight of the Earls, the battle of the Boyne, the advent of French Republican influence among the peasants, and the onset of the modern period. The influence of French Republicanism,

Yeats claimed, 'woke the peasantry from the medieval sleep, gave them ideas of social justice and equality, but prepared for a century disastrous to the national intellect' (pp. 291-2). The fruit of that nineteenth century impulse towards nationalism and democracy has produced the Ireland whose desolate reality, devoid now of 'the gifts that govern men' (Yeats, 1957, p. 264), is pictured in the Old Man's question: 'Where are the jokes and stories of a house, / Its threshold gone to patch a pig sty?' (Yeats, 1966, p. 1041). The double murder of first his father, and then his son, by which the Old Man attempts to put a halt to the perceived degeneration, is revealed to have been but a further stage in the process. The sound of hoof-beats at the close of the play signifies that history can not be broken with, and the Old Man can now only plead with God for release from the pain of enduring in the present the sins of the past: 'Appease / The misery of the living and the remorse of the dead' (p. 1049).

In the light of such a poetically rendered account of the political reality of the demise of the Ascendancy, the fact that Daniel Corkery, effective laureate of the new State, gave such attention to erecting a critique of their literature could appear simply a personal idiosyncrasy. While political power might have waned, however, Yeats, in 'Under Ben Bulben' (1938), gave a poetical programme to 'Irish poets' whose implication had, of necessity, to be contested. In what can be read as a last poetic testament to Ireland, Yeats directed that writers should shun that which was now being produced by 'Base-born products of base beds' and instead:

> Sing the peasantry, and then
> Hard-riding country gentlemen,
> The holiness of monks, and after
> Porter-drinkers' randy laughter:
> Sing the lords and ladies gay
> That were beaten into the clay
> Through seven heroic centuries;
> Cast your mind on other days
> That we in coming days may be
> Still the indomitable Irishry. (Yeats, 1957, pp. 639-40)

In his own work, and that he desired to determine for the future, Yeats attempted an appropriation of culture for the class which, while now one of 'castaways', could still impress itself on the consciousness of the present through the medium of art. The well wrought urn of Yeats's poetry may well have contained only an image of that which once was, but those ashes could flare, Phoenix-like, into new life with every celebratory reading. The marginalization from the centre of Irish culture had to be both political and poetic.

Corkery was elected Professor of English Literature at University College Cork in the early 1930s, and through his two critical works, *The Hidden Ireland* (1924) and *Synge and Anglo-Irish Literature* (1931), he expounded an exclusive notion of Irishness based on 'religion', 'nationalism', and 'the land', to which writers had to conform if they wished to claim the national nomenclature (Corkery, 1931, p. 19). In *The Hidden Ireland*, he sought to establish that despite conquests, plantations, confiscations and famines, eighteenth century Ireland had witnessed the survival of the essentials of Gaelic culture which had been preserved in the few remaining Catholic gentry houses and the peasants' hovels, forming a major part of the 'unity of mind between the [Catholic Gentry] Big House and the cabin' (Corkery, 1979, p. 64 ff.). This unity of culture was propagated, argued Corkery, by bardic schools which trained the poets who were the producers and reproducers of the 'Hidden Ireland'. The schools, Corkery acknowledged, died out at the latest by the beginning of the eighteenth century (p. 75), but in a characteristic argument he maintained: 'If a great literary tradition did not result, so widespread that in course of time it must have touched every active, every unclouded mind in the community – if this did not result, then the whole endeavour was but an expense of spirit in a waste of shame – a thought that is unthinkable' (p. 94). *The Hidden Ireland* is therefore not merely an attempt at refuting the Trinity College Historian W.E.H. Lecky whose *History of England in the Eighteenth Century* Corkery took as his counter-text, but simultaneously an attack on those who, like Yeats, found in the eighteenth century a golden age of Irish culture. Corkery sought to put inverted commas around the word Irish as applied to writers like Berkeley, Swift, and Burke, and to assert that if the eighteenth century was to be studied, the *truly* Irish of the century were the poets and bards of the 'Hidden Ireland', the Ireland of 'the Gael'.

Both Sean O'Faolain, in 1936, and L.M. Cullen, in 1969, revealed that the success of Corkery's argument depended more on assertion than documentation. O'Faolain demonstrated how the 'nationalistic premisses' of the argument led to rejection of 'Anglo-Irish literature', because it 'is not an adequate interpretation of Irish life' (O'Faolain, 1936; Cullen, 1969). As O'Faolain pointed out, this argument is fully developed in Corkery's subsequent text, *Synge and Anglo-Irish Literature: A Study*, in which he sought to provide grounds for classifying Anglo-Irish Literature as the product of 'writers who, sprung from the Ascendancy, have never shared the Irish national memory, and are therefore just as un-Irish as it is possible to be' (Corkery, 1931, p. 15). Corkery identified three forms of literature currently circulating in Ireland, English, Anglo-Irish and Irish (i.e. in the Irish language). By stating that literature written for an English readership was incompatible with the needs of Irish readers, and that what was written in Irish, particularly for the young, 'was not worth taking account of' (p. 14), Corkery admitted a vital rôle for Anglo-Irish literature, defined as 'literature written in English by Irishmen' (p. 1). Corkery maintained that all 'Anglo-Irish literature, including what is being written today, may be divided into two kinds – the literature of the Ascendancy writer and that of the writer for the Irish people. Roughly, the first kind includes all the literature that lives by foreign suffrage; the second all that lives by native suffrage' (pp. 22-3). For Corkery then, the necessity was to develop the critical techniques which could identify literature produced for 'an alien market' (p. 4), from that which it would be possible to regard as 'normal, national literature' (p. 2). The test he proposed related to the three forces which, 'working for long in the Irish national being, have made it so different from the English national being ... (1) The Religious Consciousness of the People; (2) Irish Nationalism; and (3) The Land' (p. 19).

In relation to Synge, Corkery's use of this test demonstrated reliance on only two of its three limbs: religion and nationalism, for the concept of 'The Land', in the sense of either landscape or a focus for social activity, was not developed. Of the other two limbs, religion is the most fully developed; Corkery argued that: 'We may know that genuine Anglo-Irish literature has come into being when at every hand's turn ... religious consciousness breaks in upon it, no matter what the subject' (p. 20). While Corkery freely acknowledged Synge's Irish nationalism and his firm grasp of the Irish language, application of the religious limb of the test allowed him to claim that Synge, despite his 'true and deep' sympathy with the people nevertheless 'failed to give us a true reading of the people' (p. 79), because he was 'cold to the spiritual' (p. 80). In *The Aran Islands*, therefore, in the description of the funeral of a man drowned at sea (Synge, 1979, pp. 142-5), Synge is held by Corkery to be unaware of the extent to which the people's religious consciousness had been internalized: 'for him it was no easy thing to come upon the islanders' unspoken thoughts ... The lament Synge was aware of but not the unceasing and intensely earnest praying that did not declare itself' (Corkery, 1931, p. 136). By freely acknowledging Synge's 'sympathy' towards 'the people', yet at the same time regretting that even Synge had not in the end written true Anglo-Irish literature, which should in fact be regarded as 'a ... particular branch of Catholic literature' (p. 136), Corkery provided arguments for devaluing and excluding the products of an 'alien Ascendancy' from his self-defined canon of Anglo-Irish literature. As O'Faolain suggested in 1936: 'He does, I think, influence our political evangels considerably: all that is behind our system of education in the modern Ireland, much that enthuses and supports all our more fervent politics, has come out of his books and his lecturings' (O'Faolain, 1936, p. 61).

What was also important, as O'Faolain pointed out, was the fact that Corkery, in declaring the peasants of contemporary Ireland 'the descendants of greatness, and of a cultivated greatness' (p. 60), produced what appeared to be an impeccable academic validation for the linkage of the nineteenth- and twentieth-century peasantry with the Gaelic society of the seventeenth century and earlier, and thus helped culturally to sustain the primacy of countryside over city. Corkery's works were centrally important, therefore, in establishing forms of writing and criticism which marginalized two groups: most obviously the dwindling numbers of the Anglo-Irish whose culture he defined as colonial and alien but, simultaneously, the urban working class in the new State whose interests were defined as of secondary importance to those of the farmers. These urban workers were to be neglected even when De Valéra's Fianna Fáil party took office in 1932, for the programme of import substitution and industrial development which was introduced was accompanied by a policy of decentralization which ensured that rural rather than urban workers were the beneficiaries. Changes in party, then, mattered relatively little as the interests of the farmers, which Fitzpatrick identified as paramount in 1918-22, continued to dominate in Ireland/Éire (Daly, 1985, p. 185 ff.).

Corkery made a significant contribution to bolstering the forces preserving the existing balance of power, so countering the position expressed by James Connolly in 1900: 'the man who is bubbling over with love and enthusiasm for "Ireland" and can yet pass unmoved through our streets and witness all the wrong and suffering, the shame and degradation wrought upon the people of Ireland, aye, wrought by Irishman upon Irish men and women, without burning to end it, is ... a fraud and a liar in his heart, no matter how he loves that combination of chemical elements which he is pleased to call "Ireland" ' (Connolly, 1973, p. 38). It is no surprise, therefore, to find that Corkery, applying his three-limbed test of propriety to Sean O'Casey's works should conclude that the works were a 'shapeless mass' (Corkery, 1931, p. 83), and their author an expatriate writing for a foreign, not an Irish, audience (pp. 2-7).

In O'Casey's *The Plough and the Stars*, the fact that it is the slightly comic Covey who expresses the view that 'there's no such thing as an Irishman ... we're all only human bein's' (O'Casey, 1963, p. 143), distracts attention from the centrality of the internationalist opposition to nationalistic idealizations throughout the whole of O'Casey's work. The current critical consensus on the Dublin Trilogy is informed by David Krause's concept of the basic Christian humanism of O'Casey's 'anti-heroic vision' (Krause, 1960, p. 66), though the approval implied in this consensus has recently been contested by Seamus Deane's assertion that the image of the family as the source of positive values is 'An eidetic image [that is] an image from the past. To dwell in it is an example of bad faith' (Deane, 1985a, p. 110). Deane, however, does not examine the extent to which O'Casey's apparent retreat from specifically nationalist politics is counterbalanced by the implicit assertion of a politics which is necessarily founded in material conditions rather than abstractions. The Dublin Trilogy, and specifically its centrepiece *The Plough and the Stars*, is concerned with the absence of an adequate socialist programme to contest nationalist rhetoric, the plays being the expression of a 'protesting voice' which spoke not for the recently marginalized occupants of the Big House, but for those whose political need was liberation from poverty. As O'Casey wrote in 1925: 'It isn't a question of English or Irish culture with the inanimate phantasies of the tenements, but a question of life for the few and of death for the many. Irish-speaking or English speaking, they are all what they are, convalescent homes of plague, pestilence or death' (O'Casey, 1975, p. 131). The fact that this comment, like the Trilogy itself, was made in the aftermath of the attainment of independence highlights the fact that, for O'Casey, nothing had been achieved: 'Grenville Street is here to-day, a little older, but as ugly and horrible as ever' (p. 131).

Although the plays of the Trilogy advance in technical complexity and dramatic competence from *The Shadow of a Gunman* (1923), through *Juno and the Paycock* (1924) to *The Plough and the Stars* (1926), they are all dramatizations of what O'Casey saw as a protracted crisis generated by the Easter Rising which resonated throughout subsequent Irish history. The dominant set of the plays is the tenement room into which enters the disruptive force of politics. *The Plough and the Stars* ends with the entry of the British soldiers, the internment of the men, and the shooting of Bessie Burgess, *Juno and the Paycock* sees the entry of the irregulars who take away Johnny Boyle for an execution which is reported in the play's closing minutes, while *The Shadow of a Gunman* concludes with the brutal entry of the Black and Tans and the off-stage shooting of Minnie Powell. Politics, in all three plays, is an off-stage force which destructively imposes itself on the on-stage realities of the tenement dwellers whose actual needs are not to be satisfied by the call to arms which, in Act II of *The Plough and the Stars*, O'Casey has taken directly from the speeches of Pearse (O'Casey, 1963, p. 162 ff.). Abstractions, such as those which Yeats momentarily embraced in *Cathleen Ni Houlihan*, are again staged in Act II as the insurgents swear allegiance to an Ireland which is 'greater than a wife' (p. 178), but such embraces of death for an abstract ideal are swiftly undercut by the sensual promise implicit in the exit of Fluther with Rosie; the song celebrating the very sexual pleasure on whose denial nationalist rigour was dependent.

The actualities of tenement life were recorded in the findings of a Committee of Inquiry into Dublin Housing in 1913 which reported that houses initially intended for occupation by one family were sub-divided to provide one room dwellings for individual families, with the result that, in the most extreme cases, houses were occupied by nearly 100 persons. Nearly a quarter of Dublin's 400,000-strong population lived in such conditions producing, in 1911, an infant mortality higher than that of Calcutta in the same period, while tuberculosis and related diseases were responsible for a third of all reported deaths. When the Covey speaks to Corporal Stoddart it is with documentary accuracy that he asserts: 'D'ye know comrade, that more die o' consumption than are killed in th' wars? An' it's all because of th' system we're livin' undher?', and it is Stoddart's response which pin-points the essentials of O'Casey's argument: 'Ow, I know. I'm a Sowcialist moiself, but I 'as to do my dooty' (p. 208). Knowledge which does not empower action, and action which does not represent need, are at the heart of O'Casey's critique of a political movement which embraced abstraction and denied reality.

It would be erroneous, however, to conclude that O'Casey abjured nationalist politics *per se*, rather it was a question of the concept of the nation which informed the call to sacrifice. In June 1913 O'Casey could urge the readers of the *Irish Worker* to attend a pageant at St Enda's and conclude with the declaration: 'We bow to you, A Phadraig [i.e. Patrick Pearse], but we will not pass on. Our hopes are your hopes; your work shall be our work; we stand or fall together' (O'Casey, 1975, p. 28). Nine months later in a scathing attack on the Volunteer movement, he could write that 'Pearse is worse than all' in his betrayal of the struggle of the workers in the 1913 lock-out and obsession with the pomp and show of uniforms, 'while in Dublin alone twenty thousand families are wriggling together like worms in a putrid mass in horror-filled one-room tenements' (pp. 40-1). The voice of Ireland, declared O'Casey, was in 'the hunger cry of the nation's poor' (p. 41), and the only force which should act for the nation was that which represented 'the people', defined no longer as a myth-born abstraction, but as those bound together in 'the unity engendered by a common heritage of pain, oppression, and wage-slavery' (p. 39). It is with that last unifying element that O'Casey's significance lies, for he used the realities of class to fracture the concept of nation which only worked to the advantage of those who gained political power on the backs of 'the class they elect to despise and pass by' (p. 38).

Within this context of political commitment *The Plough and the Stars* becomes readily comprehensible, not as a denunciation of military action in a trilogy Krause describes as 'all pacifist plays' (Krause, 1960, p. 66), but rather as a dramatization of what O'Casey had campaigned against so vigorously. As he wrote in February 1914: 'I hold the workers beside themselves with foolishness to support any movement that does not stand to make the workers supreme, for these are the people' (O'Casey, 1975, p. 40).The union of the bricklayer Clitheroe and the chicken-butcher Brennan with the Civil Servant Langon, captures in microcosm O'Casey's perception that the principles of the Irish Citizens Army had been subordinated to those of a class who would only preserve the iniquitous system. The Covey's declaration that the Plough and the Stars 'should only be used when we're buildin' th' barricades to fight for a Workers' Republic!' is the sentiment of the lines' author (O'Casey, 1963, p. 151). O'Casey maintained his socialist sympathies through from 1913, when he drafted the manifesto and constitution of the Irish Citizen Army, to 1926 – and beyond – when *The Plough and the Stars* was first produced. A fact that is most strikingly revealed in the controversy surrounding the original Abbey Theatre production.

As with *The Playboy of the Western World* the obstensible cause of the disturbances was the insult to Irish purity and patriotism. Not only was it claimed that the Tricolour would not have been carried into the demeaning context of a public house, but the presence of prostitutes in Dublin streets, should such a thing be possible, was claimed to be the consequence of their importation by British troops. While such claims represent the more extreme expressions of the movement that was to lead to demands for censorship of the Abbey and its "shoneen" clique'

(Lowery, 1984, p. 62), the fundamental objection to the play was not, in the words of the leader of the protests, Mrs Sheehy-Skeffington, 'directed to the moral aspect of the play. It was on national grounds solely, voicing a passionate indignation against the outrage of a drama staged in a supposedly national theatre, which held up to derision and obloquy the men and women of Easter week' (O'Casey, 1975, pp. 167-8). Her letter to *The Irish Independent* of February 1926 re-echoed all of Arthur Griffith's objections to the Abbey as unworthy to be the self-styled national theatre, but was mild compared to the review in *The Catholic Bulletin* of March 1926. Taking exception not only to the play, and the Covey's claim that 'There's no such thing as an Irishman', but to all reviews remotely favourable to the piece, the reviewer described all such deviations as the expressions of 'the New Ascendancy' who were now engaged in 'pouring scorn on the ideals of Easter Week, 1916' from the comfort of a State-subsidized theatre (Lowery, 1984, pp. 95-6) and, in a phrase, crystallized the thinking within the new State. As Sean O'Faolain commented, *apropos* O'Casey's work, 'the class that came to power and influence was not a labouring class', rather it was a new middle class, speaking for and from an alliance of the farming classes and their commercial dependents, with a vested interest in the articulation of the belief that all objectives had been achieved and any critical voices were those of the last remnants of yesterday's men: 'The upshot of it was an unholy alliance betwen the church, the new businessmen, and the politicians' (Lindsay, 1969, p. 194). To dramatize the participation of the workers in the Easter Rising as an abandonment of socialist principles to nationalist piety was to undercut the very foundations of the new State, and implicitly to suggest that while Ireland may have had a Rising, it now required a Revolution. The men of Ireland, said O'Casey in response to Mrs Sheehy-Skeffington, 'can't even get a job' and instead of dealing with these actualities the only concern seemed to be 'to make of Ireland the terrible place of a land fit only for heroes to live in' (O'Casey, 1975, p. 175). The pre-echo of Brecht is striking, and O'Casey, as Brecht, saw the need for the theatre to alert audiences to the choices existing at every moment of the historical process. In Ireland, however, there seemed to be no provision of a space for the 'protesting voice', especially one whose allegiance was with the Irish dispossessed. O'Casey's response to the new philistinism in the name of nation was exile; a route which, either physically or intellectually, was to be the dominant response to the new orthodoxy of which Corkery was the ideologue.

De-mystification of the Rising, and a satirical view of its creation – the new Free State – continued through the 1920s when, as Denis Johnston observed, 'several years of intermittent and unromantic civil war had soured us all a little towards the woes of Cathleen Ni Houlihan' (Johnston, 1983, p. 20). Flamboyant gestures of blood and barricades, argues the figure of Grattan in Johnston's *The Old Lady Says* 'No!', are the product of 'omniscient young Messiahs with neither the ability to work nor the courage to wait ... It saves working, it saves waiting' (p. 36), and results, as Johnston dramatizes, in a shoddy bureaucracy whose interest in the Talent and Art through which National Dignity will be achieved is predicated upon approval of the concept of nation which art purveys. It must be, as the Chorus observes, 'Clean and pure Art for clean and pure people' (p. 55). The abstraction of idealized art is matched by the abstraction of a nation founded on racial myths, as Johnston reiterates O'Casey's view that rhetoric is not enough through the declaration of the young revolutionary: 'I tell you, we can make this country – this world – whatever we want it to be by saying so, and saying so again. I tell you it is the knowledge of this that is the genius and glory of the Gael' (p. 70). The belief in the power of words to create realities, unaided by intellect, was now seen as that which paralysed, as even those who had fought for independence came to take a Joycean perspective on the Irish sickness. As Frank O'Connor retrospectively commented on the Civil War period: 'What neither group saw was that ... what we were bringing about was a new establishment of Church and State in which imagination would play no part, and young men and women would emigrate to the ends of the earth, not because the country was poor, but because it was mediocre' (O'Connor, 1965, p. 210). Mediocrity, mendacity, and materialism were seen by writers as the distinguishing features of the new order and, paradoxically, at the heart of it all was placed the peasant, no longer the Gael whose image fuelled nationalist ideology, but a slow, suspicious, and ultimately impoverished, being whose need was still liberation; not from the colonizer of the land but from the colonizer of the spirit, the ignorance and apathy that the 'hateful rigour' of Maynooth, in Sean O'Faolain's phrase, was doing little to alleviate (O'Faolain, 1980, p. 95).

In P.L. Dickinson's contemporary view the new State was 'largely ruled by a priesthood' and dominated by the image of the Gael, 'a rung on the ladder which has long been overstepped' (Brown, 1985, p. 117). Nonetheless, the peasant, and images of rural Ireland in general, were becoming embedded in the institutions creative of national psyche at the most fundamental levels. The coinage issued in 1928 depicted images of animals and wild-life felt by the Coinage Committee's Chairman, W.B.

Yeats, to symbolize the national essence which, if not a lived experience for the majority of the population: 'provided an imaginative consolidation of the new order' as 'an integrative symbol of national identity in the early years of independence' (pp. 98-9). What had once been the dynamo of the imagination was now becoming the brake on its development as what was essentially a literary trope became a cornerstone of cultural and economic policy. The apotheosis was reached in De Valéra's 1943 St Patrick's Day broadcast when he articulated the national ideal of which he dreamed: 'the home of a people who valued material wealth only as a basis of right living, of a people who were satisfied with frugal comfort and devoted their leisure to the things of the spirit; a land whose countryside would be bright with cosy homesteads, whose fields and villages would be joyous with sounds of industry, the romping of sturdy children, the contests of athletic youths, the laughter of comely maidens; whose firesides would be the forums of the wisdom of serene old age' (p. 146). While an impoverished actuality may have reflected little of these dreams, the poetry of such as Padraic Colum and F.R. Higgins served to consolidate the idealization and exclusivity already established in Corkery's *The Hidden Ireland* with what, in Higgins, became the often explicit expression of the racism which is immanent in all such theories of racial superiority. In his notes to his collection *The Dark Breed* (1927), Higgins argued that 'The racial strength of a Gaelic aristocratic mind – with its vigorous colouring and hard emotion – is easily recognised in Irish poetry ... Like our Gaelic stock, its poetry is sun-bred ... with fire in the mind, the eyes of Gaelic poetry reflect a richness of life and the intensity of a dark people, still part of our landscape' (Loftus, 1964, p. 243). These 'sun-bred' 'dark-people' are those of the Gaelic speaking west who come to stand for the purity of a Gaelic-Catholic Ireland standing against the 'savage factions' who beat 'Their Orange drums' 'In drunken fealty to the crown' (p. 238).

The voice of the marginalized Anglo-Irish was, understandably, raised against a vision of a nation which excluded them and any modernizing intellectual influence from the State, and not just in Yeats's tones. As AE argued the case: 'If we repudiate the Anglo-Irish tradition, if we say these are aliens, how poor does our life become' (Brown, 1985, p. 123). The fact of their being on the losing side in the political struggle, he argued in 1925, was no grounds for excluding them from the body politic, and in Lennox Robinson's *The Big House*, produced at the Abbey in 1926, the note of resistance to exclusion is sounded with passion by Kate Alcock, the daughter of the Big House, who finally refuses to abdicate her own family's investment of love in Ireland. Compromise and shame are abandoned as Kate declares 'we're what we are. Ireland is not more theirs than ours' (Robinson, 1982, p. 196), and determines to fight for her home and religion for the sake of Ireland: 'I believe in Ballydonal, it's my life, it's my faith, it's my country' (p. 197). The boldness of such assertions in the 1920s was literally born of desperation, however, as what can only be described as the submission to theocracy led to the Censorship of Film Act of 1923, the legislation against divorce of 1925, and the Censorship of Publications Act of 1929; a stunting of the Irish cultural and social development which, as Terence Brown has argued, 'a protracted colonial mismanagement had left in desperate need of revival' (Brown, 1985, p. 41). By 1937 Robinson's character Judith de Lury in *Killycregs in Twilight* could make the pointed inter-textual comment: 'I wish we'd been burned out in the Troubles ... I wouldn't have behaved like that fool-girl in the play, *The Big House*. I would have never have rebuilt Killycregs, I'd have thanked God to be quit of it' (p. 17).

Exile seemed to offer the only space in which critical thinking on Ireland and its identity could occur. Certainly there was to be no acknowledgement of the right of the protesting voice as the *Dublin Review*'s assessment of *Ulysses* in September 1922 makes clear. Having greeted the price of the limited edition publication as that which would keep it out of the hands of the people, the reviewer initiated the call for a formal exclusion of the book: 'We speak advisedly when we say that though no formal condemnation has been pronounced, the Inquisition can only require its destruction or, at least, its removal from Catholic houses. Without grave reason or indeed the knowledge of the Ordinary no Catholic publicist can even afford to be possessed of a copy of this book, for in its reading lies not only the description but the commission of sin against the Holy Ghost' (Joyce, 1970, p. 201). While explicit references to the range of bodily functions offended conceptions of purity and morality, Bloom's definition of nation and nationality was litle short of political heresy: 'A nation? says Bloom. A nation is the same people living in the same place ... Or also living in different places' (Joyce, 1986, p. 272). His claim to Irish nationality based on the fact that 'I was born here', takes on a particular resonance within a state whose fundamentalist principles are satirized in The Citizen, the monocular bigot through whom Joyce derides Michael Cusack, the founder of the Gaelic Athletic Association, along with the whole Cuchulain cult of heroic acts and masculine violence. In Bloom's declaration, 'But it's no use ... Force, hatred, history, all that. That's not life for men and women, insult and hatred. And everyone knows that it's the very opposite of that that is really life ... Love, ... the opposite of hatred' (p. 273), an antidote to sacrifice is advocated which releases nations and individuals from the nightmares of the Mother who haunts Stephen because of his refusal to submit; the Mother whose deathbed demands denied life and love for Eveline in *Dubliners*. The worth of Bloom's position is paramount in a text in which Cathleen ni Houlihan, the Shan Van Vocht, has degenerated into 'a wandering crone, lowly form of an immortal', whose 'Old shrunken paps' (p. 12) promise no sustenance. When Parnell's brother addresses him as 'Illustrious Bloom! Successor to my famous brother!' (p. 394), the Nighttown setting only serves to mask the seriousness of the declaration. As one who, literally, farts on the indulgence of self-sacrifice, the Bloom to whom Molly assents in the sensual conclusion is the living antidote to all denials and exclusions; as an advocate of passion he embodies a sense of nation celebrating the sensual rather than the sacrificial and, as Jew, presents a cosmopolitan alternative to an Ireland whose sense of self was increasingly locked into the conservatism of the Gaelic homeland.

The certainty of Mollie's sibillant 'Yes' was not to be found in the literature produced within the centre of paralysis, and in 'The Broken Land' (1937), Sean O'Faolain, analyst of Corkery's critical project and one of the most trenchant critics of the new reality, poignantly evoked the physical and spiritual bleakness of a land in which 'life was lying broken and hardly breathing' (O'Faolain, 1982, p. 173). As the narrator looks out of the railway carriage window at the snow-covered land and frozen people he asks the fundamental question of those who passionately wished to advance the nation: 'What image, I wondered ... could warm them ... What image of life that would fuse and fire us all, what music bursting like spring, what triumph, what engendering love'. Struck by the apparent futility of his dream, yet recognizing the necessity of 'living splendidly, or gather up at least enough grace for a quick remove' the narrator closes on a note whose promise is as eternal as it is apparently impossible: 'In the morning, Ireland, under its snow, would be silent as a perpetual dawn' (p. 173). The need for a liberating passion is ever apparent, but where O'Faolain takes a decisive step beyond the Joycean analysis is in that which he identifies as central cause of the paralysis. The carriage has been shared with an old farmer, and in describing him the narrator almost returns to the most fundamental Anglo-centric stereotypes, only now born more of frustrated love than colonial superiority. 'Time and nature', comments the narrator, 'had engendered something no more human than a rock ... I wanted to get up and kick him. I felt that if I did he would only moo' (p. 172). 'It is therefore futile to talk of reviving or of preserving the best rural ways', argued O'Faolain,'unless one is also prepared to revive the worst rural ways' (O'Faolain, 1974, p. 81).

Yet preservation of the rural worst seemed to be the objective of literary and political idealizations which chose to ignore the fundamental inequalities of wealth and opportunity which condemned a people to the condition so powerfully indicted in Patrick Kavanagh's 'The Great Hunger' (1942) whose narrator's declaration: 'We will wait and watch the tragedy to the last curtain' (Kavanagh, 1972, p. 34), highlights the sense of the reader being exposed to a previously shrouded desolation. The professional Gaels who peopled the ministries and Leagues of the urban centres were condemned by no-one more roundly than Flann O'Brien, who described them as 'the most nauseating brigade in Europe' (Cliss-mann, 1975, p. 238), and in *The Poor Mouth* (1941) he produced a satire on the glory of the Gael made doubly effective by its being written in Gaelic. The description of the féis of Corkadoragha to which 'Crowds came from Dublin and Galway city, all with respectable, well-made clothes on them' provides the most bitter moment of O'Brien's indictment of an idealized poverty. As the self-styled urban guardians of Gaelic purity bombard the baffled inhabitants of the Gaeltacht with praise of their living heritage the people 'collapsed from hunger and the strain of listening while one fellow died most Gaelically in the midst of the assembly'; only one of a number of deaths due, as the narrator blandly comments, 'both to the fatigue caused by the revels and the truly Gaelic famine which was always ours' (O'Brien, 1973, pp. 55-7).

An 'Elysium of the roofless' was Samuel Beckett's description of a land where 'history's ancient faeces ... are ardently sought after, stuffed and carried in processions. Wherever nauseated time has dropped a nice fat turd', he continued, 'you will find our patriots, sniffing it up, on all fours, their faces on fire' (Beckett, 1973, pp. 30-1). The company of such Gaels is described in *Murphy* as 'irksome beyond endurance', and Beckett's modernist deconstruction of the narrative is equally a parody of the 'twilighters', as Beckett called them, whose Austin Ticklepenny – 'The Olympian sot' – is such a specific mockery of Austin Clarke that he was urged to bring a libel action against Beckett. While O'Faolain's story was an elegiac lament at the loss of a sustaining ideal, Beckett's novel is a sustained deflation of such concepts. The rear of the statue of Cuchulain in the Dublin Post Office is the object on which Neary attempts to brain himself – 'That Red Branch bum was the camel's back'; a will requests that the deceased's ashes be flushed away in the toilet of the Abbey Theatre, and in the description of Miss Counihan Beckett provided the ultimate demystification of she with the walk of a queen: 'Standing in profile against the blazing corridor, with her high buttocks and her low breasts, she looked not merely queenly, but on for anything' (Beckett, 1973, p. 123).

Beckett's rejection of a Dublin where 'the antiquarians, [delivered] with the altitudinous complacency of the Victorian Gael the Ossianic goods' (Bellis, 1934, p. 235), led to exile, and images of Ireland as the context of absence in which his characters such as the sand-bound Winnie in *Happy Days* – described by Vivian Mercier as 'a daughter of the Anglo-Irish gentry' (Mercier, 1977, p. 218) – exist in an immobility which embodies both the condition of the land, its people and, critically, its intellectuals. Lacking any sense of political cohesion and, crucially, divorced from the people-nation, their sense of alienation is captured in Beckett's well-known preference for 'France in war to Ireland in peace'; an expression of the sense of 'Nothing to be done' which afflicted those described by Terence Brown as 'members of the very small Irish bourgeoisie that in its urban tastes and values had been overtaken by the populist rural values of the new state' (Brown, 1985, p. 168). Such negative responses are castigated by Seamus Deane as creating 'a fetish of exile, alienation and dislocation' (Deane, 1985b, p. 58), but they were not the only responses, even if those nominally more positive were equally afflicted by the malaise created in the aftermath of revolutionary expectations.

Writing in 1940 O'Faolain declared that the future had arrived and the time was now ripe for the abandonment of the 'old symbolic words: They are as dead as Brian Boru, Granuaile, the Shan Van Vocht, Banba, Roisin Dubh, Fodhla, Cathleen ni Houlihan, the swords of light and the risings of the moon' (McMahon, 1978, p. 13). The occasion for the statement was the founding of *The Bell*, the journal dedicated to 'Life before any abstraction' to which all Irishmen 'Gentile or Jew, Protestant or Catholic, priest or layman, Big House or Small House' (p. 16) were invited to contribute as a means of liberating Ireland from a threat described by O'Faolain as 'an intellectual one' (Brown, 1985, p. 200). The intellectual flaw was, in part, that of the fabric of the nation itself, described by O'Faolain in 1949 as 'simple and uncomplex', particularly in comparison to that 'complex social life which a writer of 1915, say, could have known'. The cause of this 'thin' society is directly attributed to the cultural inadequacies of the dominant group in the new state:

'Their conventions are embryonic; their social patterns are indistinct' (O'Faolain, 1949, p. 373). Ireland's ability to engage with, and advance in the modern world was being impeded by its inadequate self-definition, for literature was 'Blandly, sentimentally, maundering to itself' while the country languished in 'the grip of the gombeen man' (O'Connor, 1942, p. 57) and, as O'Faolain observed, there were only subjects for the slight, and essentially conservative, form of the short-story in such an 'unshaped society' (O'Faolain, 1949, p. 375). The significance of *The Bell*'s attempts to introduce some radical re-appraisal of national needs and actualities is best expressed in the recollections of those such as Dermot Folley who have recorded the deeply felt need for the journal in 'Old Testament country' where libraries were seen as 'seed-beds of corruption'. His claim that 'the real crime of the state' was in leaving the people in 'the morass of ignorance they had for so long endured' (Folley, 1974, p. 210), indicted the concept of the nation which, now a disabling orthodoxy, was the triumph of a 'social revolution that never was' (Lynch, 1966, pp. 41-54), made practicable culturally by a criticism which succeeded only through defining all voices outside of a narrow clique as abnormal and unnational. In the absence of such a critique, Kavanagh's conclusion to 'The Great Hunger' stood as a testimony to its necessity as Maguire, his story done, faces the end:

He stands in the doorway of his house
A ragged sculpture of the wind,
October creaks the rotted mattress
The bedposts fall. No hope. No lust.
The hungry fiend
Screams the apocalypse of clay
In every corner of this land. (Kavanagh, 1972, p. 55)

7

Symbols adequate to our predicament

The cultural and intellectual enervation that O'Faolain and *The Bell*'s contributors attacked in the 1940s had its counterpart in virtually all sectors of the Southern State. In 1957, John Kelleher described Ireland as a society imploding on 'a central vacuity' (Brown, 1985, p. 241). Economic stagnation, and emigration which amounted to a 'human haemorrhage' of 500,000 persons between 1945 and 1961 (Lee, 1979b, p. 169), evoked no adequate response from politicians or university dons, leaving only the State's senior civil servants to manage the crisis (Neary, 1984, p. 68; Fanning, 1978, p. 407 ff.). Contemporary pessimism was documented in the White Paper, *Economic Development*, subsequently credited with heralding the end of that gloom: 'After 35 years of native government, people are asking whether we can achieve an acceptable degree of economic progress. The common talk among parents in the towns, as well as in rural Ireland, is of their children having to emigrate as soon as their education is completed in order to secure a reasonable standard of living.' (Walsh, 1979, p. 29). The economic malaise of 1950s Ireland, to which *Economic Development* proposed the cure of free trade and Keynesianism, was substantially a product of three decades of financial, economic, and social conservatism, in combination with cultural attitudes which, viewing the farmers as embodying the essence of the national ideal, sacrificed the material and cultural well-being of other groups to their interests. Hence, when Kelleher wrote of a 'central vacuity' in Irish life he described the consequences of founding a national identity on a negation of stereotypes which originated in colonialist discourses (Chatterjee, 1986, p. 30).

The change in political leadership in 1959 from the austere, aged figure of Eamon De Valéra to his successor Sean Lemass, Fianna Fáil Taoiseach from 1959 to 1966, was followed by what contemporaries regarded as an intellectual revolution. Indeed, in 1978, commenting on the public welcome for *Economic Development*, Ronan Fanning invoked the phrases of Yeats's 'Easter 1916' to talk of an atmosphere 'changed utterly' (Fanning,

1978, p. 519). In fact, although the shift from economic stagnation to growth, from conservatism to innovation, was undoubtedly stimulating for contemporaries, only a handful of people was in any way equipped to appreciate the detailed arguments for the new approach. In part, this was a reflection on the depleted numbers of the resident Irish intelligentsia (itself a product of emigration), but it was also the product of a shift in economic writing from prose to econometrics. An opponent of this trend argued that economics had 'lost some influence by ... having become esoteric, a study to be pursued by the initiate, not comprehended by the general reader' (Fanning, 1983, p. 147), but what economics lost in ready comprehension it gained in the thaumaturgic effect of a specialist vocabulary and iconography upon audiences, including politicians, who had to defer to experts with whom they could not dispute. Only members of the Statistical and Social Inquiry Society and readers of Garret FitzGerald's explanatory articles in the *Irish Times* were in a position to enter into debate on the 'new departure'. Further, since the development promised by the 'First Programme For Economic Expansion' was to start by encouraging farmers to expand their production through provision of cheap credit, all groups in Irish society could approve the changes in policy because no vital interests were threatened. Consequently, and with only a few people able to contribute to the debate, nothing approaching an 'intense labour of social criticism, of cultural penetration and diffusion' (Boggs, 1976, p. 59) accompanied the economic developments of the 1960s. Rather than superseding the founding notions of the State, epitomised in De Valéra's 1943 St Patrick's Day broadcast, the new ideas formed a veneer overlaying them. Inconsistencies between past and present policies were not debated, as amidst a flurry of approving statements writers expressed the hope that the economic changes would lead on to a social revolution (Thornley, 1965).

During the celebration of the fiftieth anniversary of the Easter Rising, in 1966, the contradictions between past and present became apparent as the tall, near-blind figure of De Valéra endorsed the aims of 1916 as synonymous with those of the State from a platform shared with the dynamo of the new policy, Sean Lemass. Had Father Francis Shaw's article 'The Canon of Irish History: A Challenge' (Shaw, 1972, pp. 113-52) been published in 1966, as intended, the reassessment of economic nationalism would have been shortly followed by that of nationalism *tout-court*. As it was, the article was held back by the editors of *Studies*, who feared that its publication would strike a sour note on the anniversary of the Rising. Father Shaw's article was not published until 1972, by which time most of the issues it raised had become impossible to ignore, but the earlier refusal to publish a critique of the founding assumptions of the State indicates the limitations inherent in an uncritical 'social revolution'. Shaw re-examined the prevailing understandings of 1916 taught by the educational system over two generations, and the teleology immanent in that understanding, which endowed a transcendent 'Ireland' with the destiny of achieving the unification of the island in one State. In particular, Shaw questioned the implications of Pearse's politics and practice and pointed to what he saw as Pearse's mobilization of Catholicism in justification of his attempted coup d'état. The temporary suppression of Shaw's views was ultimately to no avail; the disintegration of the Northern State, beginning in Autumn 1968, raised the same questions in ways that could not be suppressed. The eventual publication of Shaw's article, together with a number of other works, such as Conor Cruise O'Brien's *States of Ireland* (1972) and Garret FitzGerald's *Towards a New Ireland* (1972), signified awareness of a need to reassess issues of national identity and purpose. *Economic Development* and the subsequent Programmes for Economic Expansion had made no direct contribution to this debate, but in stemming emigration, paving the way for the expansion of education, and beginning the erosion of rural political and cultural dominance, the economic growth of the 1960s produced the conditions in which a relatively large number of contemporary Irish intellectuals were able to address themselves to Irish issues while resident in Ireland.

By the time the economic expansion of the South had begun, Northern Ireland was experiencing its second decade of Westminster-financed infrastructural development. In the North the demands of economic development spurred the Provincial Administration to expand education and, as in the South, there were attempts to overlay an older ideology with new practices dependent on free access to the skills and information necessary to development. The older ideology in the North was Ulster Unionism, a unique cross-class alliance based upon an ideology which constructed subjectivity upon an identification of Catholics as 'other' (Cairns and Richards, 1986). The history of Ulster Unionism shows that solidarity between Protestants in the face of the threat of Catholicism/Nationalism was consistently secured by discrimination in employment, in local government expenditure, and in gerrymandering, to ensure that Protestants monopolized the powers of expenditure and coercion that command of the State apparatus conferred (Buckland, 1979, pp. 17-8; Bew, Gibbon and Patterson, 1979, p. 79).

In the 1960s, Unionism's basic need for discrimination in employment, etc., to maintain itself as a cross-class sectarian alliance, conflicted with the need of economic development for an educated workforce. More fundamentally, the aim of economic development, improved standards of living for all the community, was itself a threat to a political apparatus which required, in order to show its success, differentials in standards of living and access to employment between Protestants and Catholics. Hence, having started along the path of development earlier than the South, the North was first to experience conflict between the supporters of its founding ideology and those who sought to overlay it, without replacing it, with economic liberalism. The champion of development in the North was the Prime Minister, Terence O'Neill, who signified the seriousness of his intentions by meeting not only Seán Lemass but a Cardinal (Farrell, 1980, p. 240), acts which convinced Northern Protestants that he was unsound, an impression confirmed when Northern Catholics demanded equal access to the benefits of development and the Welfare State. It is ironic, therefore, that the crisis of the Northern State which ostensibly began in Dungannon in August 1968 should have been identified with Catholic/Nationalist grievance, when its immediate cause was the incompatibility of Unionism and economic development (Nelson, 1984, p. 49 ff.; Bew, Gibbon and Patterson, 1979, p. 152 ff.). As the crisis deepened, however, some nationalists in the North saw the situation as a prelude to unification, and sought vindication in the tropes of the earlier nationalist revival for a renewed struggle against the metropolitan power and the Unionists, once again identified as its 'garrison'. Other nationalists and Catholics, however, found such a reprise morally and intellectually indefensible and, as the Northern crisis deepened, began to search systematically for new approaches.

'Nothing', wrote Seamus Deane in 1979, 'is more monotonous or despairing than the search for the essence which defines a nation' (Deane, 1979b, p. 51). Deane has been concerned to break away from 'the idea of essence – that hungry Hegelian ghost looking for a stereotype to live in' (Deane, 1986b, p. 58), but, as he and other intellectuals are aware, in order to free people from those concepts of national essence their historic origins must first be exorcized. History, so frequently the means by which Irish intellectuals sought to erect exclusive definitions of national identity, is once more on the agenda as contemporary Irish writers – North and South – engage with a process of excavation. The poetic function being defined as: 'making contact with what lies hidden ... [making] palpable what was sensed or raised' (Heaney, 1980a, p. 48).

'Between my finger and my thumb / The squat pen rests / I'll dig with it' wrote Heaney in 'Digging', but as the poem's opening simile – 'snug as gun' – implies, the act of writing is neither innocent nor divorced from the subject matter of violence which the poet brings to the light. While Seamus Heaney's 1983 rejection of the nomenclature 'British' made open declaration that 'No glass of ours was ever raised / To toast *The Queen*' as 'from the start her reign / Of crown and rose / Defined, displaced, would not combine / What I'd espouse' (Heaney, 1985, pp. 25-6), the problematic partisanship of his position was explicit in his earliest poetry. 'Requiem for the Croppies' was 'born of and ended with an image of resurrection' (Heaney, 1980a, p. 56), but as Heaney's use of the first person plural throughout the poem indicates, he intimately identified with the failed rebels of '98 whose rebirth in 1916 he intended to commemorate on the occasion of the Easter Rising's fiftieth anniversary. As the resurgence of violence in 1969 followed two months after the poem's publication, Heaney's poetic intention was sharpened into a realization of the need to go beyond an act of personal revelation as defined in 'Personal Helicon' – 'I rhyme / To see myself' – and broadened into 'a search for images and symbols adequate to our predicament' (p. 56). The use of the first person plural again locates Heaney's personal, political situation, and subsequent poetic expression, as born of the Irish Catholic experience to whose deepest historic and psychological roots he bears witness, while transcending their sectarian limitations by that very act of excavation and revelation.

The first part of *North* (1975) is Heaney's most consistent act of poetic excavation in which images of bone and bog create an intensity and density whose weight confirms the identification with the instinctual Antaeus in whose voice Heaney opens the collection: 'I am cradled in the dark that wombed me' (Heaney, 1975, p. 12). As the first part of *North* closes, Antaeus has been raised into the light of intellect by the conquering Hercules, an act of literal deracination in which the defeated is left only with 'a dream of loss'. Heaney has commented that the violence in Ulster 'is the tail-end of a struggle between territorial piety and imperial power' whose embodiments have been variants on Mother Ireland, and 'a new male cult ... whose godhead is incarnate in a rex or caesar resident in a palace in London' (Heaney 1980a, p. 57). These dualities of male and female, intellect and instinct, are found throughout his work, forming a leitmotiv whose comprehension is central to its understanding, just as its recognition appears to have been crucial to Heaney's own poetic growth.

The act of poetic composition, wrote Heaney, 'is a kind of somnambulist encounter between masculine will and intelligence and feminine clusters of image and emotion' in which 'the feminine element ... involves the matter of Ireland, and the masculine strain is drawn from the involvement with English literature' (p. 34). The feminine and sacrificial are intertwined in Irish ideology and what is clear from 'The Tollund Man' in the collection which preceded *North*, is that Heaney's identification with the victims of violence is both intimate and complex:

> I will stand a long time.
> Bridegroom to the goddess,
>
> She tightened her torc on him. ... (Heaney, 1980b, p. 78)

The weakness of the full-stop after 'time', coupled with the enjambement which spans the two stanzas, produces a reading in which Heaney is both rapturous recorder and fated victim of a violent, and sexual, sacrifice. The whole complexity is captured in the poem's closing lines: 'lost,/Unhappy and at home'.

Heaney's excavations into the psychic darkness of self and community produced difficulties of interpretation, however, when, in *North*, his historic comprehension of what he saw as the archetypal patterns of violence, coupled with his emotive identification with his 'tribe', produced the poetic expression of one paralysed between the 'civilized outrage' of modern rationality and the instinctual understanding of the 'tribal, intimate revenge' (p. 117). An historical determinism seems to result from too deep a digging in which the modern desire to engage actively in the historical process is rendered impotent by the very completeness of intellectual understanding.

Heaney's recognition that there are two modes of response to experience, one which is 'lived, illiterate and unconscious, the other learned, literate and conscious' existing in a state of tension one with the other (Heaney, 1980a, p. 131), was a recognition of states which needed to be brought into a fructifying relationship beyond recognition. In 'A New Song' from *Wintering Out* Heaney wrote:

> But now our river tongues must rise
> From licking deep in native haunts
> To flood, with vowelling embrace,
> Demesnes staked out in consonants (p. 70)

While the stanza can be read as a return of the dispossessed, the 'vowelling embrace' of 'river tongues' has more of sensuality than hostility, and the whole linguistic balance of vowel and consonant is paradigmatic of that which Heaney advocates. The objective is to create an act of union between Antaeus and Hercules in which the historical inevitabilty which sides with the latter can be enriched by 'instinctive feel' and 'illiterate pleasure' (Randall, 1979, p. 17). As he commented after the publication of *Field Work* in 1979: 'I have begun to feel a danger in that responsible adjudicating stance towards communal experience. I just feel an early warning system telling me to get back inside my own head' (p. 17). The personal response, which admitted the inheritance of his origins along with the individual, intellectual, response to that inheritance and its implications, is the desired poetic ideal.

The achievement of such a stance is problematic in the extreme, and not least because of the extent to which it relies on the re-appropriation of essentially Arnoldian categories, but, as witnessed by *Station Island* (1984), Heaney has found a way of articulating the position he wishes to adopt, even if the adoption itself is fraught with personal difficulty. In 'Making Strange' Heaney fragments himself into his two constituent parts, Antaeus and Hercules, the one 'unshorn and bewildered / in the tubs of his wellingtons', the other 'with his travelled intelligence / and tawny containment, / his speech like the twang of a bowstring', and produces a synthesis as he, Heaney as a transcendent consciousness, stands between them, advised by a 'cunning middle voice' to 'Be adept and be dialect' (Heaney, 1984, p. 32). The poem's conclusion sees Heaney, now 'adept at dialect', reciting all that he knows of his country in a way 'that began to make strange'. The concept of 'making strange' or *ostranenie* was developed by the Russian Formalist Viktor Shklovsky as a way of expressing the function of art; a clarifying of the perception of that assumed to be known. Its better known application and, in the case of Heaney, more apposite exposition, is in the *Verfremdungseffekte* of Brecht where it takes on a specifically political function in which audiences can adopt a superior and informed attitude to their moment which otherwise would obliterate their intellectual independence through assumptions as to the naturalness and inevitabilty of their situation. In Section X of 'Station Island' Heaney records a moment of distantiation experienced, fittingly enough, in a theatrical performance when an old mug from the family kitchen is seen vividly anew when used by actors as a prop. Heaney 'sat in a dark hall estranged from it' (p. 87), and when it is returned to its accustomed place it stands out with a clarity captured in 'dazzle', 'blazed', 'sun-glare'. The use of a simile derived from his own *Sweeney Astray* to compare the return of the mug to the return of the psalter of Ronan (Heaney, 1983, pp. 4-5) fuses the personal with the 'tribal' in an image of life enhancing 'excavation'. Poetry, as Heaney wrote in 1974, is 'a restoration of the culture to itself ... an attempt to define and interpret the present by bringing it into a significant relationship with the past ... [an] effort in our present circumstances that has to be urgently renewed' (Heaney 1980a, p. 60). While he concluded that to forge a poem was one thing, to forge the consciousness of the race was a daunting step beyond the realm of art, his encounter with Joyce in the final section of 'Station Island', shows Heaney moving beyond an always problematic partisanship to implicit agreement with Joyce's declaration: 'You lose more of yourself than you redeem / doing the decent thing. Keep at a tangent' (Heaney, 1984, p. 93).

To follow that 'straight walk' and flee the nets of nationality is then one aspect of Heaney's poetic programme:

> It's time to break the cracked mirror
> Of this conceit.
> It leads nowhere so why bother
> To work it out?
>
> So let's not raise a big hubbub.
> Steer between Scylla and Charyb
> A middle way that's neither glib
> Nor apocalyptic .... (Heaney, 1985, pp. 27-8)

As 'An Open Letter' demonstrates, however, Heaney is not abandoning the right to be called by his proper name of 'Irish' which becomes, rather than a restriction on possibility, a definition from which to grow. Writing to Brian Friel after the publication of *North*, Heaney said 'I no longer wanted a door into the dark – I want a door into the light' (Randall, 1979, p. 20). The objective, however, is to face both ways: 'looking back to a ramification of roots and associations and forward to a clarification of sense and meaning' (Heaney, 1980a, p. 52). The objective is equally that of the Field Day Theatre Company whose productions of *Translations* (1980) and *The Communication Cord* (1982) by Heaney's fellow Field Day director Brian Friel, express the complementary views that those who look only backwards become the victims of history, while those who abandon the past become victims of cultural collapse.

Translations was the first production of Field Day whose objective is: '[to] contribute to the solution of the present crisis by producing analyses of the established opinions, myths and stereotypes which had become both a symptom and a cause of the current situation' (Field Day Theatre

Company, 1985, p. vii). Although the play has been seen as refurbishing 'an old myth', namely 'Ballybeg as a kind of Eden', the suggestion that it is Hugh who embodies the 'play's pervasive nostalgia for "what has been lost" ' (Longley, 1986, p. 191), ignores the extent to which the play contains an auto-critique of such backward looks – a point reinforced by an analysis of *The Communication Cord* – and the centrality of Hugh as the articulator of the necessity of recognizing that history has arrived at the moment of 'Hercules'.

The play opens with Hugh absent at the christening of the baby of Nellie Ruadh; it closes with news of the baby's death and the comment: 'It didn't last long, did it?' (Friel, 1984, p. 438). Time is then central to the play's concerns; the death of a child a strikingly apt metaphor for that of the Gaelic culture which has equally not engaged in process. As the English Officer Yolland expresses it: 'It wasn't an awareness of *direction* being changed but of experience being of a totally different order. I had moved into a consciousness that wasn't striving nor agitated, but at its ease and with its own convictions and assurances' (p. 416). That which Yolland experiences is foregrounded in the character of Jimmy Jack whose easy familiarity with Latin and Greek, whose myths he speaks of as if they were contemporary events, suggests the undifferentiated historical time in which he exists. What initially appears as an admirable advantage over the monoglot English Officers is finally revealed to be a crippling disability. At the play's conclusion Jimmy Jack anounces his engagement to the goddess Athene before falling drunkenly to the floor, his back against a broken cart.

The play then dramatizes the moment of a culture's transition, or translation, from one mode of time and experience to another. That into which they are forced, and the play is explicit as to the exercise of colonial power, is a world of commerce and Empire, the whole captured in the birth date of Lancey, the English commanding Officer: '1789 ... He inherited a new world the day he was born – The Year One. Ancient time was at an end' (p. 416). Friel's dramatic objective is then not to elegize that which has passed, but to evaluate the viability of responses to that inevitability. The old culture itself, as Jimmy Jack, is rendered incapable of comprehension and the options available are essentially those presented by Hugh and his son Owen. While the latter has acted as a translator for the English, and in the process betrayed his origins, his final act sees him translating the English place names back into Gaelic. His subsequent declaration: 'I know where I live', coupled with his intention to see Doalty, is a clear statement of intent to join with Doalty and the

Donnelly twins in some form of armed resistance in support of the doomed culture. Hugh, however, takes the more highly charged decision to teach Maire Chatach English. He has recognized that 'it can happen that a civilization can be imprisoned in a linguistic contour which no longer matches the landscape of ... fact' (p. 419) and, as the hesitation before the final word suggests, it is the sense that there is a culture in which 'facts' have currency which falls with the finality of recognition. Hugh walked out of the bold venture of 1789, but his conclusion, as he holds the Name-Book, that 'We must learn where we live. We must learn to make them our own. We must make them our new home' (p. 444), articulates the initiation of the finally triumphant process of which the shade of Joyce informed Heaney: 'The English language / belongs to us. You are raking at dead fires, / ... That subject people stuff is a cod's game / infantile, like your peasant pilgrimage' (Heaney, 1984, p. 93).

Suggestions that Friel is concerned with fossilizing history are scotched by an examination of *The Communication Cord*, a farce whose setting in a converted byre complete with milking posts and chains is a parodic reprise of the setting of *Translations*. The buildings have been stocked with articles of such authenticity that falsity is the dominant note and, despite the mouthing of platitudes such as 'This is where we all come from. This is our first cathedral. This shaped all our souls' (Friel, 1983, p. 15), the use of the cottage is purely cynical, used in the time of the play as a means of personal and sexual advancement. The key moment occurs when the visiting Senator, who is to be impressed by this lovingly restored act of homage to the 'first pieties', accidentally imprisons himself in the milking chains over whose presence he has been eulogising. Held fast by the chains of the past he reacts violently to the expression of national platitudes: 'This determined our first priorities! This is our native simplicity! Don't give me that shit!' (p. 70). At the play's conclusion the principal architect of this 'authenticity' has also become trapped by the chains and, as he calls for assistance, Tim and Claire whose genuine love has survived the former's attempts to advance his career by using the cottage to impress the Senator, lean against the upright on which the whole upper floor rests. With the cry that 'the house is falling in!' the play closes in total darkness. As the cottage, and by implication the façade of 'authentic' Irishness collapses around the characters, it is perhaps difficult to see what, if anything, Friel wishes to put in its place. The overall objective is clarified, however, by reference to one of the first pamphlets produced by the Field Day Theatre Company of which Friel was a founding director: 'Everything, including our politics and our literature, has to be rewritten – i.e. re-read. That will enable new writing, new politics, unblemished by Irishness, but securely Irish' (Deane, 1985b, p. 58).

In one sense then a *tabula rasa* cleared of disabling shibboleths is being advocated as a prerequisite for the foundation of a secure Irish cultural identity which transcends disabling divisions. While history may be interrogated, however, it is not to be abandoned. Indeed 'Memory Harbour and Killala' (Paulin, 1983, p. 27) form a crucial, if disputed, point of reference for Tom Paulin, another Field Day director, for whom that sensed non-sectarian rising against colonialism in 1798 stands as a moment of the past by which to inform the present. That desire for 'a form that's classic and secular, / The risen République' (p. 68) permeates Paulin's work, becoming the dynamic of his poetry itself with a force that overrides all individual hesitancy: 'see, it takes me now, these hands stir / to bind the northern to the southern stars' (p. 45). As Paulin makes clear in his critical writings, his own 'idea of identity ... has as yet no formal or institutional existence. It assumes the existence of a non-sectarian, republican state which comprises the whole island of Ireland. It also holds to the idea of sanctuary and to the concept of "the fifth province". This other, invisible province offers a platonic challenge to the nationalistic image of the four green fields' (Paulin, 1984, p. 17). The reference to the 'fifth province' is attributed to an enterprise similar to that of Field Day undertaken by *The Crane Bag*, a cultural/literary/political journal whose short-lived career was dedicated to the creation of 'the neutral ground where things detach themselves from all partisan and prejudiced connection and show themselves for what they really are' (Hederman and Kearney, 1977, p. 10). This 'fifth province' is the location of the critical alliance of many Irish artists and intellectuals – North and South – whose involvement with both Field Day and *The Crane Bag* suggests that the detached yet concerned critical examination of the roots of the present crisis can be made a reality.

As in Friel's *The Communication Cord* the concern of intellectuals such as Declan Kiberd and Seamus Deane is to put an end to national artifice and illusion. Indeed, Kiberd argues that 'Irish people no longer live in a country of their own making', being trapped within the inherited tropes of a Revival which have become 'a downright repression' (Kiberd, 1984, pp. 11-3). Kiberd clarifies his point through reference to Lionel Trilling's distinction between 'sincerity' and 'authenticity', the former assuming a given self to which one must be true, while the latter 'recognises that the real problem is not to be true to a self but first to find a self worth being true to. It concedes that a man, or a nation, has many identities constantly remaking themselves' (p. 21). Kiberd's adoption of Trilling's terms is parallelled by Deane's use of concepts derived from the American philosopher William James: the 'Tender Minded' and 'The Tough Minded'. Deane defines the former as those who would 'favour a single point of view and have a vocabulary of conviction ... they would give their assent, even devotion, to concepts like race, nationality, faith and they would respect the past'. The latter 'would be inclined towards innovation, change, an escape from traditional pieties which they would see as restrictive and binding. Abandoning the past for a pluralist future would seem to them a desirable aim' (Deane, 1984, p. 81). Deane, like his fellow occupants of the 'fifth province', concludes that although the abstractions of race and the past created the Republic, 'The losses now outweigh the gains. It is time to change ground before it opens up and swallows us' (Deane, 1984, p. 86).

The redundancy of the once-mobilizing ideology is given no clearer expression than in Michael O'Loughlin's 'Cuchulainn':

> If I lived in this place for a thousand years
> I could never construe you, Cuchulainn.
> Your name is a fossil, a petrified tree
> Your name means less than nothing.
> Less than Librium, or Burton's Biscuits
> Or Phoenix Audio-Visual Systems –...
> ... But watching TV the other night
> I began to construe you Cuchulainn;
> You came on like some corny revenant
> In a black-and-white made for TV
> American Sci-Fi serial. (Barry, 1986, pp. 122-3)

Although some Northern Protestant writers such as Ian Adamson, and political leaders such as Andy Tyrie, are visibly attempting to by-pass both the Battle of the Boyne and The Red Hand of O'Neill and access that same mythic history now so caustically dismissed by O'Loughlin, there is every sense that, in the words of Nelson in Ron Hutchinson's play *Rat in the Skull*, they are 'pissing in the gale of history' (Hutchinson, 1984, p. 29). The strongest expression of a sense that the dominant tropes can be deconstructed without the collapse of meaning is found in Tom Murphy's *Bailegangaire*, a play which expresses more powerfully and potently than any other the potentiality of resurrection from the unending narrative of the past.

The setting of *Bailegangaire* in 'the country kitchen ... of the traditional three-roomed thatched house' (Murphy, 1986, p. 9), along with its central focus on an old woman, evokes both plays of 'peasant quality' and central images of Ireland as the Shan Van Vocht. In Murphy's play, however, the cottage is set in a village in which the Japanese-owned computer plant is being closed down and the old woman is a senile, semi-invalid, periodic drunkard. The de-mythologizing of such central tropes of nationalist culture is central to Murphy's objective, and his cultural prescription that articulated by Mary: 'And she never finishes it – Why doesn't she finish it? And have done with it. For God's sake' (p. 19).

The means by which Murphy dramatizes this national paralysis is through the brilliant device of having the old woman, Mommo, locked into a narrative whose conclusion she is incapable of facing, and her granddaughter, Mary, recognizing that only by ending the narrative will harmony return. The play revolves around the compulsive narrative of Mommo counterpointed by the conversations, full of personal anguish, of the two granddaughters, Mary and Dolly, in the course of which it is revealed that Dolly's extra-marital affairs have resulted in her pregnancy. As Mommo provides the dramatic interest Mary provides its dynamic, for she has returned determined to 'bring about change. Comfort, civilized' (pp. 19-20). As Mary forces Mommo to conclude her story, which reveals her indirect responsibility for the death of Mary's brother, the old woman is finally brought to a point of sanity and recognition. The play closes as Mary states her belief that: 'it was decided to give that – fambly of strangers another chance, and a brand new baby to gladden their home' (p. 76).

Mommo's story is a powerful and moving evocation of a desolate existence bereft of poetry and passion, in which only by laughing at their lot has survival been made feasible. There is no romanticization of peasant actuality, rather a powerful realization of 'the wretched and neglected dilapidated an' forlorn, the forgotten and tormented, the lonely an' despairing' (p. 71); yet the entrapment within the narrative of desolation, loss, and guilt, is clearly seen to have a stultifying effect on a present in which the material actuality of multi-nationals is not matched by the dominant narrative by which identity is formed. The release from the narrative of the past, and the decision to take Dolly's baby is a necessary dramatization, and perhaps realization, of the force of the argument presented by E.F. O'Doherty in 1963: 'One cannot change the economic underpinning of our way of life, our self image as a nation, and our rôle in international affairs without accepting as a necessary concomitant, radical and far reaching consequences in the structure and culture of our society.... The fear that we may be lost as a cultural or political entity in the world of the future is only too well grounded if our thinking is that we must resist or resent change and merely preserve the past. That way is impossible and that way lies stagnation and death' (O'Doherty, 1963, p. 134).

O'Doherty's invitation to engage with a future not necessarily predicated on a projection from the nationalist past was written in the first enthusiasm of the Lemass Government's commitment to economic growth and internationalism. Some twenty years later, surveying the wreckage of the South's economic hopes and the civil strife of the North, Seamus Deane pointed to the origins of both in colonialism. 'Irishness', he argued, 'is the quality by which we want to display our non-Britishness – or our anti-Britishness or, Britishness is the quality by which we display our non-Irishness. Both are forms of dependency. The idea of what is British continues to govern the idea of what is Irish' (Deane, 1984, p. 90). Acknowledging that the consequence of the longevity of the anti-colonial discourse is that its structures of 'opposing pairs' dominate attempts to think about history and literature, Deane suggested that the only certainty was that the quest for the unattainable essences of either Nationalism or Unionism was destroying the present: 'We should start from actualities, not from abstractions ... Identity is here and now, not elsewhere and at another time' (p. 91). But, as Edward Said warns, 'there is no such thing as a merely given, or simply available, starting point: beginnings have to be made for each project in such a way as to *enable* what follows from them' (Said, 1985b, p. 16). Deane's conviction that the future must be built not on *Irishness*, that is an identity constructed as the provincial 'other' of metropolitan Britishness, but on being *Irish*, requires nothing less than the re-reading of 'what it is that constitutes the Irish reality' through the past 500 or so years of Ireland's 'long colonial concussion' (Deane, 1985b, p. 58). The hope must be that such a re-reading will represent the starting point of 'an intense labour of social criticism, of cultural penetration and diffusion' (Boggs, 1976, p. 59), making what 'was secondary and subordinate – or even incidental ... the nucleus of a new ideological and theoretical complex' (Gramsci, 1971, p. 195). Thus displaced from contemporary duty, the seductive rhetoric and visions of Yeats and Pearse *et al.* may be re-assessed and their values recuperated in new ideological formations.

This Yeatsian ideal of a 'system of culture which will represent the whole of this country' (Cullingford, 1981, p. 177) stalks contemporary debate; the same end, if not the same means, is implicit in the concept of 'the fifth province'. As Brian Friel stated in 1982: 'I think out of that cultural state, a possibility of a political state follows. That is always the sequence' (O'Toole, 1982, p. 23). The extent to which the sequence from culture to politics is, as implied, natural and inevitable, is brought into penetratingly clear focus by Said's description of the crucial next phase: 'connecting these more politically vigilant forms of interpretation to an ongoing political and social praxis. Short of making that connection, even the best-intentioned and the cleverest interpretative activity is bound to sink back into the murmur of mere prose' (Said, 1985a, p. 158).

For some among Ireland's intelligentsia, to attempt such a connection is a serious misreading of the process of artistic production and its relationship to its social and historical moment. As Edna Longley, one of the most forceful articulators of this position, commented: 'Poetry and politics, like church and state, should be separated' (Longley, 1986, p. 185). More wittily, Paul Muldoon has expressed the view that any idea that art has influence on its social moment is, as in the case of Yeats's 'posturing' on the mobilizing power of *Cathleen ni Houlihan*, merely crass rhetoric:

> Did that play of mine
> send out certain men (*certain* men?)
>
> the English shot ...?
> the answer is 'Certainly not'.
> If Yeats had saved his pencil-lead
> would certain men have stayed in bed?
>
> For history's a twisted root
> with art its small, translucent fruit
>
> and never the other way round. ('7, Middagh Street', Muldoon, 1987, p. 39)

It is Sir Samuel Ferguson's 1833 declaration, however, which is the most explicit expression of the practice of subsequent Irish intellectuals: 'We must fight our battle now with a handful of types and a composing-stick, pages like this our field, and the reading public our arbiter of war' (Ferguson, 1833b, p. 592). The belief in the efficacy of art in the creation of a national consciousness remains, albeit that the contemporary expression of this belief has abandoned the desire to consolidate sectarian exclusivism and moved to the advocacy of democratic pluralism.

The expansion of this political and cultural activity is now the urgent requirement, and not only in Ireland. As Declan Kiberd has observed: 'The current crisis has prompted most Irish people to re-examine some of their deepest historical assumptions, but it has as yet given rise to no similar self-questioning in England' (Kiberd, 1985, p. 104). The relationship of England and Ireland, colonizer and colonized, Unionist and Nationalist, within a small western European archipelago has to be re-thought and re-read, and art and culture on all dimensions and levels of complexity must seek to provide the single-word spark to an inextinguishable thought. As G.B. Shaw stated the case for art as action: 'social questions never get solved until the pressure becomes so desperate that even governments recognize the necessity for moving. And to bring the pressure to this point, the poets must lend a hand to the few who are willing to do public work in the stages at which nothing but abuse is to be gained by it' (Shaw, 1964, p. 975).

Bibliography

Guide to further reading

Reading the cultural-political in a colonial context should start with Edward Said's *Orientalism* (Said, 1985b), Ashis Nandy's *The Intimate Enemy* (Nandy, 1983) and Albert Memmi's *The Colonizer and the Colonized* (Memmi, 1974). On discourse, Michel Foucault's *The History of Sexuality Vol. 1: An Introduction* (Foucault, 1984) is essential, and on praxis Gramsci's *Selections From The Prison Notebooks* (Gramsci, 1971) presents a profusion of hints and allusions for the reader of the cultural-political – in both colonial and metropolitan contexts.

Of the general introductions to Ireland's literatures covering the period from the sixteenth century Seamus Deane's *Short History of Irish Literature* (Deane, 1986) can be recommended as absorbing and informative.

For the sixteenth century Nicholas Canny's 'The Formation of the Irish Mind' (Canny, 1982) provides a good starting point, to be followed up by Bernadette Cunningham's 'Native Culture and Political Change in Ireland 1580-1640' (Cunningham, 1986) and Tom Dunne's 'The Gaelic Response to Conquest and Colonisation: The Evidence of the Poetry' (Dunne, 1980). Stephen Greenblatt's *Renaissance Self-Fashioning: From More to Shakespeare* (Greenblatt, 1980) offers a wider perspective on the cultural political of the sixteenth century, Stephen Ellis's *Tudor Ireland: Crown, Community and the Conflict of Cultures* (Ellis, 1985) gives a detailed historical survey, informed by current research, of this complex moment, while Philip Edwards' *Threshold of a Nation* (Edwards, 1979) considers the colonizer in the process of colonization.

W.J. McCormack's *Ascendancy and Tradition in Anglo-Irish Literature* (McCormack, 1985) covers the whole of the period from the beginning of the eighteenth century to the twentieth, with a wealth of insight. On the later eighteenth and early nineteenth centuries Marilyn Butler's *Maria Edgeworth: A Literary Biography* (Butler, 1972) is an excellent introduction to the social dimension of Ascendancy life while Anthony Malcolmson's *John Foster: The Politics of the Anglo-Irish Ascendancy* (Malcolmson, 1978) provides a detailed political account of its final years. Marianne Elliot's *Partners in Revolution: The United Irishmen and France* (Elliott, 1982) is an indispensable guide to radical politics in Ireland in the later eighteenth century and Séan Connolly's *Priests and People in Pre-Famine Ireland* and *Religion and Society in Nineteenth century Ireland* (Connolly, 1982, 1985) are essential reading for all students of the making of the cultural-political in modern Ireland.

There is an abundance of material on the later nineteenth and twentieth centuries. F.S.L. Lyon's *Ireland Since The Famine* (Lyons, 1971) is still probably the best all-round historical survey. On the literary dimension, George Watson's *Irish Identity and the Literary Revival* (Watson, 1979) is the best starting point complementing F.S.L. Lyons' *Culture and Anarchy in Ireland 1890-1939* (Lyons, 1979). Declan Kiberd's *Synge and the Irish Language* (Kiberd, 1979) offers a secure guide to an aspect of the 1890s Revival students neglect at their peril and Seamus Deane's *Celtic Revivals: Essays in Modern Irish Literature 1880-1980* (Deane, 1985a) provides challenging critical analyses of nodal figures. On Yeats the best introduction is Denis Donoghue's volume in the Fontana Modern Masters series (Donoghue, 1971) while the wealth of information in John Kelly's footnotes and appendices in the *Collected Letters* (Yeats, 1986) make them an essential point of reference for all students of the the poet and the period. Wayne Hall's *Shadowy Heroes* (Hall, 1980) and W.I. Thompson's *Imagination of an Insurrection* (Thompson, 1967) both trace elements of relationship between the Revivals of the 1890's and the subsequent Easter Rising and can be read with profit. On Pearse, Ruth Dudley Edward's biography *Patrick Pearse: The Triumph of Failure* (Dudley Edwards, 1979) is a sure guide, not only to Pearse but to the politics of the Gaelic League and the I.R.B. before 1916. Any reader considering the seminal period 1913-22 will benefit from reading David Fitzpatrick's *Politics and Irish Life 1913-21. Provincial Experience of War and Revolution* (Fitzpatrick, 1977).

For the period since 1922, students are fortunate: Terence Brown's *Ireland: A Social and Cultural History 1922-1985* (Brown, 1985) can be recommended without hesitation and provides the nucleus for reflection on post-Treaty Ireland. Deane's *Celtic Revivals* and *A Short History of Irish Literature* provide much useful and stimulating discussion on this period; both Brown and Deane deal with Ireland North and South.

For the contemporary moment the *Crane Bag Book of Irish Studies* (ed. Hederman and Kearney, 1982) and the Field Day Theatre Company's *Ireland's Field Day* (Hutchinson, 1985) provide a rich abundance of criticism and cultural polemic conveying some of the current ferment in and among Ireland's intellectuals.

Michael Adams (1968) *Censorship: The Irish Experience*, Alabama: University of Alabama Press.

Louis Althusser (1971) *Lenin And Philosophy and Other Essays* (transl. B. Brewster), London: New Left Books.

– (1979) *For Marx*, (transl. B. Brewster), London: Verso Books.

K. Andrews, N. Canny and P.E.H. Hair (eds.) (1978) *The Westward Enterprise: English Activities in Ireland, The Atlantic and America, 1480-1650*, Liverpool: University of Liverpool Press.

Anon. (1833a) 'Ireland No. I', *Blackwood's Edinburgh Magazine*, Vol. XXXIII, No. CCIII (January), pp. 66-87.

– (1833b) 'The Good Old Cause', *Dublin University Magazine*, Vol. II, No. IX. (September), pp. 241-7.

Conrad M. Arensberg and Solon T. Kimball (1968) *Family and Community In Ireland*, Cambridge (Mass.): Harvard University Press.

Matthew Arnold (1962) *Lectures and Essays in Criticism* (ed. R.H. Super), Ann Arbor: University of Michigan Press.

– (1965) *Culture and Anarchy With Friendship's Garland and Some Literary Essays* (ed. R.H. Super), Ann Arbor: University of Michigan Press.

– (1973) *English Literature and Irish Politics* (ed. R.H. Super), Ann Arbor: University of Michigan Press.

Ronald Ayling (ed.) (1969) *Seán O'Casey: Modern Judgements*, London: Macmillan.

Chris Baldick (1983) *The Social Mission of English Criticism 1848-1932*, Oxford: Clarendon Press.

Francis Barker and Peter Hulme (1985) 'Nymphs and reapers heavily vanish: the discursive con-texts of *The Tempest*', in Drakakis.

Sebastian Barry (ed.) (1986) *The Inherited Boundaries: Younger Poets of The Republic of Ireland*, Dublin: Dolmen.

M.R. Beames (1975) 'Peasant Movements in Ireland 1785-95', *Journal of Peasant Studies*, Vol. 2, No. 4, pp. 562-6.

Samuel Beckett (1973a) *First Love*, London: Calder and Boyars.

– (1973b) *Murphy*, London: Picador.

Andrew Bellis (pseud. Samuel Beckett) (1934) 'Recent Irish Poetry', *The Bookman*, No. 86. (August), pp. 235-6.

Sir Isaiah Berlin (1980) *Vico and Herder: Two Studies in the History of Ideas*, London: Chatto and Windus.

Paul Bew (1978) *Land and The National Question in Ireland 1858-1882*, Dublin: Gill and Macmillan.

Paul Bew, Peter Gibbon and Henry Patterson (1979) *The State in Northern Ireland: Political Forces and Social Classes*, Manchester: Manchester University Press.

Homi Bhabha (1983) 'The Other Question', *Screen*, Vol. 24, No. 6, pp. 18-36.

– (1984) 'Of Mimicry and Man: The Ambivalence of Colonial Discourse', *October*, No. 28, pp. 125-33.

Carl Boggs (1976) *Gramsci's Marxism*, London: Pluto Press.

D. George Boyce (1982) *Nationalism in Ireland*, London: Croom Helm.

E.A. Boyd (1916) *Ireland's Literary Renaissance*, Dublin: Maunsel.

Brendan Bradshaw (1978) 'Native Reaction to The Westward Enterprise: A Case Study in Gaelic Ideology', in Andrews, Canny and Hair.

Ciaran Brady (1986) 'Spenser's Irish Crisis: Humanism and Experience in the 1590's', *Past and Present*, No. 111, pp. 16-49.

Ciaran Brady and Raymond Gillespie (eds.) (1986) *Natives and Newcomers: Essays On the Making of Irish Colonial Society, 1534-1641*, Dublin: Irish Academic Press.

Stopford Brooke (1893) *The Need and Use of getting Irish Literature into the English Tongue*, London: T. Fisher Unwin.

Malcolm Brown (1972) *The Politics of Irish Literature: From Thomas Davis To W.B. Yeats*, London: Allen and Unwin.

– (1973) *Sir Samuel Ferguson*, Lewisburg: Bucknell University Press.

Paul Brown (1985) 'This Thing of Darkness I Acknowledge Mine: *The Tempest* and the Discourse of Colonialism', in Dollimore and Sinfield, pp. 48-71.

Terence Brown (1975) *Northern Voices: Poets From the North of Ireland*, Dublin: Gill and Macmillan.

– (1985) *Ireland: A Social and Cultural History 1922-1985*, London: Fontana.

Patrick Buckland (1979) *The Factory of Grievances: Devolved Government in Northern Ireland, 1921-39*, Dublin: Gill and Macmillan.

Richard Burnham and Robert Hogan (eds.) (1984) *Lost Plays of the Irish Renaissance Vol. III: The Cork Dramatic Society*, New York: Proscenium Press.

Marilyn Butler (1972) *Maria Edgeworth: A Literary Biography*, Oxford: Clarendon Press.

David Cairns and Shaun Richards (1986) 'Pissing in the Gale of History: Contemporary Protestant Culture and the "Ancient Curse" ', unpublished paper, *Conference on the Feasibility of Consensus in Ireland*, University of Keele, April 1986.

Giraldus Cambrensis (1978) *The Conquest of Ireland* (transl. A.B. Scott and F.-X. Martin), Dublin: Royal Irish Academy.

– (1982) *The History and Topography of Ireland* (transl. J.O'Meara), Mountrath: Dolmen.

Nicholas P. Canny (1973) 'The Ideology of English Colonization: From Ireland to America', *William and Mary Quarterly*, Vol. 30, pp. 575-98.

– (1982) 'The Formation of The Irish Mind: Religion, Politics and Gaelic Irish Literature 1580-1750', *Past and Present*, No. 95, pp. 91-116.

Andrew Carpenter (1977) *Place Personality and the Irish Writer*, Gerrards Cross: Colin Smythe.

Daniel J. Casey and Robert E. Rhodes (1977) *Views of the Irish Peasantry 1800-1916*, Hamden (Conn.): Archon Books.

Partha Chatterjee (1986) *Nationalist Thought and The Colonial World: A Derivative Discourse*, London:

Zed Books.
Samuel Clark (1979) *Social Origins of the Irish Land War*, Princeton: Princeton University Press.
Randall Clarke (1942) 'The Relations between O'Connell and the Young Irelanders' *Irish Historical Studies*, Vol. III, pp. 18-30.
Anne Clissmann (1975) *Flann O'Brien: A Critical Introduction to His Work*, Dublin: Gill and Macmillan.
James Connolly (1973) *Selected Writings* (ed. P. Berresford Ellis), Harmondsworth: Penguin.
Seán Connolly (1982) *Priests and People in Pre-Famine Ireland, 1780-1845*, Dublin: Gill and Macmillan.
– (1985) *Religion and Society in Nineteenth Century Ireland. Studies in Irish Economic and Social History*, Dundalk: Economic and Social History Society of Ireland.
P.J. Corish, (1979) 'Gallicanism at Maynooth. Archbishop Cullen and the Royal Visitation of 1853', in Cosgrove and MacCartney, pp. 176-89.
Daniel Corkery (1931) *Synge and Anglo-Irish Literature*, Cork: Cork University Press.
– (1979) *The Hidden Ireland: A Study of Gaelic Munster in The Eighteenth Century*, Dublin: Gill and Macmillan.
Robert W. Corrigan (ed.) (1964) *The Modern Theatre*, New York: Macmillan.
Art Cosgrove and Donal MacCartney (eds.) (1979) *Studies in Irish History Presented to R. Dudley Edwards*, Dublin: University College Dublin.
Archbishop Croke (1884) *The Nation* (27 December).
Raymond Crotty (1986) *Ireland in Crisis: A Study in Capitalist Colonial Undevelopment*, Dingle: Brandon Book Publishers.
L.M. Cullen (1969) 'The Hidden Ireland: Reassessment of a Concept', *Studia Hibernica*, Vol. 9, pp. 7-47.
Elizabeth Cullingford (1981) *Yeats Ireland and Fascism*, London: Macmillan.
Bernadette Cunningham (1986) 'Native Culture and Political Change in Ireland, 1580-1640', in Brady and Gillespie, pp. 148-70.
L.P. Curtis Jnr (1968) *Anglo-Saxons and Celts: A Study of Anti-Irish Prejudice In Victorian England*, Connecticut: Conference on British Studies, University of Bridgeport.
– (1970) 'The Anglo-Irish Predicament', *20th. Century Studies*, November, pp. 37-63.
– (1971) *Apes and Angels: The Irishman in Victorian Caricature*, Newton Abbot: David and Charles.
G.F. Dalton (1974) 'The Tradition of Blood Sacrifice to the Goddess Éire', *Studies*, Vol. LXII, pp. 343-54.
Mary E. Daly (1981) 'Late Nineteenth and Early Twentieth Century Dublin', in Harkness and O'Dowd, pp. 221-52.
– (1982) 'The Social Structure of the Dublin Working Class, 1871-1911', *Irish Historical Studies*, Vol. XXIII, No. 90, pp. 121-33.
– (1985) 'An Alien Institution? Attitudes Towards The City in Nineteenth and Twentieth Century Irish Society', *Études Irlandaises*, Vol. 10, pp. 181-94.
D.J. O'Neill Daunt (1842) *The Nation* (13 May)
Thomas Davis (1842a) 'Our Present Policy'. *The Nation* (13 May)
– (1842b) *The Nation* (17 December)
– (1843a) *The Nation* (1 April)
– (1843b) *The Nation* (30 December).
Thomas Davis (1869) *National and Historical Ballads, Songs and Poems By Thomas Davis*, Dublin: James Duffy.
– (n.d) *Thomas Davis: Selections From His Prose and Poetry* (ed. T.W. Rolleston), Dublin: Talbot Press, Every Irishman's Library.
– (1914) *Essays Literary and Historical By Thomas Davis* (ed. D.J. O'Donoghue), Dundalk: W. Tempest, Dundalgan Press.
Seamus Deane (1982) 'Postscript', *The Crane Bag*, Vol. 3, No. 2 (1979), in Hederman and Kearney, pp. 512-14.
– (1983) 'Editorial', *The Crane Bag*, Vol. 3, No. 1, in Hederman and Kearney, pp. 339-40.

– (1984) 'Remembering the Irish Future', *The Crane Bag*, Vol .8, No. 1, (The R.T.E./U.C.D. Lectures), pp. 81-6.
– (1985a) *Celtic Revivals: Essays in Modern Irish Literature 1880-1980*, London: Faber and Faber.
– (1985b) 'Heroic Styles: The Tradition of an Idea', in Field Day Theatre Company, pp. 45-58.
– (1986) *A Short History of Irish Literature*, London: Hutchinson.
Liam De Paor (1986) *The Peoples of Ireland: From Prehistory to Modern Times*, London: Hutchinson.
John Denvir (1972) *Life Story of an Old Rebel*, Dublin: Irish University Press.
Jonathan Dollimore and Alan Sinfield (eds.) (1985) *Political Shakespeare: New Essays In Cultural Materialism*, Manchester: Manchester University Press.
Denis Donoghue (1971) *Yeats*, London: Fontana.
– (1983) 'Ideas and How to Escape From Them', *The Crane Bag*, Vol. 7, No. 2, pp. 21-8.
– (1985) 'Afterword', in Field Day Theatre Company, pp. 107-20.
J.S. Donnelly (1978) 'The Whiteboy Movement 1761-5', *Irish Historical Studies*, Vol. XX, pp. 20-54.
John Drakakis (ed.) (1985) *Alternative Shakespeares*, London: Methuen.
Edward Dudley and Maximilian E. Novak (eds) (1972) *The Wild Man Within: An Image in Western Thought From The Renaissance to Romanticism*, Pittsburg: University of Pittsburg Press.
Sir Charles Gavan Duffy (1881) *Young Ireland: A Fragment of Irish History 1840-1850*, New York: Appleton Press; (1973) reprint New York: Da Capo Press.
– (1894) 'What Irishmen May Do For Irish Literature', in Duffy, Sigerson, Hyde, pp. 9-33.
Sir Charles Gavan Duffy, Dr George Sigerson, Dr Douglas Hyde (1894) *The Revival of Irish Literature: Addresses by Sir Charles Gavan Duffy, Dr. George Sigerson Dr. Douglas Hyde*, London: Fisher Unwin; (1973) reprint New York: Lemma Publishing.
Tom Dunne (1980) 'The Gaelic Response to Conquest and Colonisation: The Evidence of The Poetry', *Studia Hibernica*, Vol. XX, pp. 7-30.
Terry Eagleton (1971) 'History and Myth in Yeats's "Easter 1916" ', *Essays in Criticism*, Vol. 21, No. 3, pp. 248-60.
Philip Edwards (1979) *Threshold Of A Nation*, Cambridge: Cambridge University Press.
Robert Dudley Edwards (1947) 'The Contribution of Young Ireland to The Development of the Irish National Idea', in S. Pender (ed.) *Feilschríbhinn Torna*, Cork: University College Cork, pp. 115-33.
Ruth Dudley Edwards (1979) *Patrick Pearse: The Triumph of Failure*, London: Faber and Faber.
John Eglinton (1899) *Literary Ideals in Ireland*, Dublin: Fisher Unwin; (1973) reprint New York: Lemma Publishing.
Marianne Elliott (1978) 'The Origins and Transformation of Early Irish Republicanism', *International Review of Social History*, Vol. XXIII, No. 3, pp. 405-28.
– (1982) *Partners in Revolution: The United Irishmen and France*, London: Yale University Press.
Steven G. Ellis (1985) *Tudor Ireland: Crown, Community and The Conflict of Cultures*, London: Longman.
Richard Ellman (1966) *James Joyce*, Oxford: Oxford University Press.
Ronan Fanning (1978) *The Irish Department of Finance 1922-58*, Dublin: Institute of Public Administration.
– (1983) 'Economists and Governments: Ireland 1922-52', *Hermathena*, Vol. CXXV, pp. 138-56.
Franz Fanon (1965) *The Wretched of the Earth*, London: Macgibbon and Kee.
Michael Farrell (1980) *Northern Ireland: The Orange State*, London: Pluto Press.
M. Feeney (1982) 'Print For the People: The Growth in Popular Writings and Reading Facilities in Ireland 1820-1850', unpublished. M.Litt Thesis, Trinity College, University of Dublin.
William J. Feeney (ed.) (1980) *Lost Plays of the Irish Renaissance Vol II: Edward Martyn's Irish Theatre*, New York: Proscenium Press.
Lady Ferguson (1896a) *Sir Samuel Ferguson in The Ireland of His Day Vol. I*, Edinburgh, London: William Blackwood.
– (1896b) *Sir Samuel Ferguson in The Ireland of His Day Vol. II*, Edinburgh, London: William

Blackwood.
Sir Samuel Ferguson (1833a) 'An Irish Garland', *Blackwood's Edinburgh Magazine* Vol. XXXIII, No. CCIII (January), pp. 87-8.
– (1833b) 'A Dialogue Between the Head and Heart of an Irish Protestant', *Dublin University Magazine*, Vol. II, No.XI (November), pp. 586-93.
– (1834a) 'Hardiman's Irish Minstrelsy– No.I', *Dublin University Magazine*, Vol. III, No. XVI (April), pp. 465-77.
– (1834b) 'Hardiman's Irish Minstrelsy– No. II', *Dublin University Magazine*, Vol. IV, No. XX (August), pp. 152-67.
– (1834c) 'Hardiman's Irish Minstrelsy– No. III', *Dublin University Magazine*, Vol. IV, No. XXII (October), pp. 447-67.
– (1834d) 'Hardiman's Irish Minstrelsy– No. IV', *Dublin University Magazine*, Vol. IV, No. XXIII (November), pp. 514-42.
– (1836) 'Attractions of Ireland No. III', *Dublin University Magazine*, Vol VIII (December), pp. 658-75.
Field Day Theatre Company (1985) *Ireland's Field Day*, London: Hutchinson.
Garret FitzGerald (1972) *Towards a New Ireland*, Dublin: Gill and Macmillan.
David Fitzpatrick (1977) *Politics and Irish Life, 1913-21. Provincial Experience Of War and Revolution*, Dublin: Gill and Macmillan.
– (1980) 'The Disappearance of the Irish Agricultural Labourer. 1841-1912', *Irish Economic and Social History*, Vol. VII, pp. 66-92.
– (1983) 'Irish Farming Families Before the First World War', *Comparative Studies in Society and History*, Vol. 25, No. 2, pp. 339-73.
Dermot Folley (1974) 'A Minstrel Boy with a Satchel of Books', *Irish University Review*, Vol.4, No.2, pp. 204-17
Alan Ford (1986) 'The Protestant Reformation in Ireland', in Brady and Gillespie, pp. 50-74.
Hal Foster (ed.) (1985) *Postmodern Culture*, London: Pluto Press.
Michel Foucault (1967) *Madness and Civilization: A History of Insanity In the Age of Reason*, London: Tavistock Press.
– (1970) *The Order of Things*, London: Tavistock Press.
– (1972) *The Archaeology of Knowledge*, London: Tavistock Press.
– (1978) 'Politics and the Study of Discourse', *Ideology and Consciousness*, Vol. 3, pp. 7-26.
– (1980) *Power/Knowledge: Selected Interviews and Other Writings 1972-1977* (ed. Colin Gordon), Brighton: Harvester Press.
– (1981) 'The Order of Discourse', in Young, pp. 48-78.
– (1984) *The History of Sexuality. Volume I: An Introduction* (transl. R. Hurley), Harmondsworth: Penguin.
Brian Friel (1983) *The Communication Cord*, London: Faber and Faber.
– (1984) *Selected Plays of Brian Friel*, London: Faber and Faber.
W.P. Fryer (1964) 'Romantic Literature and the European Age of Revolutions', *Renaissance and Modern Studies*, Vol.8, pp. 53-74.
Ernst Gellner (1983) *Nations and Nationalism*, Oxford: Basil Blackwell.
Maud Gonne (see Maud Gonne MacBride).
Antonio Gramsci (1971) *Selections From The Prison Notebooks* (transl. Q. Hoare and G. Nowell Smith), London: Lawrence and Wishart.
E.R.R. Green (1973) 'The Fenians Abroad', in T.D. Williams (1973), pp. 79-89.
Stephen Greenblatt (1980) *Renaissance Self-Fashioning: From More To Shakespeare*, London: University of Chicago Press.
Lady Gregory (1900) 'The Felons of Our Land', *Cornhill Magazine*, No.47, pp. 622-34.
– (1901) (ed.) *Ideals in Ireland*, London: At The Unicorn VII Cecil Court.
– (1972) *Our Irish Theatre*, Gerrards Cross: Colin Smythe
– (1974) *Poets and Dreamers: Studies and Translations From the Irish*, Gerrards Cross: Colin Smythe.
Eamon Grennan (1982) 'Language and Politics: A Note on Some Metaphors in Spenser's *View*

of the Present State of Ireland', *Spenser Studies*, Vol. 3, pp. 99-110.
Trevor R. Griffiths (1983) 'This Island's Mine': Caliban and Colonialism', *The Yearbook of English Studies*, 13, pp. 159-80.
Wayne E. Hall (1980) *Shadowy Heroes*, Syracuse: Syracuse University Press.
D. Harkness and M. O'Dowd (1981) *The Town in Ireland*, Belfast: Appletree Press.
Seamus Heaney (1975) *North*, London: Faber and Faber.
– (1980a) *Preoccupations: Selected Prose 1968-1978* London: Faber and Faber.
– (1980b) *Selected Poems, 1965-1975*, London: Faber and Faber.
– (1983) *Sweeney Astray*, London: Faber and Faber.
– (1984) *Station Island*, London: Faber and Faber.
– (1985) 'An Open Letter', in Field Day Theatre Company, pp. 23-30.
Mark Patrick Hederman and Richard Kearney (1977) 'Editorial', *The Crane Bag*, Vol. 1, No. 1, in Hederman and Kearney, 1982.
Mark Patrick Hederman and Richard Kearney (eds.) (1982) *The Crane Bag Book of Irish Studies*, Dublin: Blackwater Press.
D.N. Hempton (1980) 'The Methodist Crusade in Ireland', *Irish Historical Studies*, Vol. XXII, No. 85, pp. 33-48.
F.R. Higgins (1927) *The Dark Breed*, London: Macmillan.
Jacqueline Hill (1975) 'Nationalism and the Catholic Church in the 1840's: Views of Dublin Repealers', *Irish Historical Studies*, Vol.XIX, No.76, pp. 371-94.
– (1980) 'The Intelligentsia and Irish Nationalism in the 1840's', *Studia Hibernica*, No. XX, pp. 73-109.
– (1984) 'National Festivals, The State and "Protestant Ascendancy" in Ireland, 1790-1829', *Irish Historical Studies*, Vol. XXIV, No. 93, pp. 30-51.
Robert Hogan and James Kilroy (eds.) (1970) *Lost Plays of the Irish Renaissance*, New York: Proscenium Press.
– (1975) *The Modern Irish Drama. A Documentary History Vol. I: The Irish Literary Theatre 1899-1901*, Dublin: Dolmen Press.
– (1976) *The Modern Irish Drama. A Documentary History Vol. II: Laying the Foundations 1902-1904*, Dublin: Dolmen Press.
– (1978) *The Modern Irish Drama A Documentary History Vol. III: The Abbey Theatre: The Years of Synge*, Dublin: Dolmen Press.
K.T. Hoppen (1977) 'Landlords, Society and Electoral Politics in Mid-Nineteenth Century Ireland, 1848-1904', *Past and Present*, No. 75, pp. 62-93.
– (1979) 'National Politics and Local Realities in Mid-Nineteenth Century Ireland' in Cosgrove and MacCartney, pp. 190-227.
J.J. Horgan (1948) *Parnell To Pearse*, Dublin: Browne and Nolan.
Ron Hutchinson (1984) *Rat in the Skull*, London: Methuen.
Douglas Hyde (1894) 'The Necessity For De-Anglicising Ireland', In Duffy, Sigerson, Hyde, pp. 117-61.
– (1974) *The Twisting of the Rope*, in Lady Gregory.
A.N. Jeffares (1968) *A Commentary on the Collected Poems of W.B. Yeats*, London: Macmillan.
A.N. Jeffares and K.G.W. Cross (eds.) (1965) *In Excited Reverie: A Centenary Tribute To W.B. Yeats*, London: Macmillan.
A.N. Jeffares and A.S. Knowland (1975) *A Commentary on the Collected Plays of W.B. Yeats*, London: Macmillan.
Denis Johnston (1983) *Selected Plays of Denis Johnston*, Gerrards Cross: Colin Smythe.
Dora M. Jones (1900) ' "The Celtic Twilight" The Poems of W.B. Yeats', *London Quarterly Review*, Vol. XCIV, pp. 61-70.
James Joyce (1960) *Portrait of the Artist as A Young Man*, Harmondsworth: Penguin.
– (1964) *James Joyce: The Critical Writings* (eds. Ellsworth Mason and Richard Ellman), New York: Viking Press.
– (1970) *James Joyce: The Critical Heritage* (ed. Robert H. Deming), London: Routledge and Kegan

Paul.
– (1975) *Selected Letters of James Joyce* (ed. Richard Ellman), London: Faber and Faber.
– (1977a) *Dubliners*, London: Granada.
– (1977b) *Stephen Hero*, London: Granada.
– (1986) *Ulysses: The Corrected Text*, Harmondsworth: Penguin.
Patrick Kavanagh (1972), *Collected Poems*, London: Martin, Brian & O'Keeffe.
John V. Kelleher (1950) 'Matthew Arnold and the Celtic Revival', in H. Levin (ed.), pp. 197-221.
– (1957) 'Ireland: Where Does She Stand?', *Foreign Affairs*, No. 3, p. 495.
John S. Kelly (1976) 'The Fall of Parnell and the Rise of Anglo-Irish Literature: An Investigation', *Anglo-Irish Studies*, Vol. II, pp. 1-23.
Patrick Kelly (1985) ' "A Light To The Blind": The Voice of the Dispossessed Élite In the Generation after The Defeat at Limerick', *Irish Historical Studies*, Vol. XXIV, No. 96, pp. 431-62.
Malcolm Kelsall (1975) 'Synge in Aran', *Irish University Review*, Vol. 5, No. 2, pp. 254-70.
Frank Kermode (1966) *The Sense of An Ending*, London: Oxford University Press.
Declan Kiberd (1979) *Synge And The Irish Language*, London: Macmillan.
– (1984) 'Inventing Irelands', *The Crane Bag*, Vol. 8, No. 1 (The R.T.E./U.C.D. Lectures), pp. 11-23.
– (1985) 'Anglo-Irish Attitudes' in Field Day Theatre Company, pp. 83-105..
– (1986) *Men and Feminism in Modern Literature*, London: Macmillan.
Robert Kilroy (1971) *The Playboy Riots*, Dublin: Dolmen.
Mary C. King (1985) *The Drama of J.M. Synge*, London: Fourth Estate.
A.S. Knowland (1983) *W.B. Yeats: Dramatist of Vision. Irish Literary Studies Vol.* 17, Gerrards Cross: Colin Smythe.
David Krause (1960) *Sean O'Casey: The Man and His Work*, New York: Macmillan.
Peter Kuch (1986) *Yeats and AE: The Antagonism That Unites Dear Friends*, Gerrards Cross: Colin Smythe.
Jacques Lacan (1977) *Écrits: A Selection* (transl. A. Sheridan), London: Tavistock Press.
Ernesto Laclau (1979) *Politics and Ideology in Marxist Theory: Capitalism, Fascism, Populism*, London: Verso.
Michael Laffan 1971 'The Unification of Sinn Féin in 1917', *Irish Historical Studies*, Vol. XVII, pp. 353-79.
James Fintan Lalor (1947) *Collected Writings*, Dublin: Talbot Press.
Emmet Larkin (1984) *The Historical Dimension of Irish Catholicism*, New York: Catholic University Press.
Joseph Lee (1973) *The Modernisation of Irish Society 1848-1918*, Dublin: Gill and Macmillan.
– (1978) 'Women and the Church Since The Famine', in MacCurtain and Ó Corrain, pp. 37-45.
– (ed.)(1979a) *Ireland 1945-1970*, Dublin: Gill and Macmillan.
– (1979b) 'Continuity and Change in Ireland, 1945-70', in Lee, 1979a.
Colm Lennon (1986) 'The Counter-Reformation in Ireland, 1542-1641', in Brady and Gillespie, pp. 74-92.
H. Levin (ed.) (1950) *Perspectives in Criticism No. 20: Harvard Studies in Comparative Literature*, Cambridge (Mass.): Harvard University Press.
Jack Lindsay (1969) 'Seán O'Casey as A Socialist Artist', in Ayling, pp. 192-203.
Richard Loftus (1964) *Nationalism in Modern Anglo-Irish Poetry*, Madison and Milwaukee: University of Wisconsin Press.
Edna Longley (1986) *Poetry in the Wars*, Newcastle-upon-Tyne: Bloodaxe Books.
Uri M. Lotman (1978) 'On The Semiotic Mechanism of Culture', *New Literary History*, Vol. IX, No. 2, pp. 211-31.
Robert G. Lowery (1984) *A Whirlwind in Dublin: 'The Plough and the Stars' Riots*, London: Greenwood Press.
F.S.L. Lyons (1970) 'James Joyce's Dublin', *Twentieth Century Views*, No. 4, pp. 6-35.

– (1971) *Ireland Since The Famine*, London: Fontana.
– (1977) 'The Parnell Theme in Literature', in Carpenter, pp. 69-95.
– (1979) *Culture and Anarchy in Ireland 1890-1939*, Oxford: Oxford University Press.
Patrick Lynch (1966) 'The Social Revolution That Never Was', in T. Desmond Williams (1966), pp. 41-54.
Maud Gonne MacBride (1970) *Dawn*, in Hogan and Kilroy, pp. 73-84.
Colin MacCabe (1978) *James Joyce And The Revolution Of The Word*, London: Macmillan.
Norman McCord (1970) 'The Fenians and Public Opinion in Great Britain', in M. Harmon (ed.) *Fenians and Fenianism*, Dublin: Scepter Books, pp.40-55.
W.J. McCormack (1985) *Ascendancy and Tradition in Anglo-Irish Literature*, Oxford: Clarendon Press.
Margaret MacCurtain and Donncha Ó Corrain (eds.) (1978) *Women In Irish Society: The Historical Dimension*, Dublin: Arlen House.
Oliver MacDonagh, W.F. Mandle, Pauric Travers (eds.) (1983) *Irish Culture And Nationalism, 1750-1950*, London: Macmillan.
Thomas MacDonagh (1908) *When The Dawn is Come*, Dublin: Maunsel & Co.
– (1916) *Literature in Ireland: Studies Irish and Anglo-Irish*, Dublin: The Talbot Press.
Thomas MacDonagh (1980) *Pagans*, in Feeney.
Hugh A.MacDougall (1982) *Racial Myth in English History: Trojans, Teutons And Anglo-Saxons*, Montreal: Harvest House.
R.B. McDowell (1952) *Public Opinion and Government Policy in Ireland 1801-1846. Studies in Irish History Vol. V*, London: Faber; (1975) Connecticut: Greenwood Press.
– (1979) *Ireland in the Age of Imperialism and Revolution*, Oxford: Clarendon Press.
Kevin MacGrath (1948) 'Writers in *The Nation*, 1842-5', *Irish Historical Studies*, Vol. VI, pp. 189-223.
Alf MacLochlainn (1977) 'Gael and Peasant– A Case of Mistaken Identity?', in Casey and Rhodes, pp. 17-35.
J.A. MacMahon O.F.M. (1981) 'The Catholic Clergy and the Social Question in Ireland, 1891-1916', *Studies*, Vol. LXX, No. 280, pp. 263-88.
S. MacMahon (ed.) (1978) *The Best From The Bell*, Dublin: The O'Brien Press.
Terence MacSwiney (1984) *The Last Warriors of Coole: A Heroic Play in One Act*, in Burnham and Hogan, pp. 61-77.
Anthony P.W. Malcolmson (1978) *John Foster: The Politics of the Anglo-Irish Ascendancy*, Oxford: Institute of Irish Studies, Queen's University Belfast, Oxford University Press.
Dominic Manganiello (1980) *Joyce's Politics*, London: Routledge and Kegan Paul.
Phillip L. Marcus (1970) *Standish O'Grady*, Lewisburg: Bucknell University Press
Karl Marx (1977) *Karl Marx: Selected Writings* (ed. David McLellan), Oxford: Oxford University Press.
Albert Memmi (1974) *The Colonizer and the Colonized*, London: Souvenir Press.
Vivian Mercier (1977) *Beckett/Beckett*, New York: Oxford University Press.
D.W. Miller (1973) *Church State and Nation in Ireland 1898-1921*, Dublin: Gill and Macmillan.
Ralph Miliband (1973) *Parliamentary Socialism*, London: Merlin.
T.W. Moody (1966) 'Thomas Davis and the Irish Nation', *Hermathena* (autumn), pp. 5-31.
George Moore (1914) *The Untilled Field*, London: Heinemann.
– (1976) *Hail and Farewell A Trilogy* (ed. Richard Cave), Gerrards Cross: Colin Smythe.
David P. Moran (n.d) [1905] *The Philosophy of Irish Ireland*, Dublin: J. Duffy, M.H. Gill, *The Leader*.
Paul Muldoon (1987) *Meeting the British*, London: Faber and Faber.
J.A. Murphy (1969) 'Priests and People in Modern Irish History', *Christus Rex*, Vol. 23, pp. 235-59.
Thomas Murphy (1986) *Bailegangaire*, Dublin: Gallery Press.
R. Munck (1983) 'At the Very Doorstep: Irish Labor and the National Question', *Éire/Ireland*, Vol. XVIII, No. 2, pp. 36-51.
Ashis Nandy (1980) *At The Edge of Psychology: Essays in Politics and Culture*, Delhi: Oxford University Press.
– (1983) *The Intimate Enemy: Loss and Recovery of Self Under Colonialism*, Delhi: Oxford University

Press.
Peter Neary (1984) 'The Failure of Economic Nationalism', *The Crane Bag*, Vol.8, No.1 (The R.T.E./U.C.D. Lectures), pp. 68-81.
Sarah Nelson (1984) *Ulster's Uncertain Defenders: Loyalists and the Northern Ireland Conflict*, Belfast: Appletree.
David Norris (1979) 'Imaginative Response Versus Authority Structures. A Theme of the Anglo-Irish Short Story', in Rafroidi and Brown, pp. 38-59.
Kevin B. Nowlan (1973) 'The Fenians At Home', in T. Desmond Williams (1973), pp. 90-99.
Kevin B. Nowlan and T. Desmond Williams (1969) *Ireland in The War Years and After: 1939-51*, Dublin: Gill and Macmillan.
Conor Cruise O'Brien (1965) 'Passion and Cunning: An Essay on the Politics of W.B. Yeats', in Jeffares and Cross, pp. 207-78.
– (1972) *States of Ireland*, London: Hutchinson.
– (1985) 'Willie and Augusta', *The Observer*, 19 May, p. 27.
Flann O'Brien (1973) *The Poor Mouth*, New York: Viking.
Margaret O'Callaghan (1981) 'Language and Religion: The Quest For Identity in The Irish Free State', unpublished M.A. thesis, University College, Dublin.
– (1983) 'Religion and Identity. The Church and Irish Independence', *The Crane Bag*, Vol. 7, No. 2, pp. 65-76.
Seán O'Casey (1963) *Three Plays*, London: Macmillan
– (1975) *The Letters of Seán O'Casey 1910-1941* (ed. David Krause), London: Cassell.
Frank O'Connor (1942) 'The Future of Irish Literature', *Horizon*, Vol. V, No. 25, pp. 55-63.
– (1965) *An Only Child*, London: Macmillan.
E.F. O'Doherty (1963) 'Society, Identity and Change', *Studies*, Vol. LII, pp. 125-35.
F.H. O'Donnell (1972) 'Souls For Gold: A Pseudo-Celtic Drama in Dublin', in Lady Gregory, Appendix VIII.
Mary O'Dowd (1986) 'Gaelic Economy and Society', in Brady and Gillespie, pp. 120-47
Robert O'Driscoll (1976) *An Ascendancy of the Heart: Ferguson and The Beginnings of Modern Irish Literature in English*, Dublin: Dolmen Press.
Seán O Faolain (1936) 'Daniel Corkery', *The Dublin Magazine*, Vol. XI, No. 2, pp. 49-61.
– (1949) 'The Dilemma of Irish Letters', *The Month*, Vol. 2, pp. 366-79.
– (1982) *Midsummer Night's Madness and Other Stories*, Harmondsworth: Penguin.
– (1974) *The Irish*, Harmondsworth: Penguin.
Standish O'Grady (1878) *History of Ireland Volume I: Heroic Period*, Dublin: E. Ponsonby; (1970) reprint New York: Lemma Publishing.
– (1879) *Early Bardic Literature: Ireland*, Dublin: E. Ponsonby; (1970) reprint New York: Lemma Publishing.
– (1882) *The Crisis in Ireland*, Dublin: E Ponsonby.
– (1886) *Toryism and the Tory Democracy*, London: Chapman and Hall.
– (1896) 'Introduction' to Sir George Carew *Pacata Hibernica Or A History Of the Wars in Ireland*, London: Downey and Co.
– (1897) 'The New Irish Movement', *Fortnightly Review*, No. 67 (February), pp. 170-9.
– (n.d.) [1918] *Standish O'Grady: Selected Essays and Passages* (Intr. E.A. Boyd), Dublin: The Talbot Press.
John O'Riordan (1984) *A Guide To O'Casey's Plays*, London: Macmillan.
Fintan O'Toole (1982) 'The Man From God Knows Where' (Interview with Brian Friel), *In Dublin*, No. 165, 28 October, pp. 20-3.
Seán Ó Tuama and Thomas Kinsella (1981) *An Duanaire 1600-1900: Poems of the Dispossessed*, Dublin: Dolmen Press.
Gearoid O Tuathaigh (1972) *Ireland Before The Famine*, Dublin: Gill and Macmillan.
Edd Winfield Parks and Aileen Wells Parks (1967) *Thomas MacDonagh, The Man, The Patriot, The Writer*, Athens (Ga.): University of Georgia Press.
Tom Paulin (1983) *Liberty Tree*, London: Faber and Faber.

– (1984) *Ireland and the English Crisis*, Newcastle-upon-Tyne: Bloodaxe Books.
Patrice Pavis (1982) 'The Aesthetics of Theatrical Reception', in *Languages of the Stage: Essays in the Semiology of the Theatre*, New York: Performing Arts Journal Publications.
R.R. Pearce (1961) *The Senate Speeches of W.B. Yeats*, London: Faber and Faber.
Patrick Pearse (n.d) *Patrick Pearse: Political Writings and Speeches* (ed. D. Ryan), Dublin: Maunsel and Co.
– (1979) *The Literary Writings of Patrick Pearse*, Cork: Mercier Press.
Patrick Rafroidi and Terence Brown (eds.) (1979) *The Irish Short Story*, Gerrards Cross: Colin Smythe.
James Randall (1970) 'An Interview with Seamus Heaney', *Plough Shares*, Vol. 5, No. 3, pp. 7-22.
Bernard Ransom (1980) *Connolly's Marxism*, London: Pluto Press.
J.M. Reilly (n.d.) 'The Threatening Metempsychosis of A Nation', *Gaelic League Pamphlets No. 24*, Dublin: The Gaelic League.
Ernest Renan (1897) *The Poetry of the Celtic Races* (transl. W.G. Hutchinson), London: Walter Scott.
Irving Ribner (1979) *The English History Play in the Age of Shakespeare*, New York: Octagon Books.
Lennox Robinson (1918) *The Lost Leader*, Dublin: Thomas Kiersey.
– (1982) *Selected Plays of Lennox Robinson Vol. I*, Gerrards Cross: Colin Smythe.
William Rooney (n.d.) [1909] *Prose Writings by William Rooney*, Dublin: M.H. Gill.
Desmond Ryan (1963) *The 1916 Poets*, Westport (Conn.): Greenwood Press.
Michael T. Ryan (1981) 'Assimilating New Worlds in The Sixteenth and Seventeenth Centuries', *Comparative Studies in Society And History*, Vol. 23, No. 4, pp. 519-38.
Ann Saddlemyer (1982) *Theatre Business: The Correspondence of the first Abbey Theatre Directors*, Oxford: Blackwell.
Edward Said (1985a) 'Opponents, Audiences, Constituencies and Community', in Foster, pp. 135-59.
– (1985b) *Orientalism*, Harmondsworth: Penguin.
Francis Shaw S.J. (1972) 'The Canon of Irish History: A Challenge', *Studies*, Vol.LXI (summer), pp. 113-52.
G.B. Shaw (1964) 'The Problem Play - A Symposium', in Corrigan (ed.).
Dr. George Sigerson (1894) 'Irish Literature: Its Origin, Environment and Influence', in Duffy, Sigerson, Hyde, pp. 63-114.
Edmund Spenser (1934) *A View of the Present State of Ireland* (ed. W.L.Renwick), London: Eric Partridge.
– (1965) *The Faerie Queene* (ed. P.C. Bayley), Oxford: Oxford University Press.
John Storey (1985) 'Matthew Arnold: The Politics of an Organic Intellectual', *Literature and History*, Vol. 11, No. 2, pp. 217-28.
John M. Synge (1958) *Plays, Poems and Prose*, London: Dent.
– (1979) *The Aran Islands*, Oxford: Oxford University Press.
– (1983) *The Collected Letters of J.M. Synge* (ed. Anne Saddlemyer), Oxford: Clarendon Press.
E.P. Thompson (1985) *Whigs and Hunters: The Origin of the Black Act*, Harmondsworth: Penguin.
W.I. Thompson (1967) *The Imagination of an Insurrection: Dublin 1916*, London: Oxford University Press.
David Thornley (1965) 'Ireland: The End of an Era?', *Tuairim Pamphlet No.12*.
W.E. Vaughan (1984) *Landlords and Tenants in Ireland 1848-1904. Studies in Irish Economic and Social History No. 2*, Dundalk: Economic and Social History Society of Ireland.
Brendan Walsh (1979) 'Economic Growth and Development, 1945-1970', in Lee, 1979a, pp. 27-37.
Margaret Ward (1983) *Unmanageable Revolutionaries: Women and Irish Nationalism*, London: Pluto Press.
George J. Watson (1979) *Irish Identity and the Literary Revival*, London: Croom Helm.
Jeffrey Weeks (1982) 'Foucault For Historians', *History Workshop Journal*, No.14, pp. 106-19.
Hayden White (1972) 'The Forms of Wildness: Archaeology of An Idea', in Dudley and

Novak, pp. 3-38.
John Whyte (1960) 'The Influence of the Catholic Clergy on Elections in Nineteenth Century Ireland', *English Historical Review* Vol. LXXXV, pp. 239-59.
Martin Williams (1983) 'Ancient Mythology and Revolutionary Ideology in Ireland, 1878-1916', *Historical Journal*, Vol. XXVI, No. 2, pp. 307-28.
T. Desmond Williams (ed.) (1966) *The Irish Struggle 1916-1926*, London: Routledge and Kegan Paul.
– (1973) Secret Societies in Ireland, Dublin: Gill and Macmillan.
W.B. Yeats (1937) *A Vision*, London: Macmillan.
– (1939) *On The Boiler*, reprinted 1971, Dublin: Cuala Press.
– (1954) *Letters* (ed. Allan Wade), London: Rupert Hart Davis.
– (1955) *Autobiographies*, London: Macmillan.
– (1957) *The Variorum Edition of the Poems of W.B. Yeats* (eds. Peter Allt and Russell K. Alspach), New York: Macmillan.
– (1961) *Essays and Introductions*, London: Macmillan.
– (1962) *Explorations*, London: Macmillan.
– (1966) *The Variorum Edition of the Plays of W.B. Yeats* (ed. Russell K. Alspach), London: Macmillan.
– (1970) *Uncollected Prose by W.B. Yeats Vol. 1.* (eds. John P. Frayne and Colton Johnson), London: Macmillan.
– (1974) *Selected Plays* (ed. A.N. Jeffares), London: Pan.
– (1975) *Uncollected Prose by W.B. Yeats Vol. 2* (eds. John P. Frayne and Colton Johnson), London: Macmillan.
– (1978) *A Critical Edition of Yeats' 'A Vision' (1925)* (eds. George Mills Harper and Walter Kelly Hood), London: Macmillan.
– (1980) *Selected Criticism* (ed. A.N. Jeffares), London: Pan Books.
– (1986) *The Collected Letters of W.B. Yeats* (ed. J.S. Kelly, associate ed. Eric Domville), Oxford: Clarendon Press.
W.B. Yeats and Thomas Kinsella (1970) *Davis, Mangan, Ferguson?: Tradition and the Irish Writer*, Dublin: Dolmen Press.
Robert Young (1981) *Untying The Text: A Post-Structuralist Reader*, London: Routledge and Kegan Paul.
Carol B. Ziener (1971) 'The Beleaguered Isle: A Study of Elizabethan and early Jacobean Anti-Catholicism', *Past and Present*, No. 51, pp. 27-61.
Alex Zwerdling (1965) *Yeats and the Heroic Ideal*, London: Peter Owen.

Glossary

Anglo-Irish Persons resident in Ireland of English stock and generally communicants of the Anglican Church of Ireland. Also includes some Presbyterian and other Protestant nonconformist sects.

Anglo-Normans Persons of Norman descent who had settled for a time in England or on its borders after the Conquest.

Ascendancy Members of the Anglo-Irish (q.v.) who enjoyed access to political power in Ireland during the later seventeenth and eighteenth centuries. The Ascendancy comprised an amalgam of New English families, together with a few of the Old English (q.v.) who had conformed to Anglicanism and a very much larger number of descendants of colonists who had arrived during the Commonwealth (1649–60) or the subsequent Williamite/Jacobite struggles.

Boycotting The procedure used, particularly in the Land Wars, to apply pressure on individuals in rural communities to follow a particular political or social line. It involved social ostracism, in conjunction with the withdrawal of that host of mutually supportive activities upon which rural producers and their dependents relied, such as at harvest time. It took its name from a County Mayo landlord, Captain Charles Boycott, whose subjection to such coercion in 1880 was widely reported.

Catholic Emancipation The removal in 1829 of the requirement that certain office holders and all MPs should subscribe to a declaration denouncing the Roman Catholic Church and affirming support for the Anglican Church. This opened high offices in the judiciary, bureaucracy and armed forces to Catholics and made it possible for Catholics to take seats in Parliament if elected. Emancipation was achieved by the contruction of a mass movement led by a Catholic Barrister, Daniel O'Connell, and frequently administered locally by Catholic parish priests.

Civil society The sphere of private relations between citizens, as distinct from the relations of the citizen(s) and the state.

Coercion The term commonly applied to measures which sought in the nineteenth century to make the conviction or neutralization of suspected agitators or politically motivated persons easier. Coercion Acts frequently dispensed with the need for juries in trials, created new offences and imposed new scales of punishment for those offences.

Confederation of Kilkenny A union of Old English and the Native Irish, formalized in 1642, which sought to use the occasion of the conflict between Charles I and Parliament to reverse confiscations of property and to reassert the rights of Catholicism.

Counter hegemony A leadership position, elaborated as a challenge to the hegemony (q.v.) of the currently leading group and not infrequently based upon a critique of their ideological and cultural positions.

Defenders A Catholic secret agrarian society which functioned in the later eighteenth century in and around County Armagh, seeking to protect Catholic tenants from victimization by landlords and from attacks by Protestant secret societies (Steelboys, Whiteboys and Peep O'Day Boys). It spread throughout Ireland after the suppression of the United Irishmen partially in response to the growth of militant Protestant societies, particularly Orange societies (q.v.). In the 1798 Rising outside Belfast, most of the insurrectionaries were Defenders rather than members of the Society of United Irishmen.

Discourse A group of statements which together constitute and delimit a particular area of concern and which is given coherence by a set of internal rules and procedures.

Dublin Castle The seat of government administration in Ireland during the Union.

Episteme Literally, 'knowledge'. As used by Foucault the term refers to the underlying code of knowledge employed in a given period in particular discourses and which, as one of its effects, produces an isomorphism between discourses.

Fenians Alternative, popular, name for the Irish Republican Brotherhood, a secret revolutionary organization, founded in 1858, dedicated to achieving an Irish Republic by armed struggle.

Gaelic Athletic Association An organization founded by Michael Cusack in 1884, with substantial Fenian involvement, dedicated to developing Irish sports and pastimes and to countering the spreading influence of the (English) Amateur Athletics Association.

Gaelic League An organization founded by Eoin MacNeill in 1893 to promote the restoration of the Irish language. Douglas Hyde was its President from its foundation until 1915.

Gombeen Man A rural usurer, usually a shopkeeper or publican.

Grattan's Parliament The period from 1782 to 1800 during which the Irish Parliament enjoyed legislative independence from the supervision of the Westminster Parliament. Widely regarded in the nineteenth century and after as a 'golden age' during which the Irish economy thrived, freed from British interference.

Habeas Corpus The doctrine, founded upon the right to apply for a writ of Habeas Corpus, which guarantees the citizen under Common Law against arbitrary arrest and imprisonment without due cause.

Hegemony The usual English translation for the Italian *egemonia*, the term which Gramsci uses to indicate that the political 'leadership' of a particular group is frequently more or less willingly accepted by those led or ruled, rather than imposed. It takes two main forms: 'expansive hegemony', in which the leadership of a particular group advances the interests of all those who are led and 'transformist hegemony', where a particular class or class fraction is benefited, possibly at the expense of the remaining member groups of the class alliance.

Hierarchy The Conference of Bishops which served and serves as a form of national ecclesiastical organization for the Catholic Church in Ireland.

Ideological State Apparatuses (ISAs) Those apparatuses which, according to Althusser, operate in civil society (q.v.) and are the principal agencies by which the constitution of the subject takes place through the process of interpellation (q.v.). They include the family, the churches, trade unions, cultural organizations and culture generally, civil legal relations and the political parties.

Internal colonialism Concept developed by Lenin, in his *The Development of Capitalism in Russia*, to convey the notion that relations of domination and subservience may exist between regions within a state analogous to those between a colony and the metropolitan state.

Interpellation The process whereby individuals acquire awareness of themselves as subjects. In Althusser's formulation this process is likened to being 'hailed', or called to, in that the person hailed accepts that she or he has been located and identified. The process may also be termed 'the constitution of the subject'.

Irish Citizen Army Formed in November 1913 during the Dublin Lock-Out in response to attacks on strikers by the Dublin Metropolitan Police. Until Autumn 1914 its secretary was Sean O'Casey. He resigned from the organization in opposition to Countess Markiewicz continuing to be a member, while simultaneously being a member of nationalist organizations, particularly the Irish Voluntéers. After Jim Larkin left for America in Autumn 1914, the I.C.A. was led by James Connolly.

Irish Parliamentary Party Under a series of titles, a distinct Irish parliamentary presence, working for some form of autonomy, operated at Westminster from 1870. In that year Isaac Butt, a Protestant barrister, founded the Home Government Association, after led by Charles Stewart Parnell under the title of the Home Rule Confederation of Great Britain and, after 1900, the United Irish League.

Irish Volunteers A Volunteer militia founded by Eoin MacNeill in November 1913 as a response to the formation in January 1913 of the Ulster Volunteers.

Jansenism A form of Catholic doctrine held to originate with Jansenius (1585–1638), Bishop of Ypres, and Duvergier de Hauranne (1581–1643), Abbé de St Cyran, condemned as heretical in 1653, in which an important element was the belief that the world, being irredeemably corrupt, posed a terrible threat to the possibility of salvation. Vice and sensuality must be spurned and the imaginative arts, being seductive and vainglorious, were particularly dangerous.

Land League The organization, founded by Michael Davitt, a Fenian, and after taken over by Parnell, which initiated a campaign in the wake of the agrarian crisis of 1879 to resist landlord seizure of tenants' land for non-payment of rent.

Maynooth A Catholic seminary founded and endowed in 1795 by the British Government to obviate the necessity for candidates for the priesthood to study on the Continent where they might acquire Jacobin ideas. It remained Ireland's leading seminary in the nineteenth century and the powerhouse of Cullen's 'devotional revolution'.

Mere Irish *See* 'Native Irish'.

National Schools A state-controlled and financed elementary level education system for Ireland founded in 1831.

Native Irish Gaelic speaking persons, the descendants of the various pre-Norman invaders of Ireland and its original inhabitants.

New English English colonists arriving in Ireland during the sixteenth century and early part of the seventeenth century. Usually adherents to the Anglican Church of Ireland.

Old English English and Anglo-Norman colonists who had settled in Ireland before the sixteenth century. Usually stayed within the Roman Catholic Church.

Orange Order An exclusively Protestant society founded in 1795 and formalised with quasi-masonic ritual in 1797. It began as a popular society but gentry members very rapidly came to dominate it and it became a powerful means of welding together Protestants (usually Anglican) of all social ranks in opposition to Catholic claims and progress. The leaders of the Order dissolved it to forestall Government suppression in the wake of revelations of its widespread penetration of the army in 1836. It resumed activity in 1845 and has since played a significant if intermittent role in Irish and Northern Ireland politics.

Organic intellectuals Intellectuals who elaborate the bases for hegemony and who either come from – or identify with – the class for which they speak.

Penal Laws Measures enacted in the early eighteenth century to deny Catholics access to political power and in particular to fragment Catholic estates.

Political society The sphere of social and political relations dominated by the state and its apparatuses: the criminal law and the judiciary, the bureaucracy, the police, the armed forces, the administration and legislature.

Recusants Persons who refused to participate in the rites of the Anglican Church after the Reformation.

Reform Bill The 1832 Reform Act amended some of the more glaring examples of political corruption of contemporary Britain and redistributed seats to reflect some of the changes caused by industrialization. It made modest inroads into the power of the great landed families but contemporary critics feared that it heralded the beginning of a process which would lead to French-style radical republicanism.

Repeal Movement A movement initiated and led by Daniel O'Connell in 1840 to campaign for the repeal of the 1800 Act of Union and the re-establishment of the Irish Parliament.

Repressive State Apparatuses *See* Political Society.

Sinn Féin ('Ourselves'.) The party founded on Arthur Griffith's political ideas which, in 1908, united a number of smaller groups to campaign for Irish independence on a policy of economic self-reliance and abstention from Westminster. Popularly and erroneously believed to have instigated the Easter Rising.

Strategic formation An ensemble of texts, part-texts and genres which, grouped together, may be read as mutually informing one another and which supply explanations and justifications for 'strategic locations' (q.v.).

Strategic location The position that an author adopts within a text *vis-à-vis* the material written upon.

Structured in dominance Term employed by Tony Bennett to convey the notion that there is a gradient on the terrain of political and social relations and that those possessing power enjoy superior positions upon that terrain and their dominance thence becomes part of the structure of a given society or order.

United Irish League An organization founded in 1898 by William O'Brien to campaign for the buying out of landlords, by compulsory purchase, in the interests of the tenants. In 1901 it had almost 100,000 members and formed a powerful base for the Parliamentarians to re-unite upon.

United Irishmen A radical political society founded in Dublin and Belfast in 1791, which was non-sectarian and rationalist. Influenced by the development of French political thought, the Society forged an alliance with leaders of the Catholic community to demand the widening of the franchise and an end to the political and civil disabilities of Catholics. Suppressed in 1794, the Society's demands grew more radical as it operated underground, eventually entering into alliance with French forces and with the aim of concerting a French invasion with an Irish insurrection. The various attempts that the Society's adherents made at insurrection, together with the French invasion, were signal failures providing the justification for the Act of Union of 1800 which incorporated Ireland in a new United Kingdom.

War of manoeuvre The struggle which takes place following the 'war of position' (q.v.) in which the contending class forces struggle openly through political and more direct means.

War of position The long drawn-out struggle between groups vying for leadership of a class-alliance or seeking to supplant the rule of one class-alliance with that of another. It takes place principally, according to Gramsci, in the sphere of 'Civil society' (q.v.) and must be successfully concluded before a new would-be hegemonic group can secure state power.

Index